IMAGES
of America

NASHVILLE'S JEWISH COMMUNITY

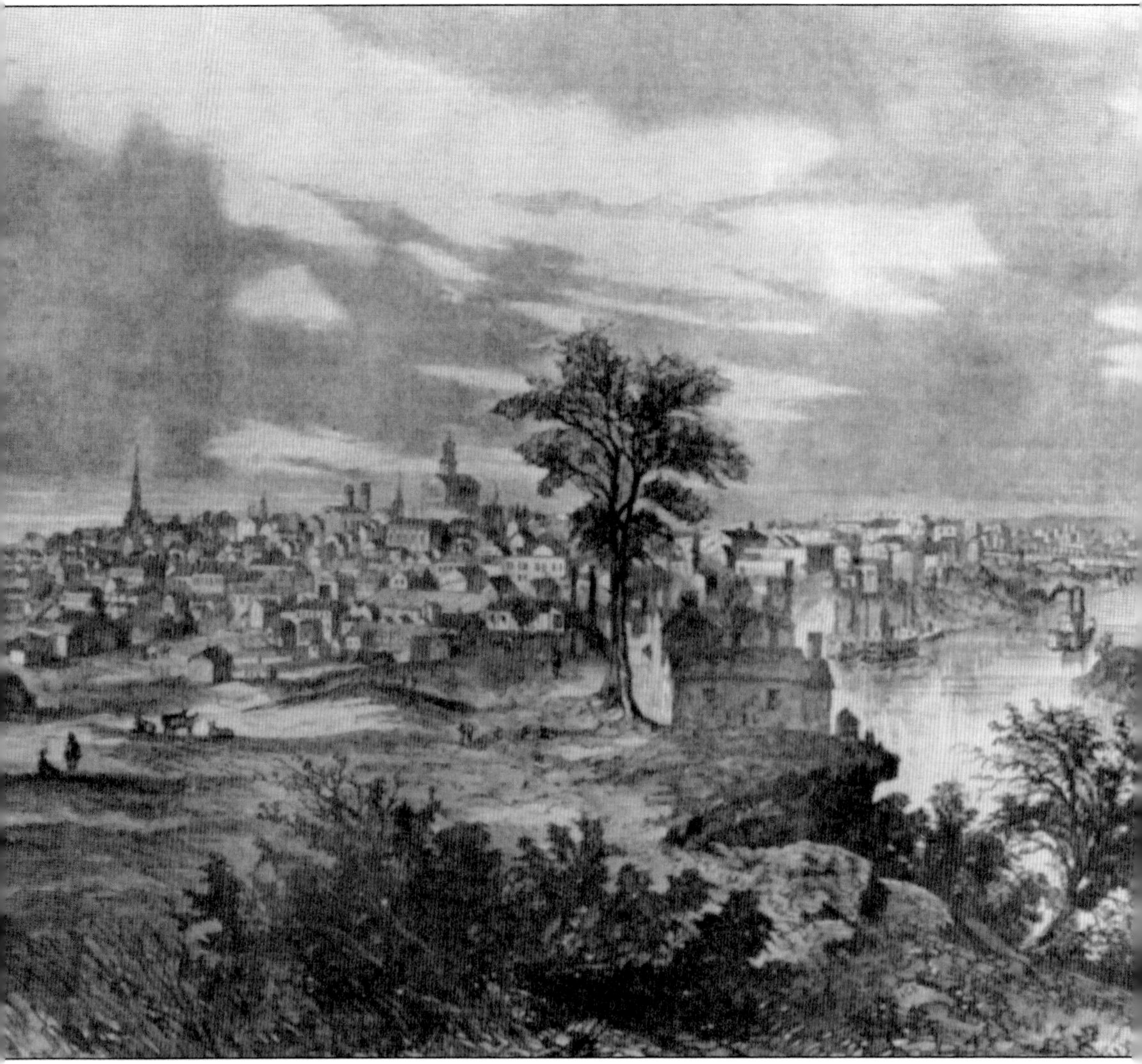

This is Nashville as it looked in 1854, when the earliest Jewish settlers began arriving. Building outward from the Cumberland River, the state capitol building can be seen in the middle of the photograph, on the city's highest elevation. (Courtesy of Tennessee State Archives.)

On the Cover: The N. Hirsch Store was one of Nashville's largest and earliest Jewish-owned businesses. It was opened in 1870 by Nathan Hirsch, who had emigrated with his wife and sons from Waldgrune, Germany, to the United States in the 1860s. About the same time that he started his business, two of his sons, Sigmund and Joseph, opened their own store. By 1875, N. Hirsch and Company had outgrown its building on Union Street and merged with the store owned by son Samuel and son-in-law Sam Lowenstein. By 1880, the store had begun to decline, and it moved into smaller quarters. In 1886, the business failed, and Samuel, Sigmund, and Sam Lowenstein went to work for L. Jonas and Company. (Courtesy of Jewish Federation Archives.)

IMAGES
of America

NASHVILLE'S JEWISH COMMUNITY

Lee Dorman

ARCADIA
PUBLISHING

ISBN 978-0-7385-6680-1
Published by Arcadia Publishing
Charleston, South Carolina

Printed in the United States of America

Library of Congress Control Number:2009934187

For all general information contact Arcadia Publishing at:
Telephone 843-853-2070
Fax 843-853-0044
E-mail sales@arcadiapublishing.com
For customer service and orders:
Toll-Free 1-888-313-2665

Visit us on the Internet at www.arcadiapublishing.com

This book is dedicated to my parents, Sol and Betty Dorman, who helped instill in me a love of Judaism and a thirst for knowledge. In working on this project, I was constantly reminded of my father's passion for learning. One of the indelible images I have from my childhood is seeing him reading Commentary *and* Atlantic Monthly *magazines, then writing his opinions of the articles. But he never took it beyond that, never shared his writings, and never wrote for publication. With this book, I feel like I am finishing something he started.*

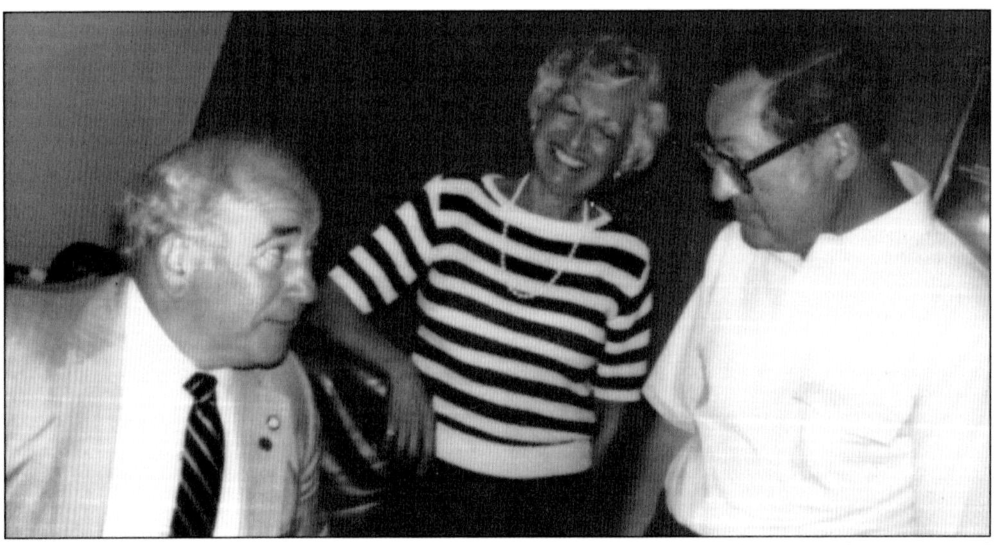

When the author was general manager of WLAC radio in 1983, actor and activist Ed Asner visited the station to be interviewed on one of the talk shows. Knowing his parents had always admired Asner and his character Lou Grant, Lee told them they could meet Asner if they came to the station while he was there. They did, and it was a special moment they always treasured. (Author's collection.)

Contents

ACKNOWLEDGMENTS

Many people helped make this book a reality, sharing their photographs, family histories, and favorite stories handed down by parents and grandparents. Particular thanks go to Barbara Balch, Teddy Bart, David Blumen, Julie Boehm, Betsy Chernau, Paul Cohn Jr., Beth Davidson, Mike Dorman, Phyllis and Stanley Frank, Joel Gordon, Susan Gordon, Melanie Hirt, Marvin Koch, Lee Kraft, William Kuhn, Carolyn and Larry Levine, Leon May, David Raybin, Carla Rich, Gayle Rosen, Terry and Bernie Rosenblum, Barbara Schwartz, Richard Schweid, Willy Stern, Sally Wolfe, and Jeff Zander. Without the assistance of Annette Levy Ratkin, Lynn Fleischer, and Steve Edelstein, the book would still be only an idea. With the exceptions noted in the captions of photographs provided by various individuals, most of the images in this book were obtained from the extensive collection of the archives of the Jewish Federation of Nashville and Middle Tennessee. The research and writings of Fedora Frank some 30 years ago were of enormous value. Thanks also to my wife, Faye, for both her help and her patience, and to my editor at Arcadia, Maggie Bullwinkel, who always had, or found, the answers to all my questions.

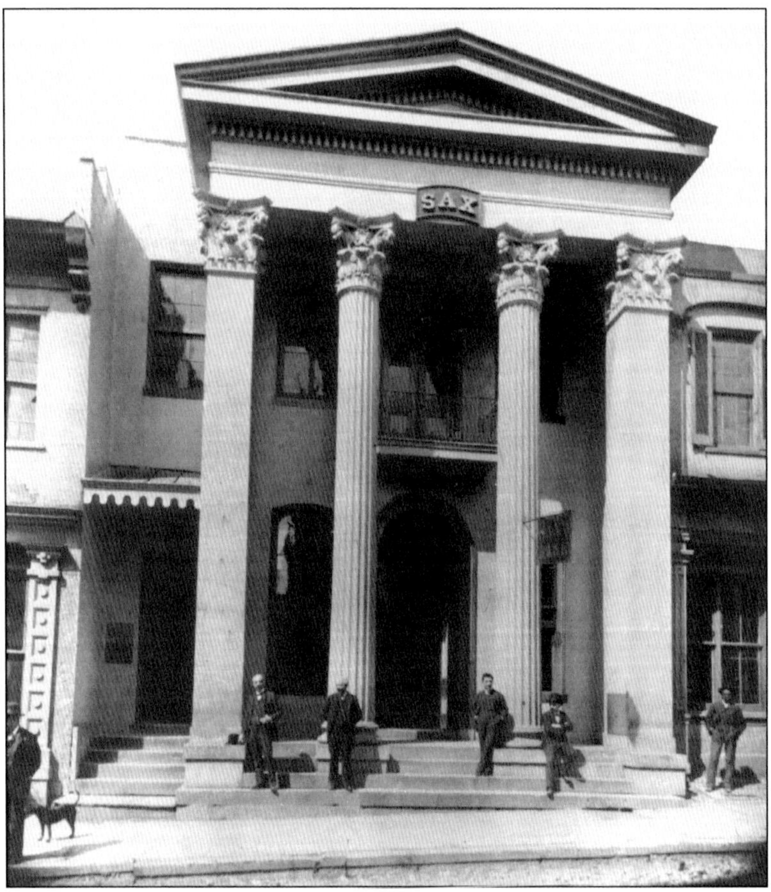

Julius and Max Sax, born in Prussia in the 1830s, chartered Nashville's first Jewish-owned bank, the Nashville Savings Bank, in 1863. Successful for three decades, the bank suffered severe financial losses during the panic of 1893 and failed, causing many Nashvillians to lose their life savings. Although the brothers had been active in the Vine Street Temple, B'nai B'rith, and the Concordia and Standard Clubs, both families moved to New York after the bank failed.

Why an Archives?

The farther backward you can look, the farther forward you are likely to see.

—Winston Churchill

In 2009, the Jewish Museum in New York featured an exhibit of paintings of an artist's memories of his childhood in Opatow (Apt), Poland, before the Holocaust. The Gordon Jewish Community Center Library has a small collection of *yizkor* (memorial) books of life in Jewish communities in Europe prior to their destruction in the Holocaust. One of the books is a memorial to Apt, and the late Alvin Dembsky was thumbing through it some years ago in the library. Suddenly he shouted, "There's a picture of my grandfather!"

These memorial books vary in quality, cobbled together by survivors of cities whose Jewish populations were destroyed in the Holocaust. In 1978, as I looked at them in the library of the old Jewish Community Center on West End Avenue, I realized the need for a repository for documents and photographs of the vibrant Nashville Jewish community, first organized in 1851 by "five families and eight young men," the title of the late Fedora Frank's first history of Nashville's Jews. Mrs. Frank had a small archives collection in the safe at The Temple, Congregation Ohabai Sholom. She shared that collection with the new Jewish Federation Archives, opened in 1979 with the help of a grant from the National Historical Publications and Records Commission. Over 30 years of actively collecting the records of the institutions, businesses, and individuals of the Nashville Jewish community has preserved their documents, minutes, bulletins, photographs, and oral histories, and they are available for researchers to use.

What should you collect? You may have a box of family photographs in the hot, dry attic, or in the damp basement. Or there are a few brittle scrapbooks, with fading newsprint, yellowing tape, and rusting paper clips. You can start safely protecting your family records with a little advice from such organizations as the Metro Archives and Tennessee State Library and Archives. You can get a genealogy computer program and start entering all the names and dates you know, and ask family members or check cemetery tombstones for others. Then your family information will be preserved. You can encourage your church or synagogue, book or garden club, to start saving their minutes, bulletins, and photographs.

These are just a few ways to write history. Most of the photographs in this book are from the Annette Levy Ratkin Jewish Community Archives. The individual Jewish family sagas, business successes, and organizations responding to community, national, and international needs make up this history. It's like going to a supermarket instead of a produce stand: one-stop shopping for history. Your life experiences are a part of history. Start an archive, or donate your records to an existing one.

—Annette Levy Ratkin

INTRODUCTION

The history of Nashville's Jewish community, as pointed out by Annette Levy Ratkin, has been chronicled twice in the last 50 years with the publication of two books by Fedora Frank: *Five Families and Eight Young Men* in 1962 and *Beginnings on Market Street* in 1976. Future books are in the works, and the story of Nashville and its Jewish community continues to be told.

Because history is made on a daily basis, no account can ever be complete. This treatment is meant to cover the years 1850 to 1950. In the final chapter, several more recent events and people have been included so as to not omit important parts of the story, but by and large, the details of the last 50 years have been left for a future project.

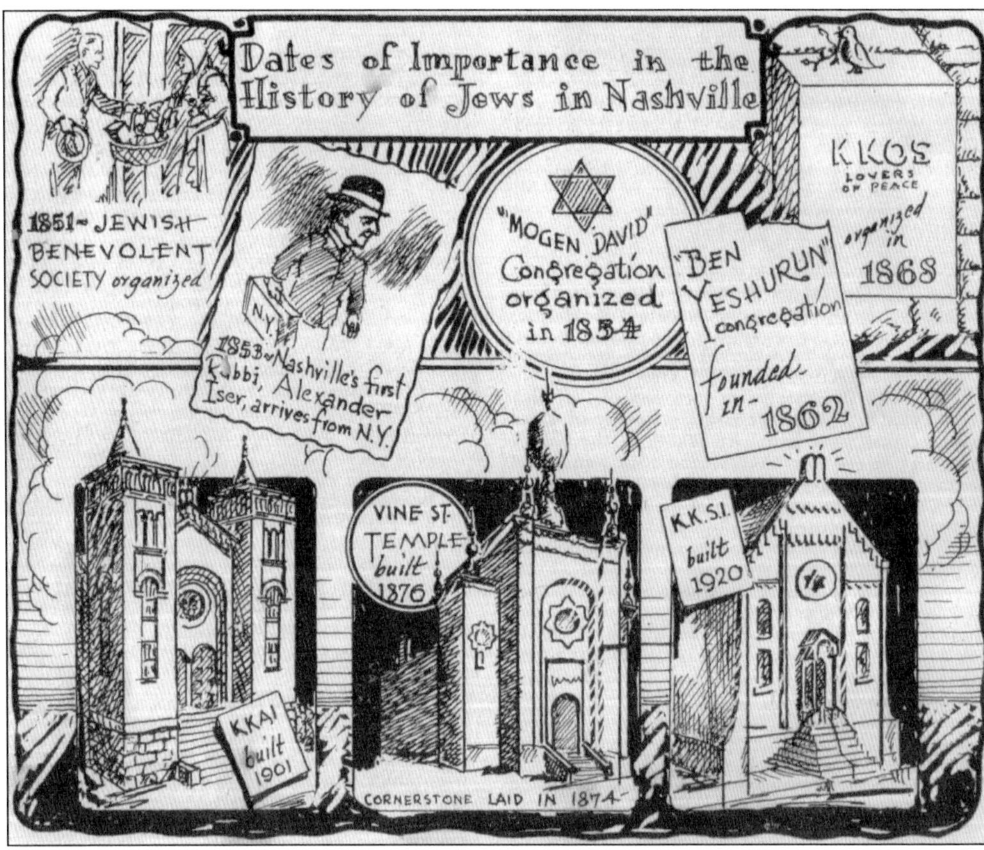

This (approximate) time line is the work of artist and illustrator Meyer Wolfe, who grew up in Nashville. It has been reproduced numerous times over the years, first appearing in an early edition of the *YMHA News*, the monthly newsletter put out by the Young Men's Hebrew Association (YMHA) and the predecessor to the Jewish community newspaper, the *Observer*.

One

The First Jewish Settlers

When America won its independence, the Jewish population was only 2,500. Tennessee, originally part of North Carolina, did not become a state until 1796. The first Jewish residents were trappers and traders who came across the mountains from North and South Carolina and settled in the Knoxville area. In 1748, Scottish lawyer Sir Alexander Cuming proposed that Britain allow 300,000 Jewish families to settle on Cherokee Indian territory in western North Carolina and East Tennessee. However, King George, Lord Halifax, and the Parliament did not think too highly of Cuming's idea, and it was never implemented.

According to the census of 1790, only 32 of the nearly 32,000 persons living in Tennessee were anything other than English, Irish, Scotch, Dutch, French, or German—including "Hebrews." The first birth of a Jewish child here was that of Sarah Myers, the daughter of Benjamin and Hannah Myers, in 1795. There are no records to show why they came to Middle Tennessee or how Benjamin earned his living, and they stayed just one year before moving to Virginia.

Because of a lack of detailed record keeping and the absence of established Jewish synagogues or temples in those early days, whether or not someone was Jewish was often determined years later and was sometimes based on whether or not a person's name "sounded Jewish." A. Shymanski, the area's first dental surgeon; H. W. Abrams, who opened a private school for both males and females; and Z. Rosendrah are believed to be among the first Jewish settlers in Nashville in the late 1700s and early 1800s. Andrew Smolniker, who came from Austria, received his American citizenship in Davidson County Circuit Court in 1841, as did Simon Pollock, a doctor, in 1843. While the number of Jewish individuals and families remained relatively small between 1820 and 1860, that began to change as the Civil War came to an end and Reconstruction began. Jewish peddlers and merchants, some of whom had followed the Union troops south during the war years, settled in Nashville, started businesses, married, and had families, and the Jewish population of the city began to grow.

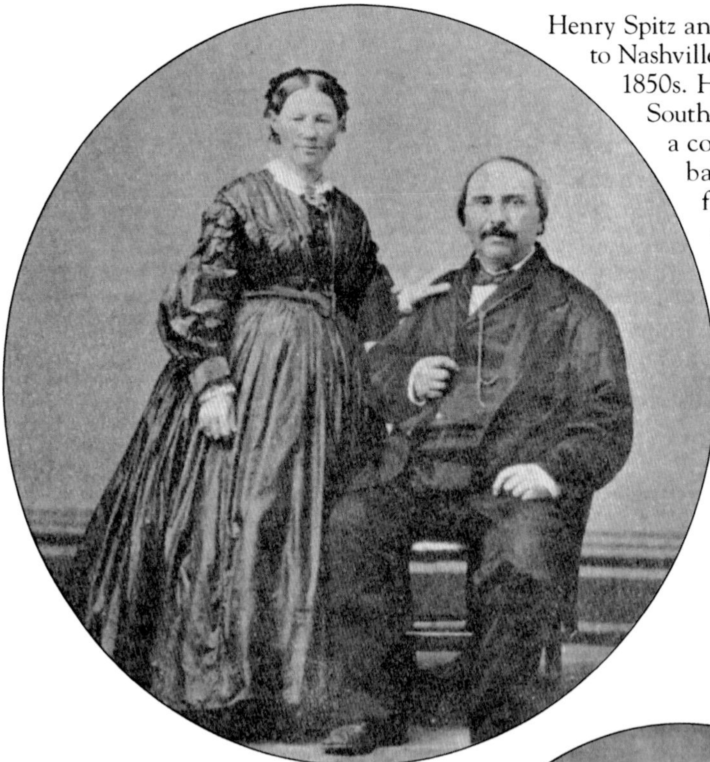

Henry Spitz and his wife, Caroline, came to Nashville from Georgia in the early 1850s. Henry opened a bakery on South Market Street, later adding a confectionery. In addition to baked goods, he also sold fruit, wine, and preserves and advertised catering for parties and weddings.

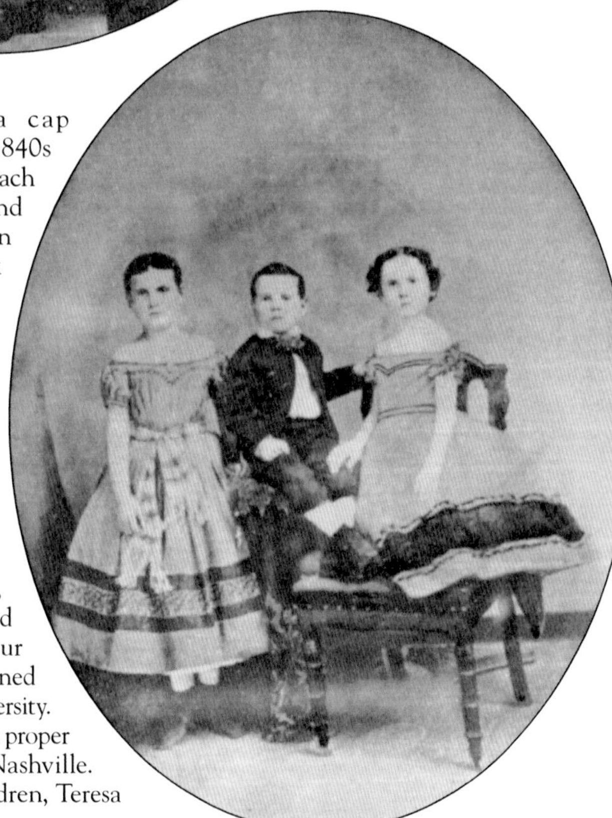

Aaron Lande established a cap manufacturing company in the 1840s and was a partner in the Lande-Elsbach Store on North Market Street and the Lande-Schlessinger Store on the Public Square. Tragedy struck the Lande family in 1861, when his wife, Esther, died after a six-week illness. Lande was president of Congregation Mogen David from 1865 to 1867 and a year later was the first president of Ohavai Sholom. He was also one of the founders of the Young Men's Hebrew Relief Society. In January 1863, Spitz discovered the body of Lt. Julius Lettman, a Union soldier, at a local funeral parlor. The two had prayed together during Yom Kippur when Lettman's regiment was stationed on the campus of the Nashville University. Lande saw that the soldier received a proper burial in the Jewish cemetery in Nashville. Shown here are Lande's three children, Teresa (left), Solomon, and Rebecca.

Israel and Isaac Barker were brothers. Isaac was first a peddler, and then he went into the clothing business, while Israel operated a saloon. Israel's daughter, Carrie, married R. D. Blum's son, Joseph (see page 18). Carrie and Joseph's daughter, Tessie, married David Lowenheim (see page 18). Isaac had several sons, two of whom moved to Cuba and settled there, marrying non-Jewish Cuban women. One of those sons was the father of Watergate burglar Bernard Barker.

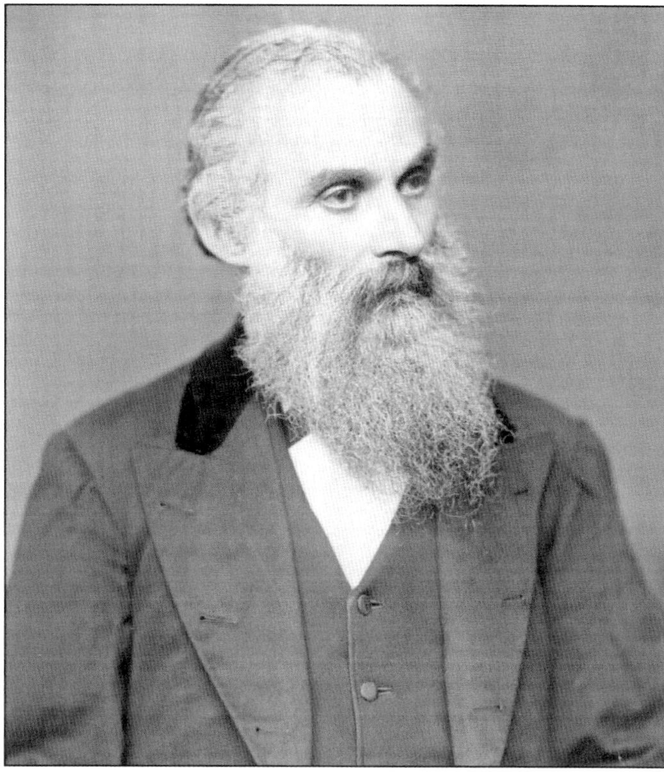

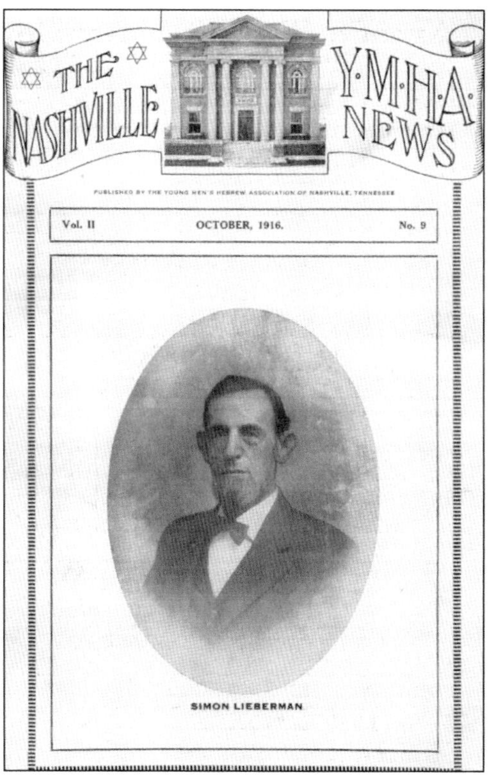

THE NASHVILLE Y.M.H.A. NEWS

PUBLISHED BY THE YOUNG MEN'S HEBREW ASSOCIATION OF NASHVILLE, TENNESSEE

Vol. II OCTOBER, 1916. No. 9

SIMON LIEBERMAN

Simon Lieberman was one of the founders of the Young Men's Hebrew Association (YMHA), president of B'nai B'rith, and treasurer of B'nai Yeshurun congregation. Although he started in the boot and shoe business, in 1878, he and Adolph Loveman created Lieberman, Loveman, and O'Brien Lumber Company. He later served as chairman of the Nashville Board of Education.

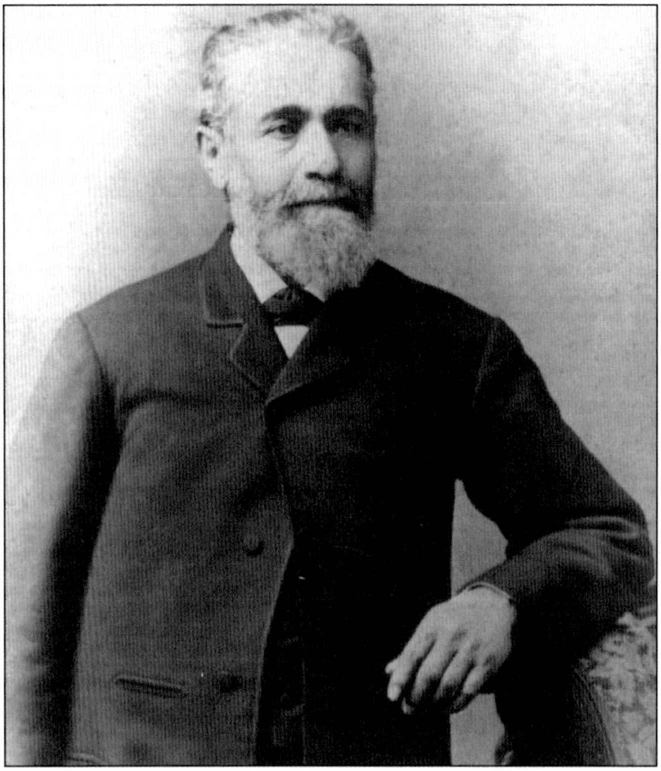

Jacob Bloomstein came to Nashville from Poland in the 1850s, first owning and operating a cigar manufacturing business and then grocery and dry goods stores. In 1863, he was arrested and sent to a federal prison in Alton, Illinois, charged with smuggling goods to the Confederate army. He was released after four months when his wife sent an appeal to Tennessee's military governor, Andrew Johnson. Years later, Bloomstein's daughter explained that her father's "smuggling" consisted of feeding and clothing Confederate prisoners working in a stone quarry near his home. In the 1870 census, Bloomstein was listed as Nashville's wealthiest Jewish citizen.

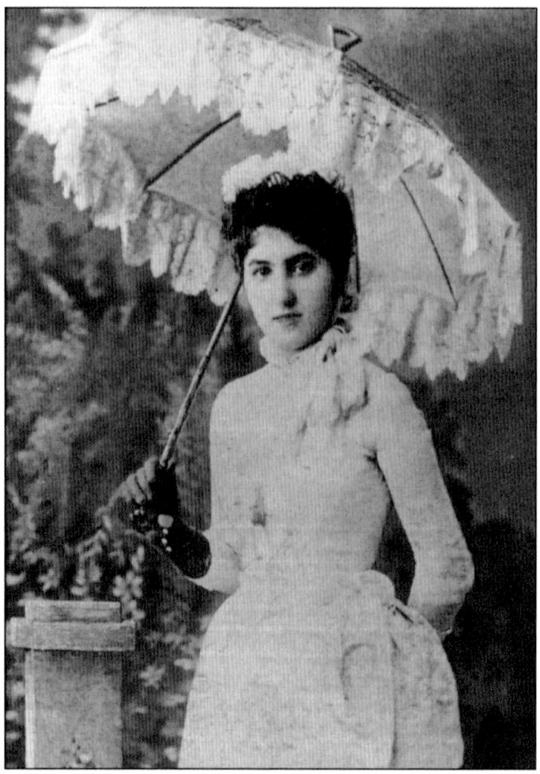

Jennie Goldammer was the daughter of Julius Goldammer, rabbi at Ohavai Sholom from 1878 to 1886. She married Judah Bloomstein, one of Jacob's sons, who is believed to be the first Jewish Nashvillian to receive a college degree. He was a physician in Nashville by 1870 and in 1878 added a degree in pharmacy from Vanderbilt, opening Bloomstein's Pharmacy on Union Street. Judah's brother Max, also a pharmacist, is said to have introduced the milk shake to Nashville at their drugstore.

Emanuel Lebeck was born near Frankfort, Germany in 1819. He and his wife, Caroline, arrived in Nashville in 1892 following his retirement from the iron and steel business. They were the parents of Mike, Sam, and Louis Lebeck.

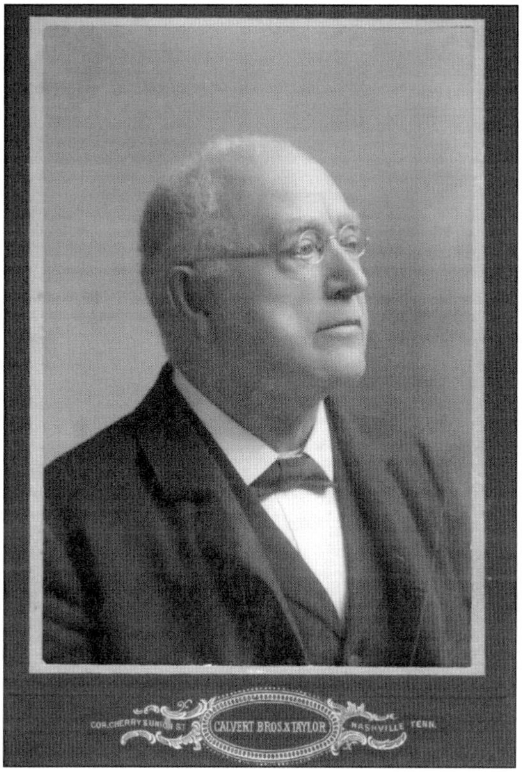

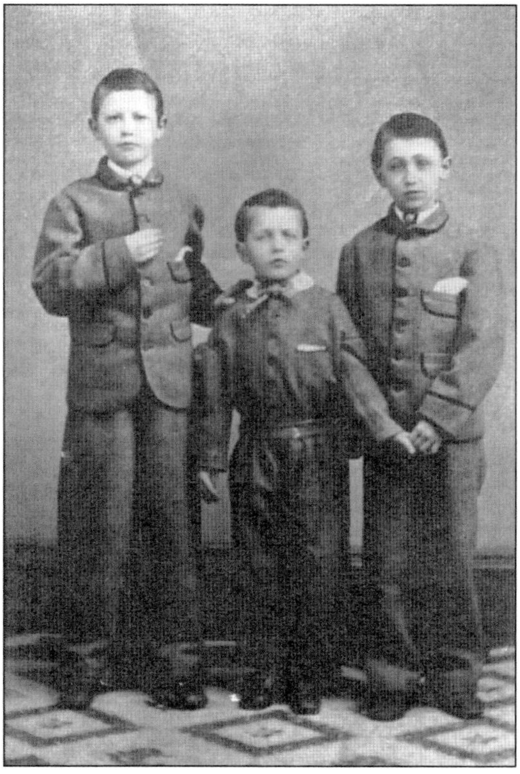

Here are Michael, Sam, and Louis Lebeck in 1864, when Mike (left) was nine, Sam (center) was six, and Louis was eight. All worked together at Lebeck's Department Store, building it into one of the largest and most successful stores in Nashville.

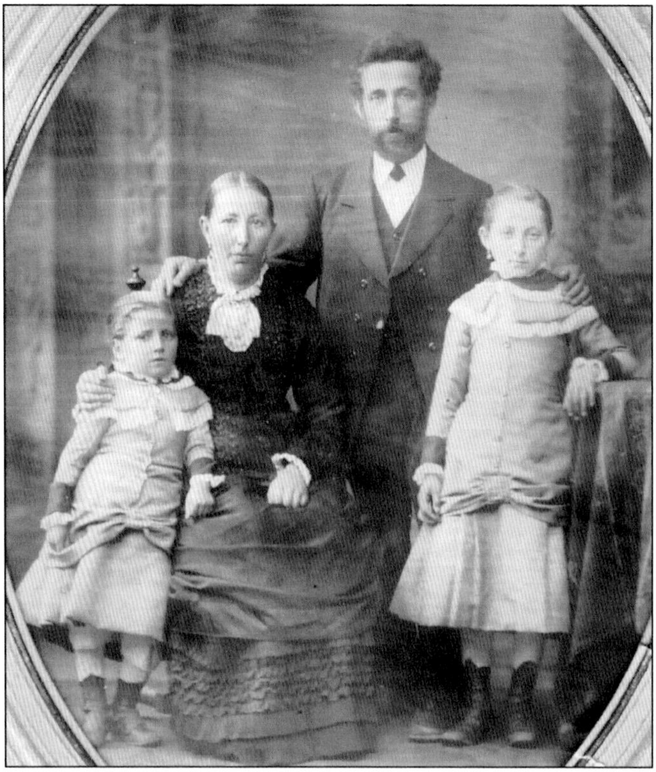

Abraham Leiser was a sergeant in the Union's 7th Cavalry during the Civil War, fighting in Kentucky, Tennessee, and Mississippi. When the war ended, he settled in Nashville. He is shown here in Germany, before he immigrated to the United States, with his wife, Bettie, and their two daughters.

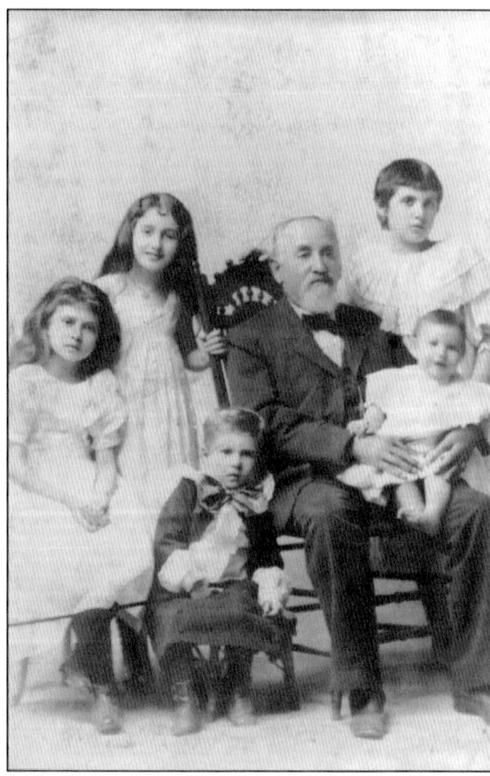

Emanuel Wolf was born in 1823 in Friedelsheim, a village on the Rhine in Germany, and came to the United States at the age of 10. He arrived in Nashville in 1850 and lived here until his death in 1896, owning and operating Wolf's Clothing Store. He founded Nashville's B'nai B'rith chapter, Maimonides Lodge Number 46. He and his wife, Gertrude, had eight children. Henry Redelsheimer and his wife, Bertha, came to Nashville by covered wagon after Henry was released as a prisoner of war by Union troops in 1865. Their daughter, Clara, married Wolf's son, Isaac, and had two daughters, Birdie and Blanche. Redelsheimer started in business specializing in fire insurance and was a member of B'nai B'rith and Vine Street Temple.

Zadoc Levy was born in Bavaria in 1813 and came to Nashville in 1852. By 1855, he had opened a dry goods store on South Market Street, and four years later, he opened a second location on Broad Street, advertising that Z. Levy's specialized in "Men's and Boy's Clothing." He was married to the former Amelia Laufer and had five sons. He served as vice president of Ohavai Sholom in 1872–1873.

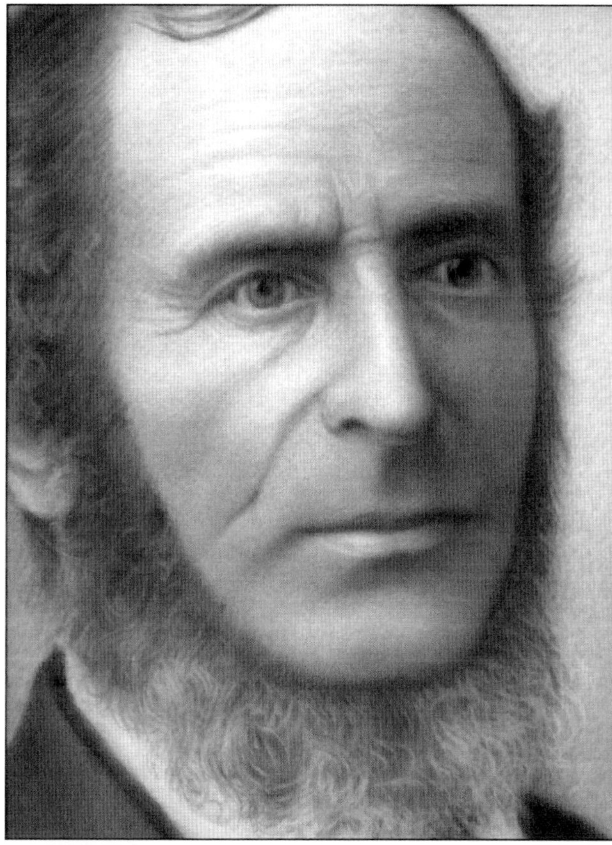

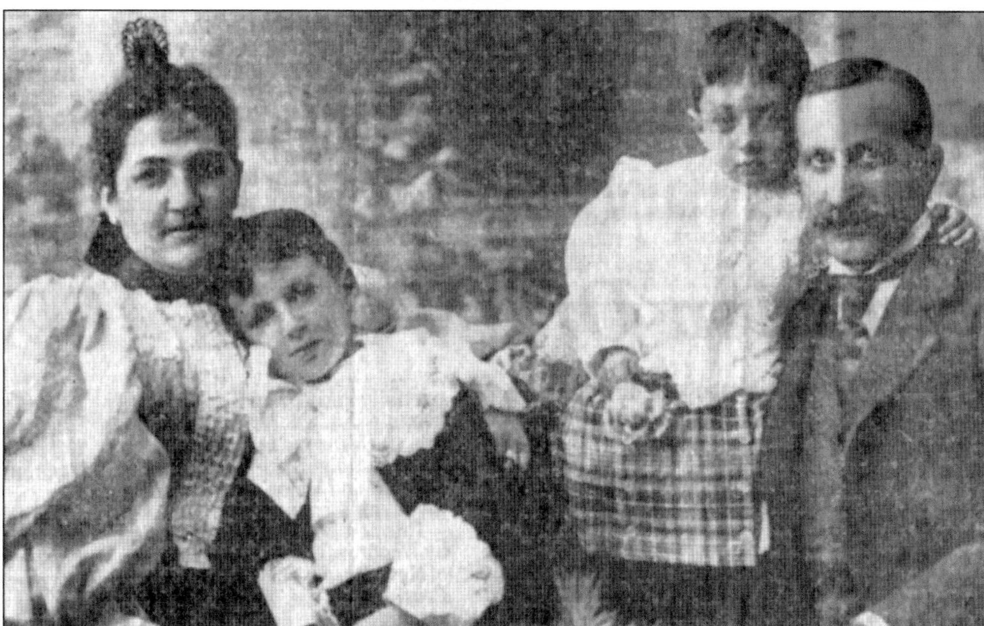

Zadoc Levy's second oldest son, Raphael Z. Levy, is seen here with his wife, Ada Jaros, and their two sons, Herbert (left) and Alfred (right).

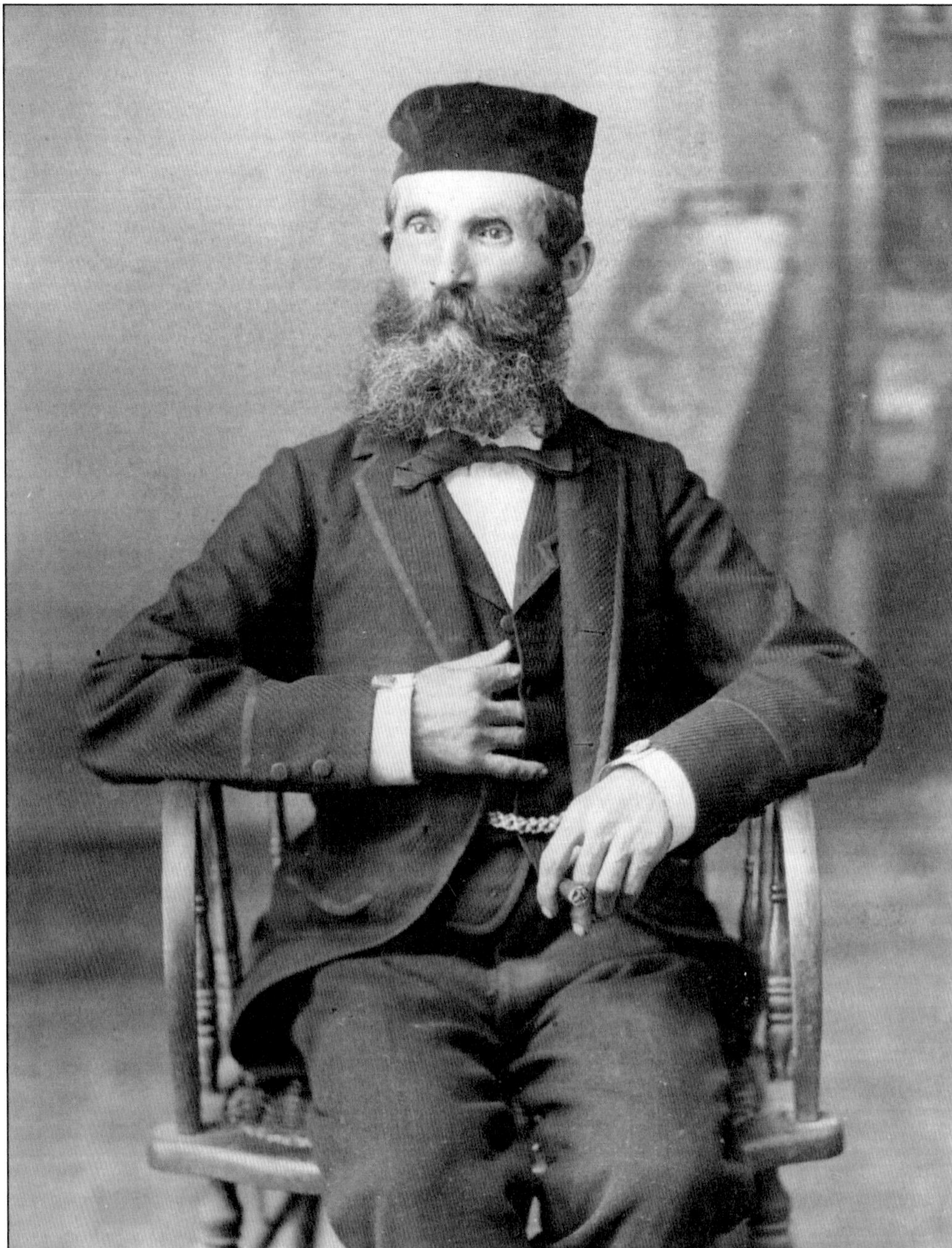

Samuel Bergeda was the father of Aaron and David Bergeda, partners in a jewelry and watch repair store in downtown Nashville. The Bergeda family came to Nashville from Bosnia in the 1890s.

Maurice Glick (center) was one of two sons of Elias and Hattie Shyer Glick (the daughter of Solomon and Henrietta Shyer). Maurice and his brother, Bert, lived in Clarksville and ran the family's store there, but both were actively involved in YMHA and other Nashville Jewish organizations.

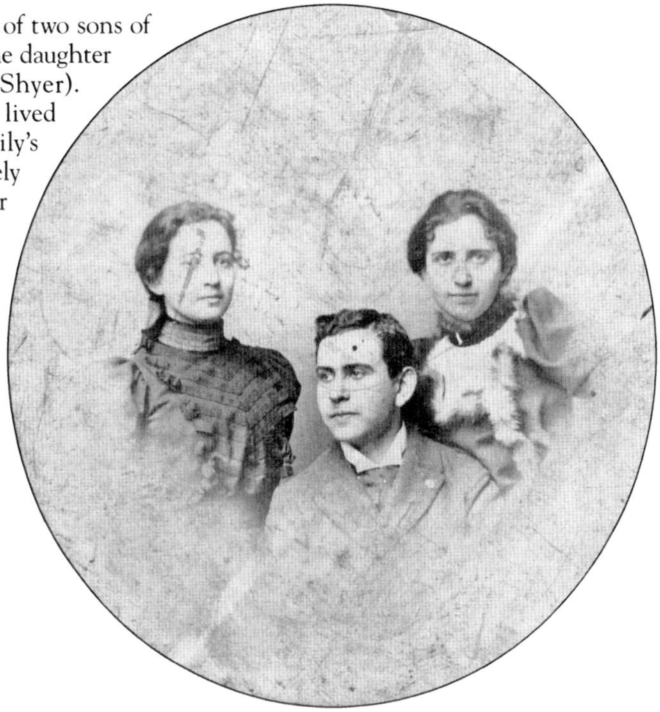

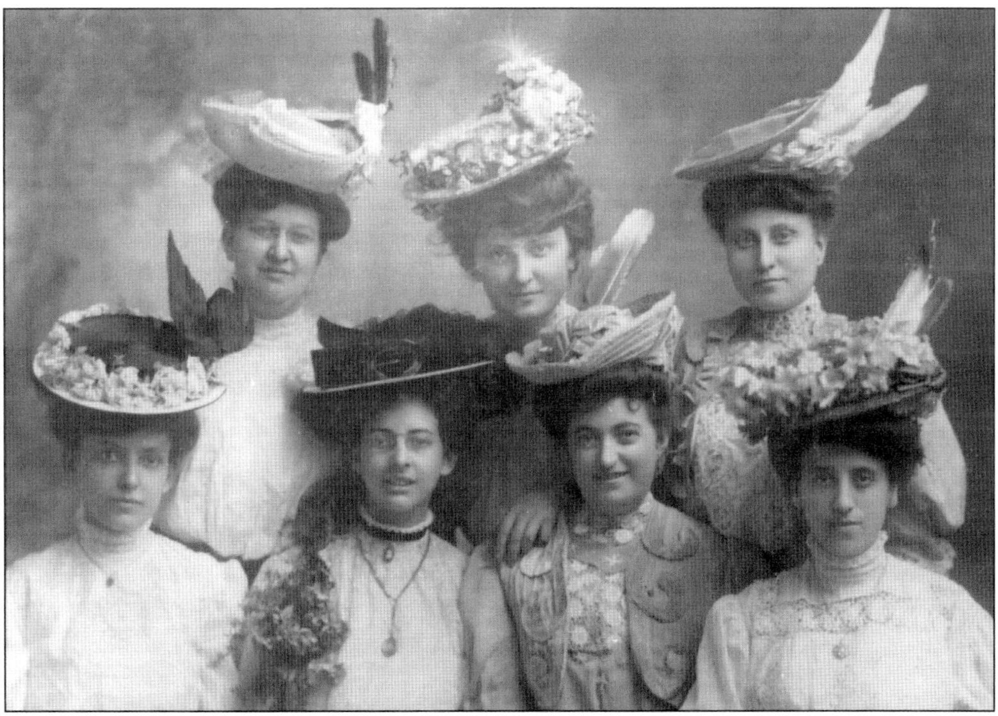

These young women, some from Nashville and others from nearby communities, were involved in Nashville's Jewish community organizations and activities in the late 1890s and early 1900s. From left to right are Mary Glick Ellis, Flora Rosensweig, Sophia Fish, Rose Rosensweig Schwartz, Stella Rich, unidentified, and Gertrude Frank Harris.

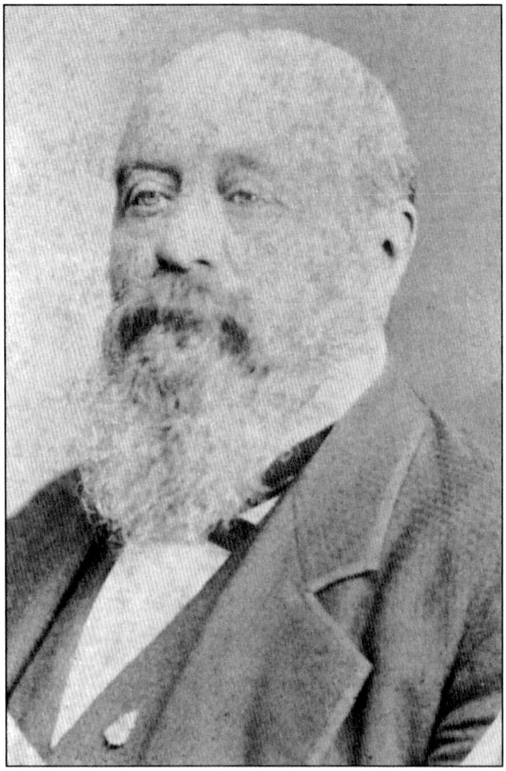

R. D. Blum, an engraver who worked with metals and stone, was considered Nashville's most gifted artist of his day. He created the tablets of the Ten Commandments, which hung above the ark at Vine Street Temple and a similar work for Mogen David. He also carved the letters on the cornerstone of the new Temple in 1874 and made the silver crown for the Torah for Vine Street's dedication service in 1876. In 1874, he was president of the Young Men's Hebrew Benevolent Society.

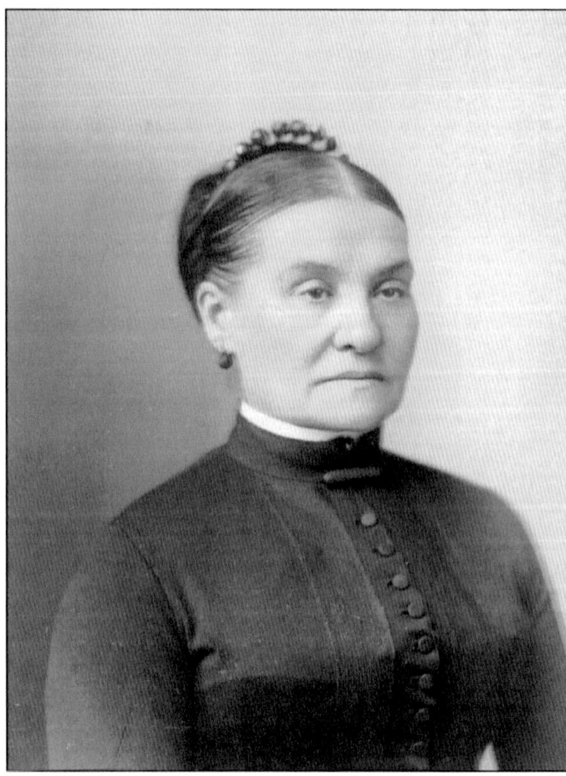

Blum was married to the former Frances Lewin. They were the parents of four daughters and one son. That son, Joseph, married Carrie Barker, the daughter of Israel Barker.

Martin Sulzbacher (right) and his wife, Dorothy (below), moved from Cincinnati to Pulaski, Tennessee, in 1849, then to Nashville in 1851. He purchased the City Clothing Store in 1853, advertising it as having "everything necessary in a gentlemen's furnishing house including Spanish cloaks, silk and satin plush vests, cravats, valises and carpet bags."

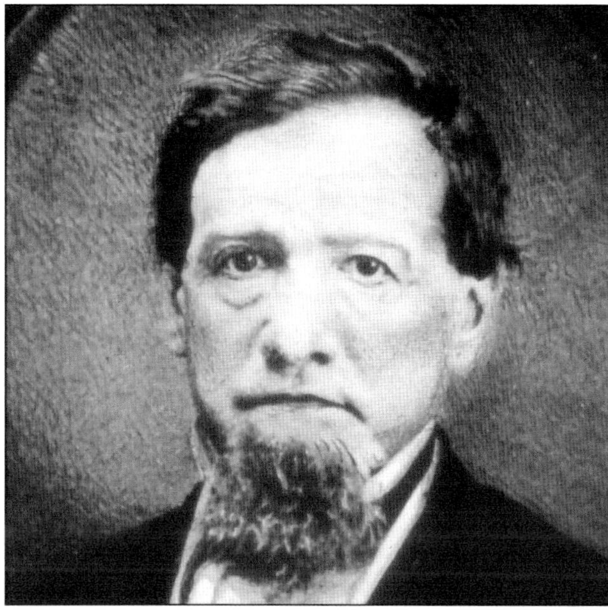

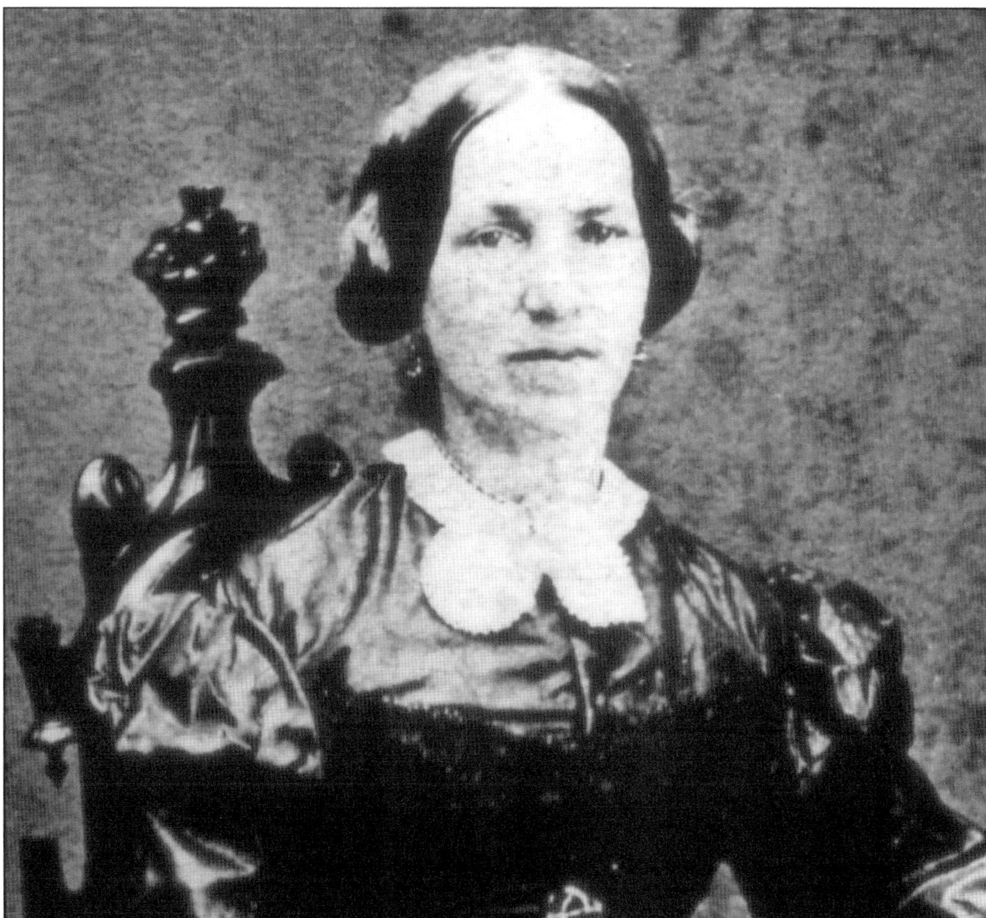

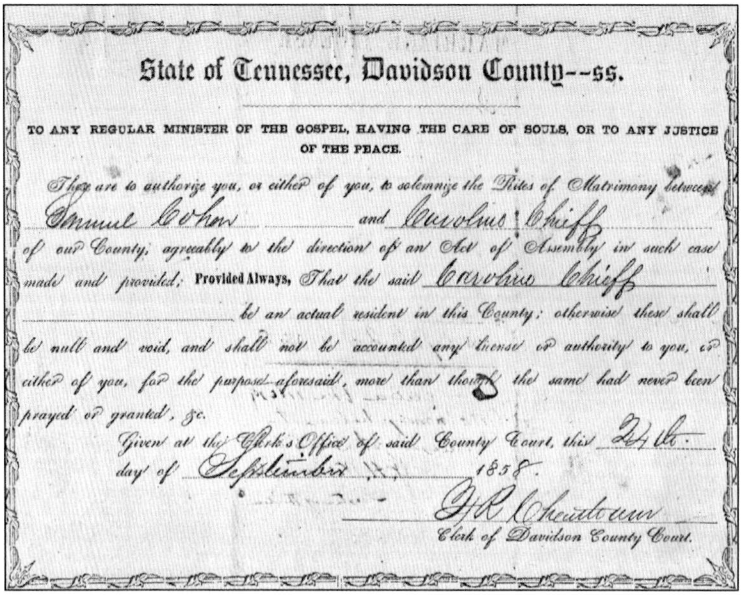

State of Tennessee, Davidson County--ss.

TO ANY REGULAR MINISTER OF THE GOSPEL, HAVING THE CARE OF SOULS, OR TO ANY JUSTICE OF THE PEACE.

These are to authorize you, or either of you, to solemnize the Rites of Matrimony between Samuel Cohen and Caroline Schiff of our County; agreeably to the direction of an Act of Assembly in such case made and provided; **Provided Always,** That the said Caroline Schiff be an actual resident in this County; otherwise these shall be null and void, and shall not be accounted any license or authority to you, or either of you, for the purpose aforesaid, more than though the same had never been prayed or granted, &c.

Given at the Clerk's Office of said County Court, this 24th day of September 1858.

[illegible]
Clerk of Davidson County Court.

Among the Jewish couples who got married in Nashville during the 1850s were Samuel Cohen and Caroline Schiff. All Jewish weddings had to be legalized by a justice of the peace until March 1879, when the Tennessee legislature authorized rabbis to legally unite two people in matrimony.

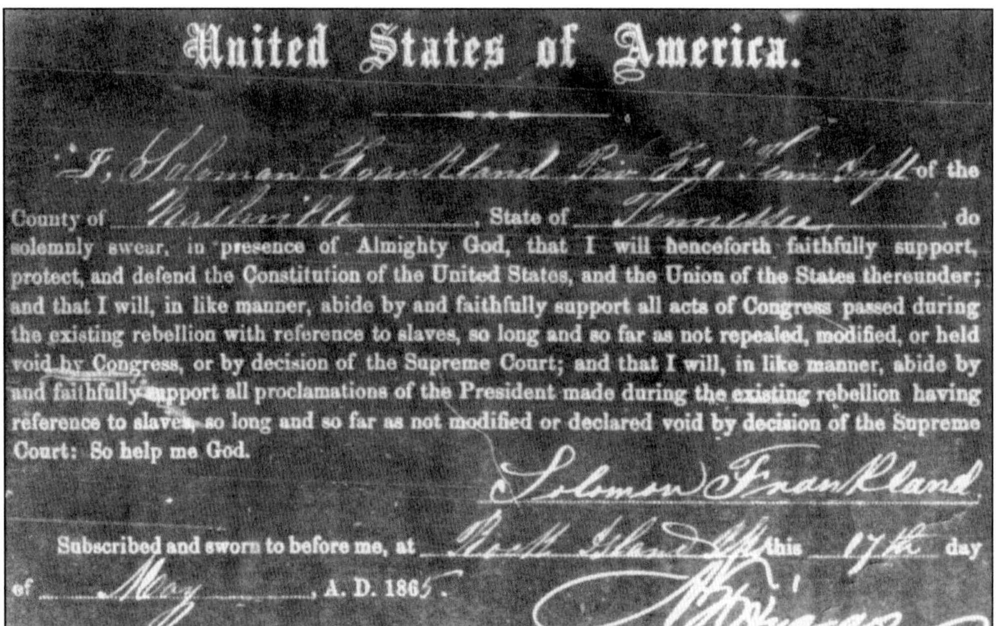

United States of America.

I, Solomon Frankland Pvt [illegible] of the County of Nashville, State of Tennessee, do solemnly swear, in presence of Almighty God, that I will henceforth faithfully support, protect, and defend the Constitution of the United States, and the Union of the States thereunder; and that I will, in like manner, abide by and faithfully support all acts of Congress passed during the existing rebellion with reference to slaves, so long and so far as not repealed, modified, or held void by Congress, or by decision of the Supreme Court; and that I will, in like manner, abide by and faithfully support all proclamations of the President made during the existing rebellion having reference to slaves, so long and so far as not modified or declared void by decision of the Supreme Court: So help me God.

Solomon Frankland

Subscribed and sworn to before me, at Rock Island Ill this 17th day of May, A. D. 1865.

[illegible]

Solomon Frankland came to Nashville from Prussia, starting as a peddler in Sumner County before opening a store in Cottontown, near Gallatin. When the Civil War began, he enlisted in the Confederate army and was captured by Union troops at Fort Donelson in 1862. Released seven months later, he was recaptured in 1863 at Missionary Ridge and was not released again until May 1865, after signing this loyalty oath. He was vice president of Vine Street Temple, and his wife, the former Henrietta Tugendrich, was an officer of the Ladies' Hebrew Working Society.

Two

Jewish Nashville's Religious Community

By 1850, Davidson County court records list approximately 160 Nashville families as being "of the Jewish faith." The first Jewish organization in Nashville was the Hebrew Benevolent Burial Association, also known as the Shield of David, which purchased 3.33 acres of land for a Jewish cemetery in 1851. The group was spearheaded by Isaac Garritsen (also Garritson), Jacob Mitchell, and Michael Powers, who paid $377.36 for the land near Buena Vista Pike, where Nashville's Jewish cemetery is still located today.

Nashville's first Jewish congregation had its unofficial beginnings in 1848, when Garritsen, Henry Harris, S. Marks, E. Wolfe, Henry Jessel, Abraham and Judah Frankland, Louis Hanf, Michael Powers, Jacob Mitchell, Sinai Nathan, Abraham Schwab, and Julius Ochs gathered for a minyan at Garritsen's home on Summer Street. For this and other reasons, Garritsen is considered by many to be the father of Nashville's early Jewish community. He was so highly though of that when his wife died in 1856 and a question arose about burying her in the Jewish cemetery (she had not been born Jewish but converted), a visiting rabbi was brought in as mediator. The rabbi ruled she could be given a Jewish burial because she had lived her life as a "faithful Jew" and died with the Shema on her lips. Isaac died eight years later, in 1864.

Nashville's first "official" house of worship came in 1853 with the creation of Congregation Mogen David. It was given its state charter one year later and had about 30 members. It hired its first rabbi, Alexander Iser, who moved to Nashville from New York, and paid him $600 a year. In 1854, the congregation changed its name to Khal Kodesh Mogen David. Over the next six years, members disagreed with one another on a variety of issues, and in 1860, Rabbi Iser established a second congregation, leaving Khal Kodesh Mogen David to begin Ohava Emes. That synagogue functioned for seven years, through the Civil War and Reconstruction, before the two congregations reunited in 1867, becoming Ohavai Sholom. In 1864, Nashville got its third Jewish congregation, with B'nai Yeshurun introducing Reform Judaism. Its first rabbi was Reverend Labshiner, who was there from 1864 to 1865. He was succeeded by David Burgheim, who led the congregation until 1869, when he left to join Ohavai Sholom. Replacing him was Rabbi Judah Wechsler, who remained until leaving for Atlanta in 1872. Rabbi Iser resigned to go into business. B'nai Yeshurun disbanded in 1876, after the Vine Street Temple was created. Vine Street was led in its early years by a series of lay leaders and visiting rabbis.

By the end of Reconstruction, there were three congregations serving the Jewish community's spiritual needs, and it would remain that way until 1992 and the creation of Congregation Micah (Reform). A fifth congregation, the Orthodox Congregation Beit Tefilah, based on the ideology of Chabad, was established in 2001.

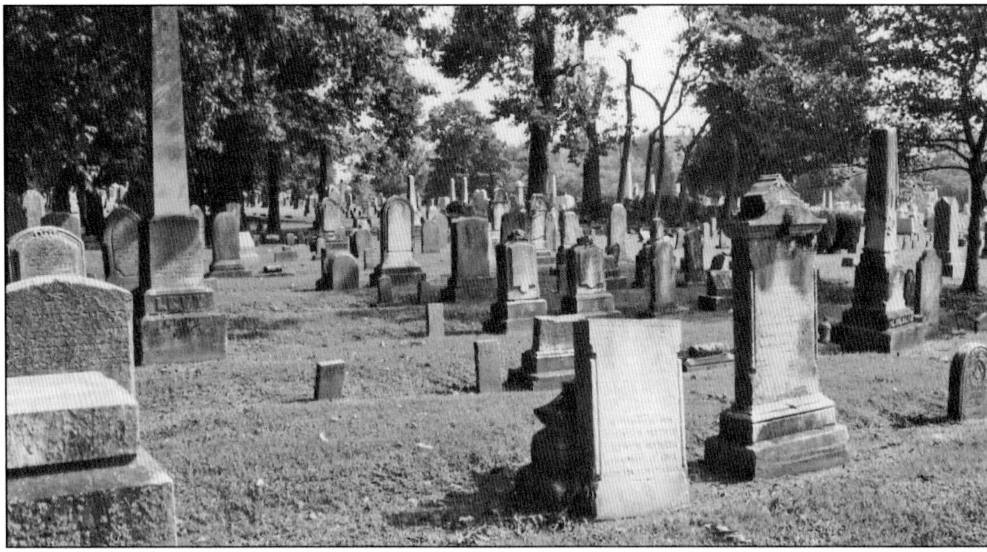

Nashville's Jewish cemetery has existed for more than 150 years in the same location, on Eighteenth Avenue North between Clay and Cass Streets. Created in 1851, when the Hebrew Benevolent Burial Society purchased slightly less than 4 acres of land, the cemetery serves five of Nashville's six Jewish congregations (Micah has its own cemetery adjacent to its facility on Old Hickory Boulevard in the Forest Hills area). The Temple cemetery, the oldest section, is on the National Register of Historic Places.

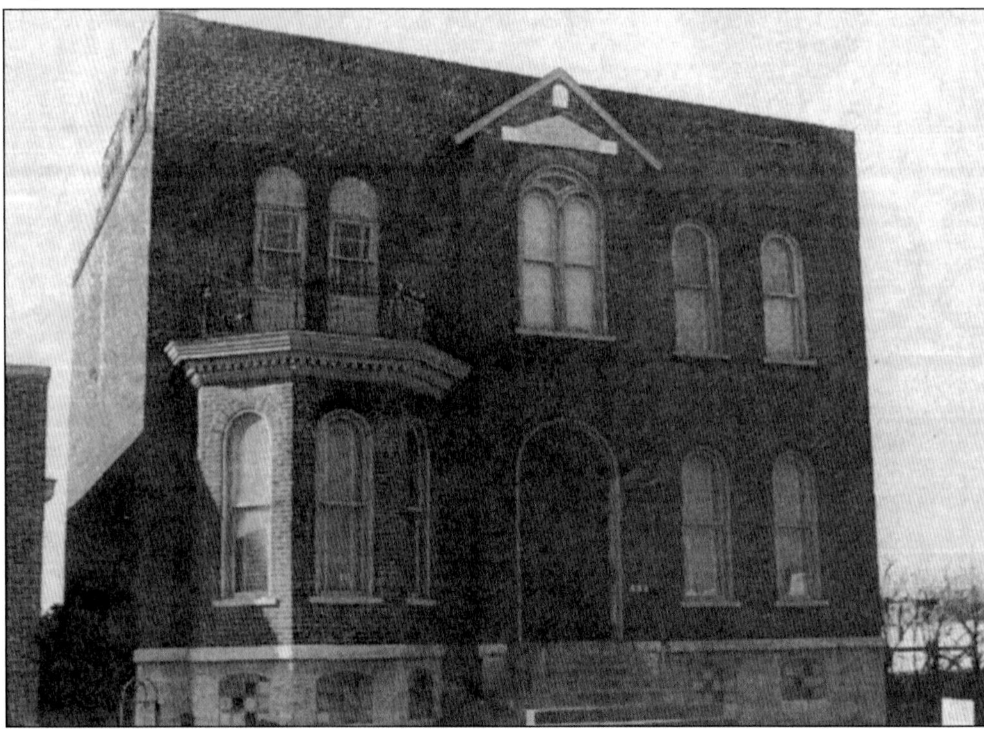

Isaac Garritsen built his home in 1859, and owners included David and Mark Elsbach, Rabbi Alexander Iser, and Jacob Bloomstein. In 1927, it was sold to the Nashville chapter of the Workmen's Circle, a Jewish fraternal and civic organization. The home still stands today.

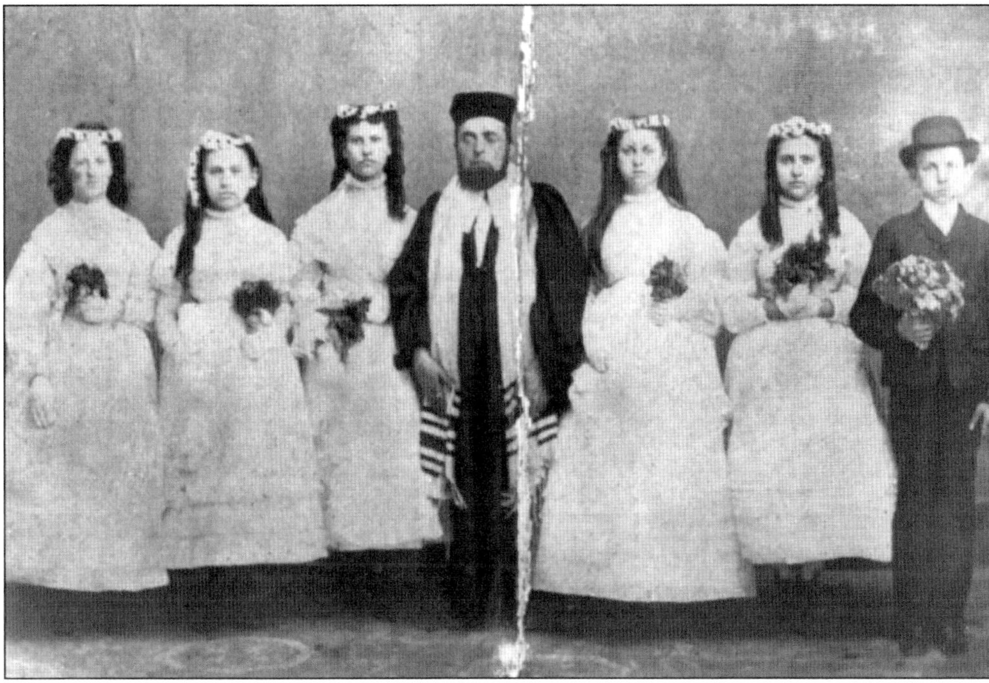

Confirmation concludes a Jewish student's religious study at a synagogue or temple's Sunday school and Hebrew school, usually at the end of 10th grade. Nashville's first confirmation was held in 1869 at B'nai Yeshurun. The confirmands, from left to right, are Hannah Spitz, Emma Feldman, Hattie Shyer, Bella Spitz, Hettie Shyer, and Sam Weil. Rabbi Judah Weschler is pictured in the center.

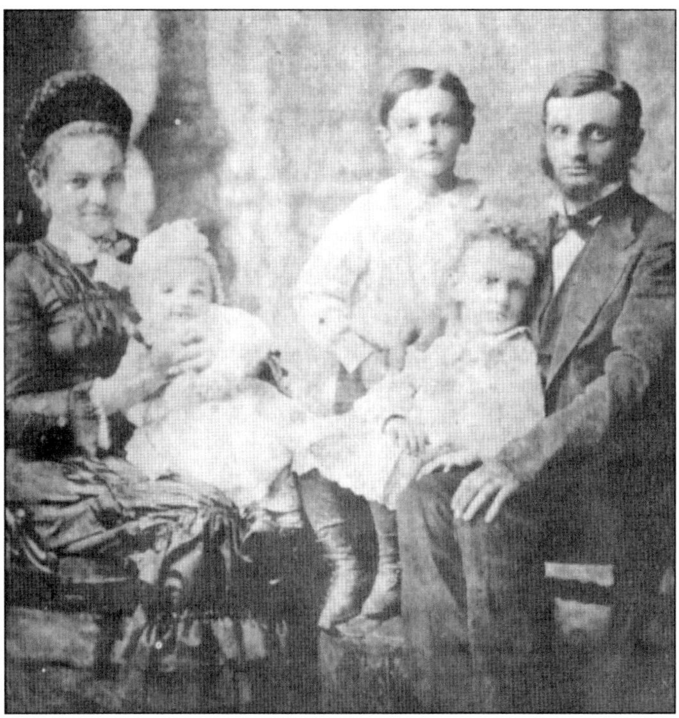

Rabbi Herman Saltzman, a native of Hungary (here with his wife and three children), was the leader of Sherith Israel from the 1890s until his death in 1928. Before that, he was assistant rabbi at Vine Street Temple and then with Congregation Adath Israel. His moves were a response to the evolving views of the congregations away traditional (Orthodox) to more modern (Reform, Conservative) Jewish customs. While serving as rabbi at Sherith Israel, Saltzman never accepted a salary, earning his living by operating a kosher butcher shop in the Market House.

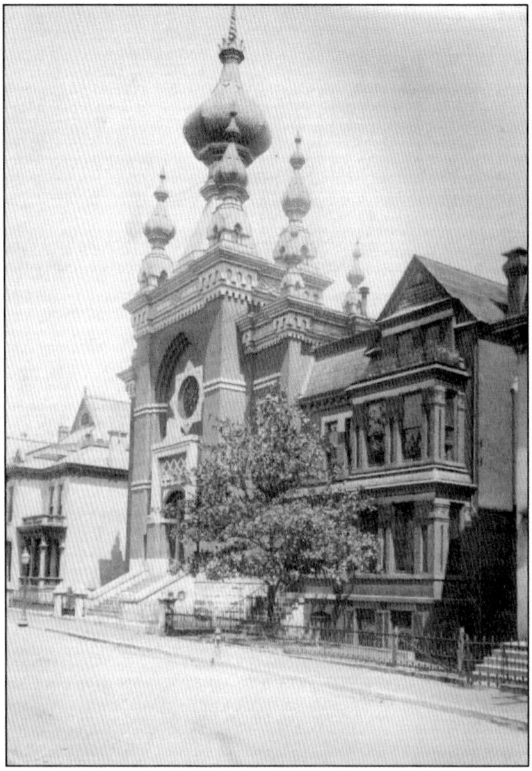

Vine Street Temple was dedicated in 1876, and its first rabbi was Isadore Kalisch. Featuring ornate domes and spires, it served the congregation for 75 years.

Isadore Lewinthal was rabbi at Vine Street Temple from 1888 until 1922. During his 34-year tenure, one of the longest with any congregation in Nashville, membership at Vine Street Temple increased from 125 to more than 200 families. Lewinthal worked tirelessly for social justice and equality for the less fortunate of society. Born near Frankfort, Germany, in 1849, the son of a rabbi, he immigrated to the United States in 1870, going to New Orleans, Mississippi, Baton Rouge, and San Antonio before coming to Nashville in 1888. Invited in 1915 to speak to the Fisk Jubilee Chorus at the Ryman Auditorium, he did exactly that, turning his back to the 5,000 people in the audience and addressing members of the chorus in such hushed tones that only they could hear him. His words remain a secret to this day.

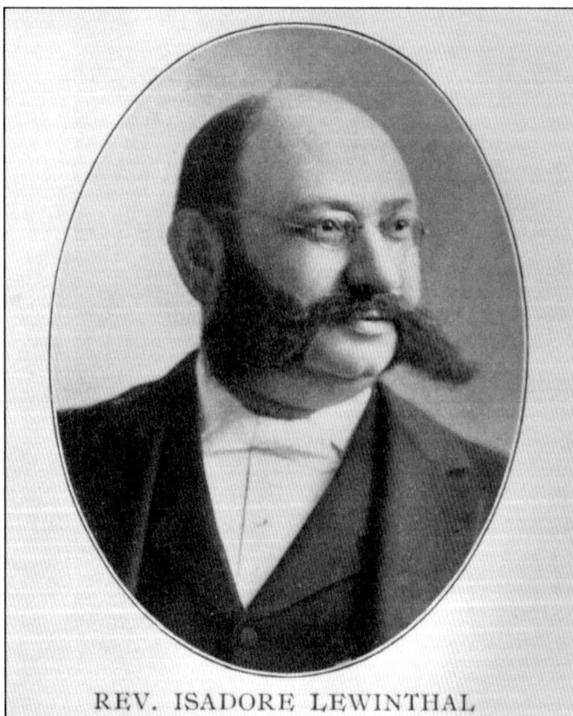

REV. ISADORE LEWINTHAL
Rabbi Vine Street Temple
Nashville

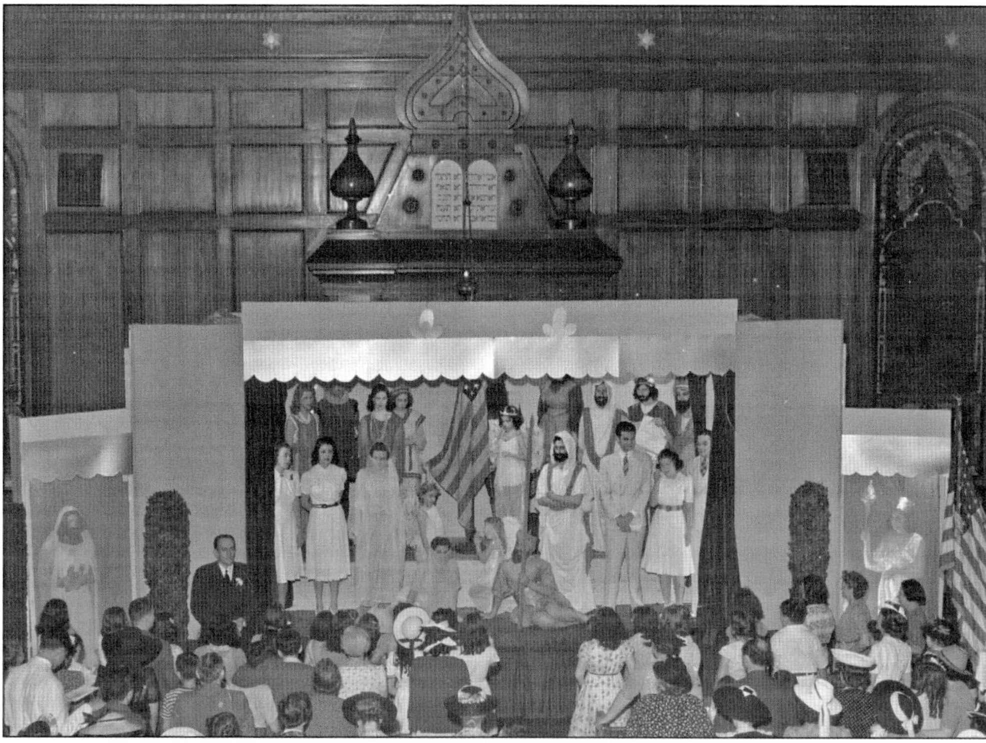

In the mid-1930s, these members of Vine Street Temple played the parts of Queen Esther, King Ahashuerus, Mordecai, and Haman in a traditional Purim play.

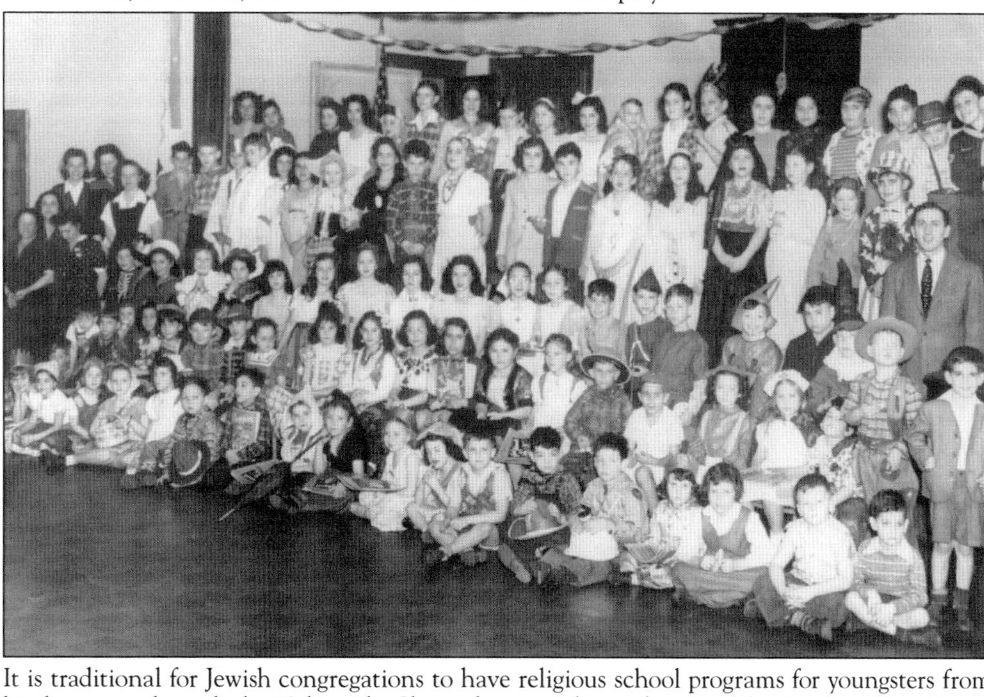

It is traditional for Jewish congregations to have religious school programs for youngsters from kindergarten through the 10th grade. Shown here are the students and faculty from Vine Street Temple in 1946.

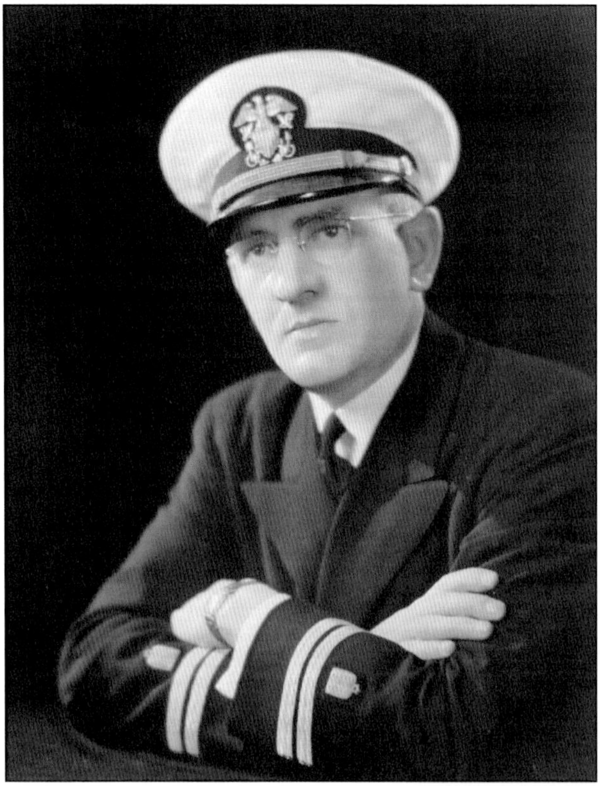

Julius Mark became rabbi at Vine Street Temple in 1926, succeeding Richard Stern, who had been in that position for just three years following Rabbi Lewinthal's death in 1922. Mark served as the congregation's leader for 22 years, taking a leave of absence from 1942 to 1945 to serve on the staff of Adm. Chester Nimitz as Jewish naval chaplain for the Pacific Fleet.

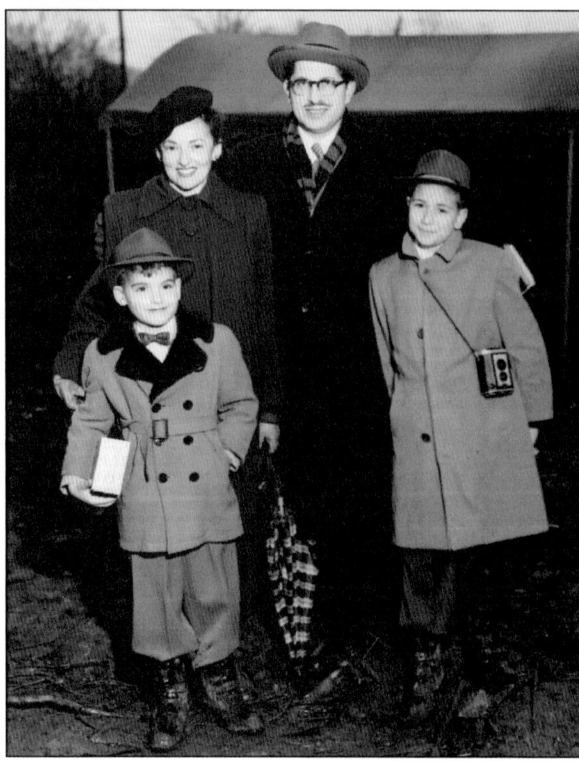

Rabbi William Silverman was hired at Vine Street Temple in 1950 and led the congregation when it moved from downtown Nashville to 5015 Harding Road in 1955. He left in 1960 and was replaced by Rabbi Randall Falk. Silverman is shown here with his wife, Pearl, and sons Eldon (left) and Joel (right).

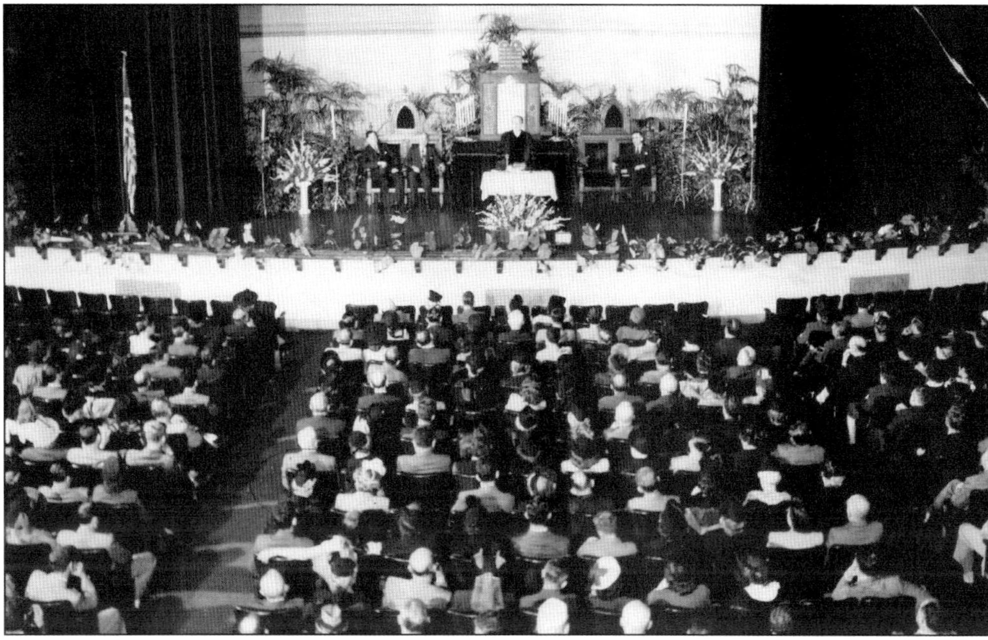

In the mid-1950s, after Vine Street Temple had grown too large for its downtown building but before it could move to its new facility on Harding Road, the congregation held High Holy Day services at the War Memorial Auditorium.

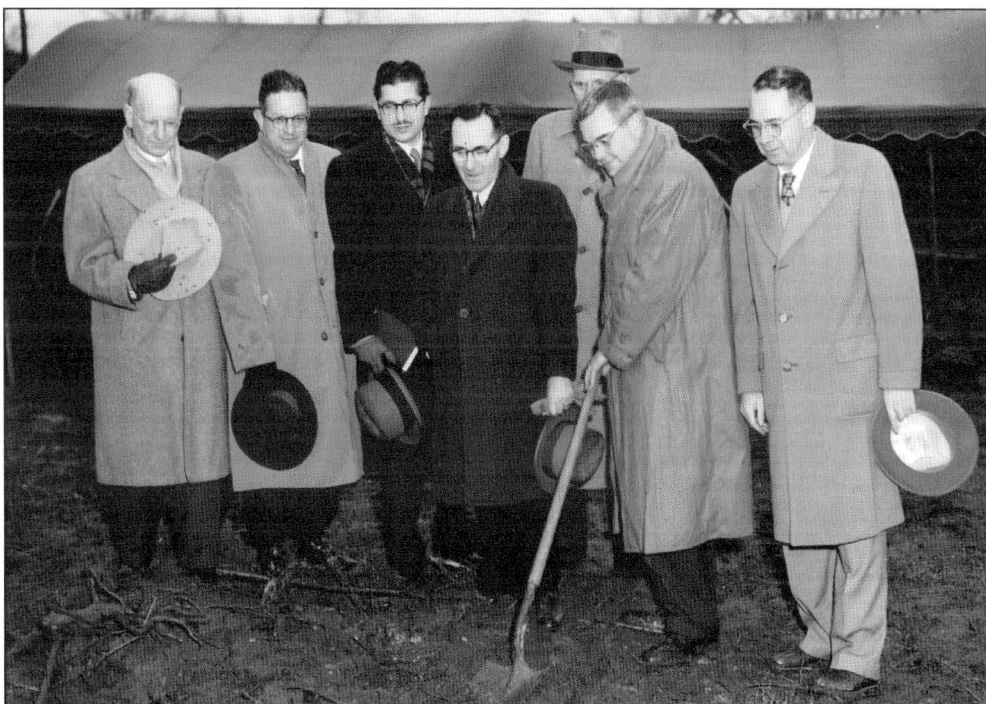

Once the temple membership decided they needed a new, larger building, plans were made for the move west. Here members of the temple board and Rabbi William Silverman (third from left) take part in the official ground-breaking ceremony in 1954.

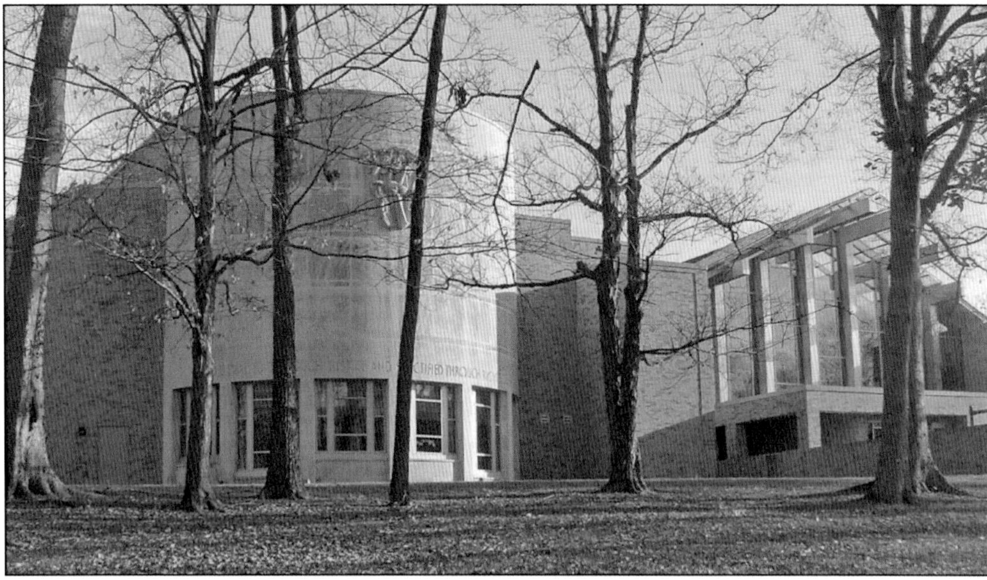

With the move from downtown, Vine Street Temple became simply The Temple, and Ohabai Sholom, Nashville's largest congregation, now had the largest building to call home.

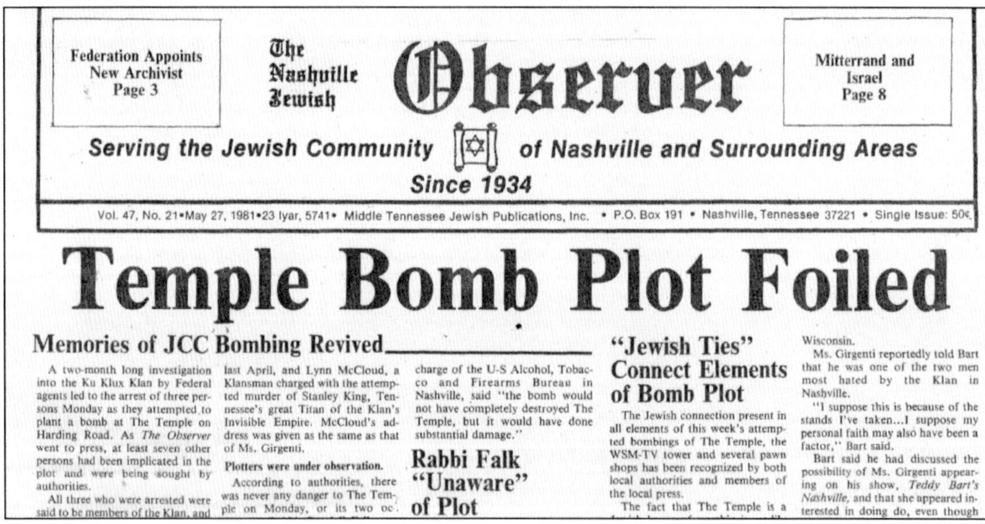

Federation Appoints New Archivist Page 3

The Nashville Jewish Observer

Mitterrand and Israel Page 8

Serving the Jewish Community of Nashville and Surrounding Areas Since 1934

Vol. 47, No. 21•May 27, 1981•23 Iyar, 5741• Middle Tennessee Jewish Publications, Inc. • P.O. Box 191 • Nashville, Tennessee 37221 • Single Issue: 50¢

Temple Bomb Plot Foiled

Memories of JCC Bombing Revived

A two-month long investigation into the Ku Klux Klan by Federal agents led to the arrest of three persons Monday as they attempted to plant a bomb at The Temple on Harding Road. As *The Observer* went to press, at least seven other persons had been implicated in the plot and were being sought by authorities.

All three who were arrested were said to be members of the Klan, and last April, and Lynn McCloud, a Klansman charged with the attempted murder of Stanley King, Tennessee's great Titan of the Klan's Invisible Empire. McCloud's address was given as the same as that of Ms. Girgenti.

Plotters were under observation.

According to authorities, there was never any danger to The Temple on Monday, or its two oc- charge of the U-S Alcohol, Tobacco and Firearms Bureau in Nashville, said "the bomb would not have completely destroyed The Temple, but it would have done substantial damage."

Rabbi Falk "Unaware" of Plot

"Jewish Ties" Connect Elements of Bomb Plot

The Jewish connection present in all elements of this week's attempted bombings of The Temple, the WSM-TV tower and several pawn shops has been recognized by both local authorities and members of the local press.

The fact that The Temple is a

Wisconsin.

Ms. Girgenti reportedly told Bart that he was one of the two men most hated by the Klan in Nashville.

"I suppose this is because of the stands I've taken...I suppose my personal faith may also have been a factor," Bart said.

Bart said he had discussed the possibility of Ms. Girgenti appearing on his show, *Teddy Bart's Nashville*, and that she appeared interested in doing do, even though

On May 25, 1981, an attempted bombing of The Temple was thwarted by the U.S. Alcohol, Tobacco, and Firearms Bureau office in Nashville. Rabbi Randall Falk was preparing to leave for the day when three members of a splinter group of the Ku Klux Klan were arrested as they drove into The Temple parking lot. Teddy Bart, a radio and television personality who is Jewish, remembers his involvement: "In April of 1981, I got a phone call from Gladys Girgenti, the adult leader of the Klan youth group, suggesting we meet at WSM so she could tell me what she does and why. [She] arrived . . . [and] I escorted her . . . down the long hall . . . around the corner to my . . . office. The meeting was brief, but, as future events would unfold, [for her] it was an intelligence gathering mini-tour of . . . WSM radio and television. On the evening of May 25th . . . John Seigenthaler, editor and publisher of the *Nashville Tennessean* . . . [called and] told me that the Nashville police had just arrested three people on the grounds of The Temple. Included was Gladys Girgenti. They had been charged in a plot to blow up WSM-TV [where I worked] and The Temple, where I worshiped."

Rabbi Randall Falk, who succeeded William Silverman in 1960, became actively involved in the fight for civil rights shortly after arriving in Nashville. He spent countless hours working with local civil rights leaders preparing young black students for the reception they would get when they began their downtown Nashville lunch counter sit-ins. He later was a founding member and chairman of the Metro Human Relations Commission.

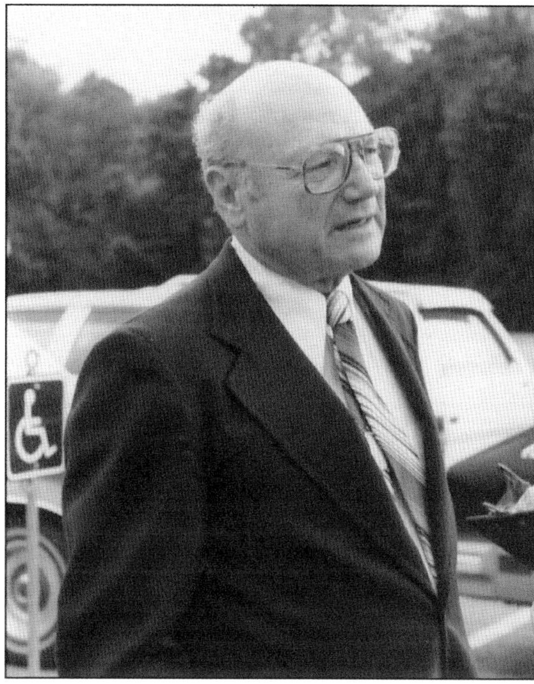

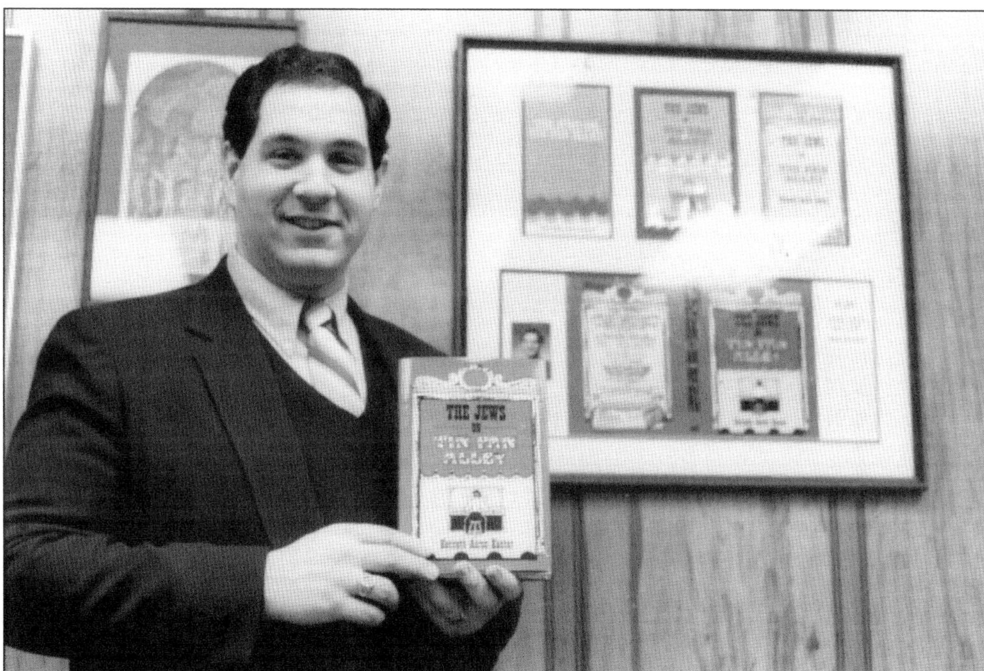

Ken Kanter, during his years in Nashville, served two different congregations as rabbi. His first job was as assistant rabbi with The Temple. He left Nashville to become rabbi at Congregation Mizpah in Chattanooga, but when a group of dissenting members decided to break away from The Temple and start a new Reform congregation in 1992, they asked Kanter to return as Congregation Micah's first rabbi. He is shown here with his first book, *The Jews of Tin Pan Alley*, which was published in 1982.

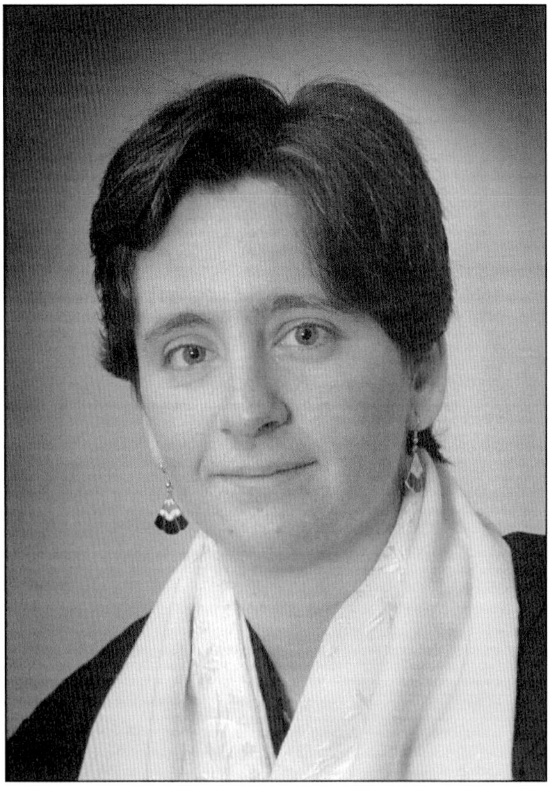

Beth Davidson became Nashville's first woman rabbi when she was hired as assistant rabbi by The Temple in 1987. She remained there for six years, leaving to become rabbi of a congregation in Port Washington, New York. She is currently rabbi at Temple Adath Yeshurun in Manchester, New Hampshire. (Courtesy of Beth Davidson.)

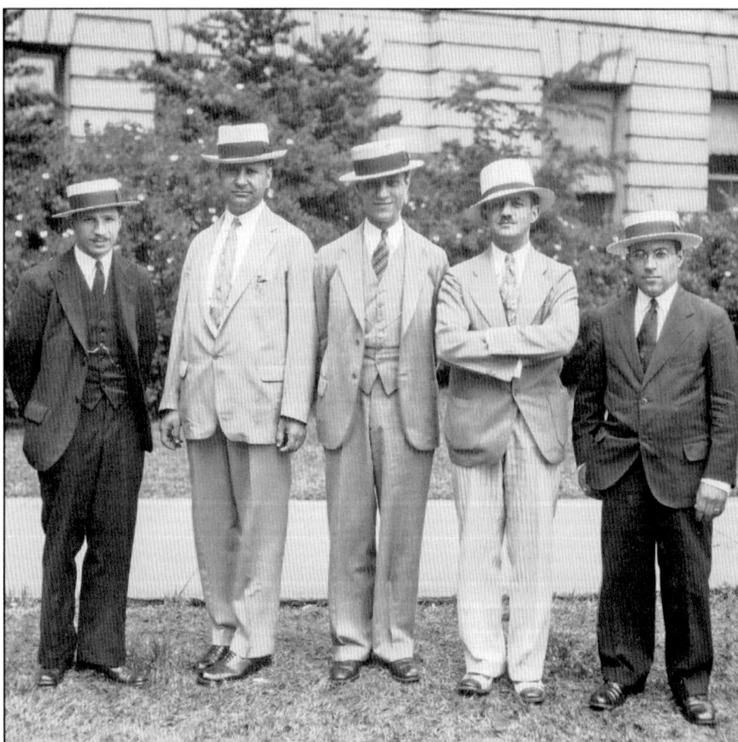

In 1929, five rabbis were invited to address the Tennessee legislature, then considering a bill to regulate the sale of kosher meat and kosher food and to define the word "kosher." Accepting the invitation were, from left to right, unidentified, Rabbi Stempfel (Memphis), Rabbi Rosen (Charleston), Rabbi Weisfeld (Savannah), and Rabbi Nisan Haifetz (Nashville's Gay Street Synagogue).

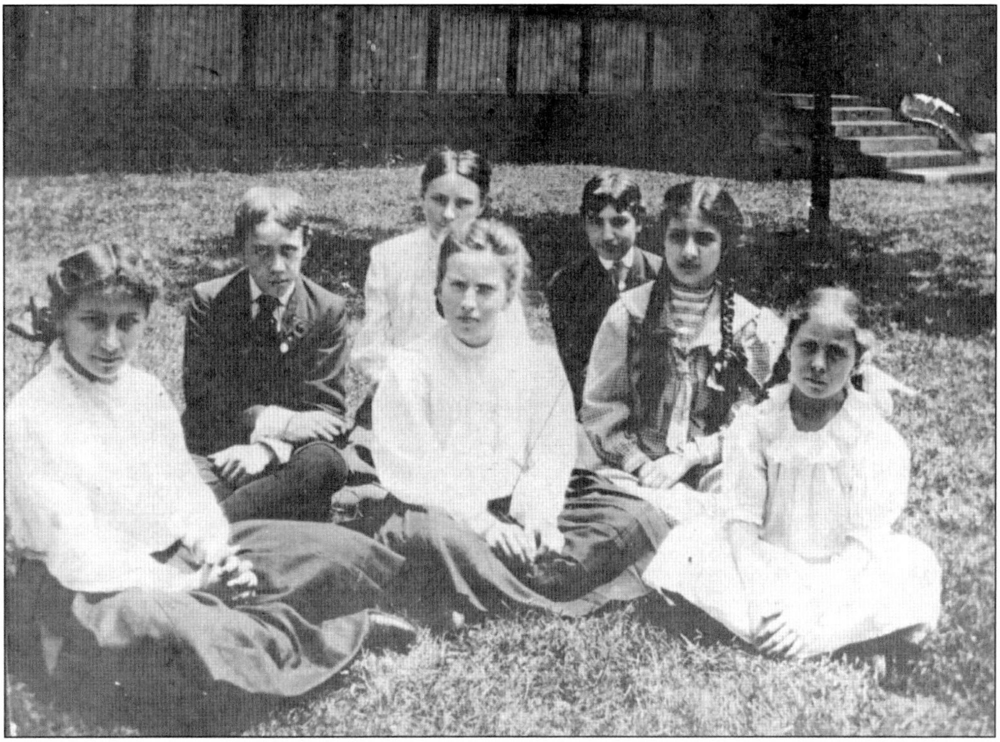

These are the Gay Street Synagogue confirmation classes of 1910 (above) and 1916 (below).

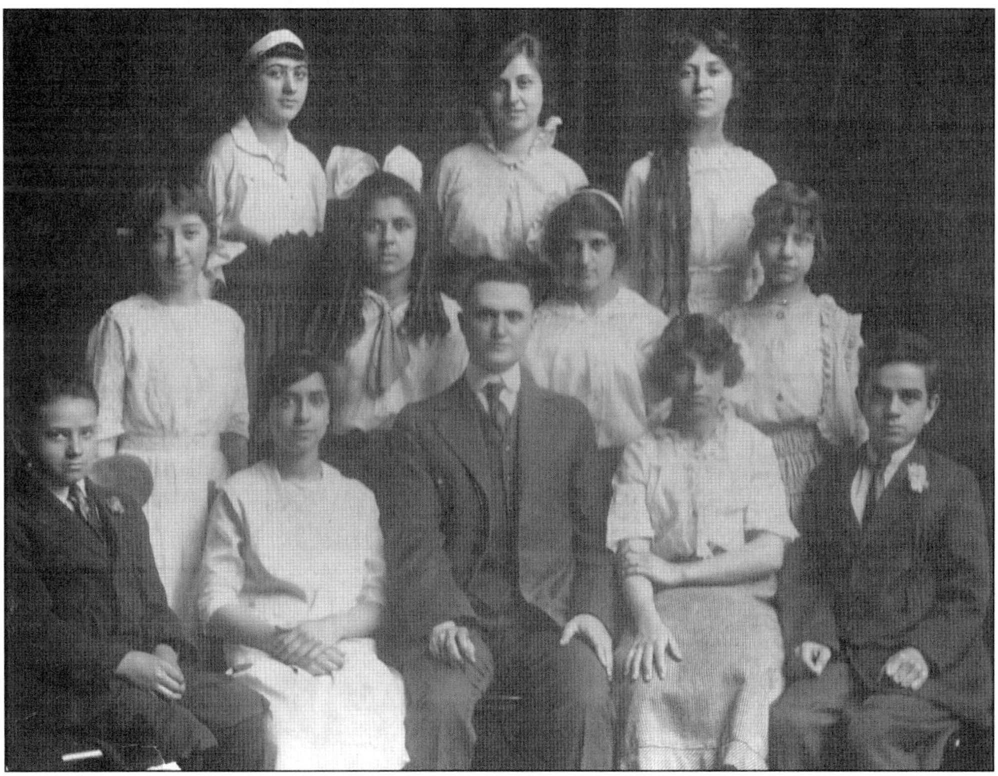

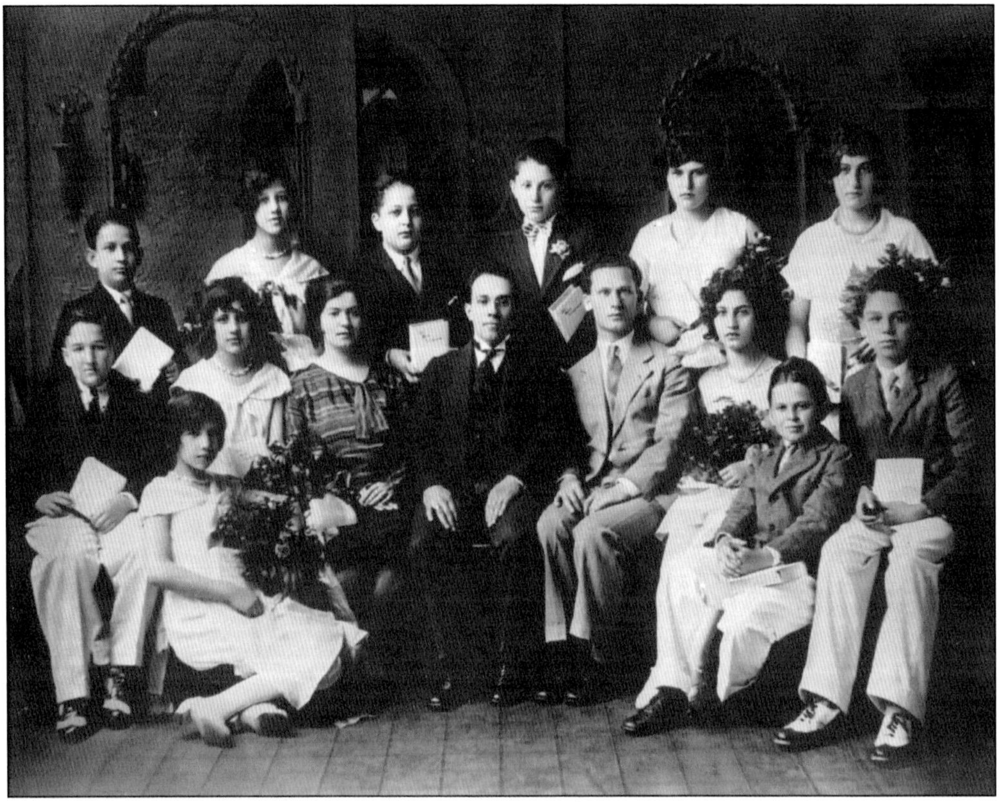

In this photograph of the confirmation class of 1928 at the Gay Street Synagogue, it is interesting to note the increasing size of the groups from 1910 to 1916 to 1928, reflecting the growth of the Nashville's Jewish community and Conservative Judaism here.

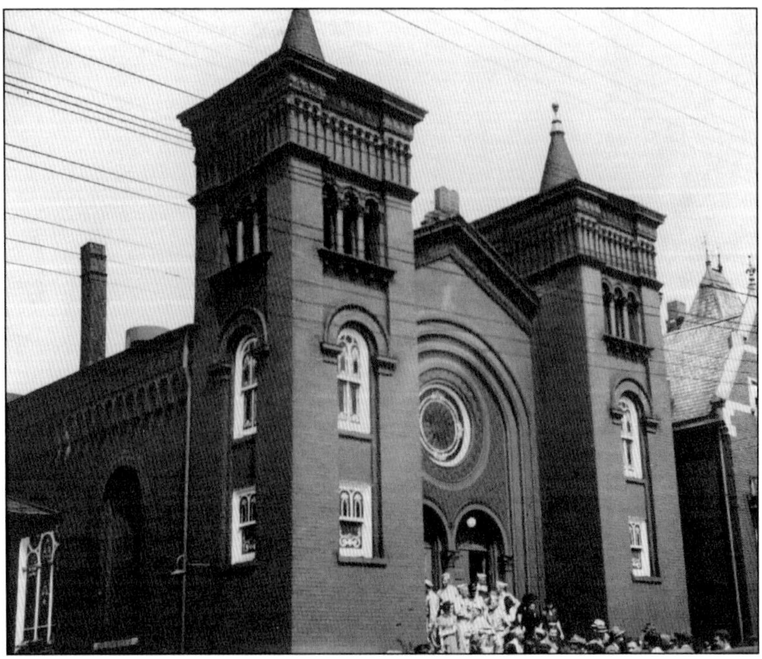

The Gay Street Synagogue, which became the official name for the Khal Kodesh Adath Israel (KKAI) congregation after it moved to that location, remained the center of Conservative Judaism in Nashville until shortly after World War II. Here young soldiers socialize with others attending services in 1942.

This is the bimah and ark, with its Torahs, at the Gay Street Synagogue in the 1940s. As in most shuls of that era, the extensive use of wood and ornate scrolls and carvings provided warmth and comfort for worshipers.

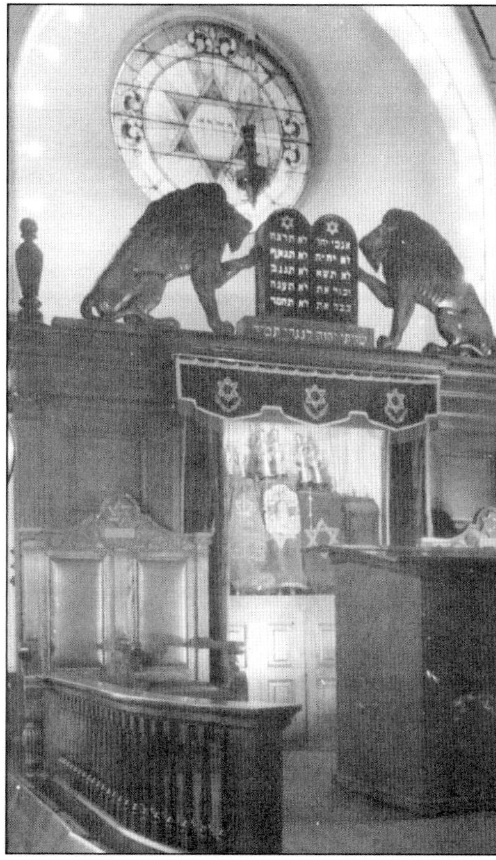

In 1947, facing urban renewal, KKAI purchased an older home at 3810 West End Avenue and moved into it while a new, modern building on an adjoining lot was under construction. In February 1951, the new facility at 3814 West End Avenue was dedicated, and the congregation was renamed West End Synagogue. For several years after moving into its new facility, the congregation used the old home for Sunday school classes, but it was eventually demolished when an addition was made to the new building.

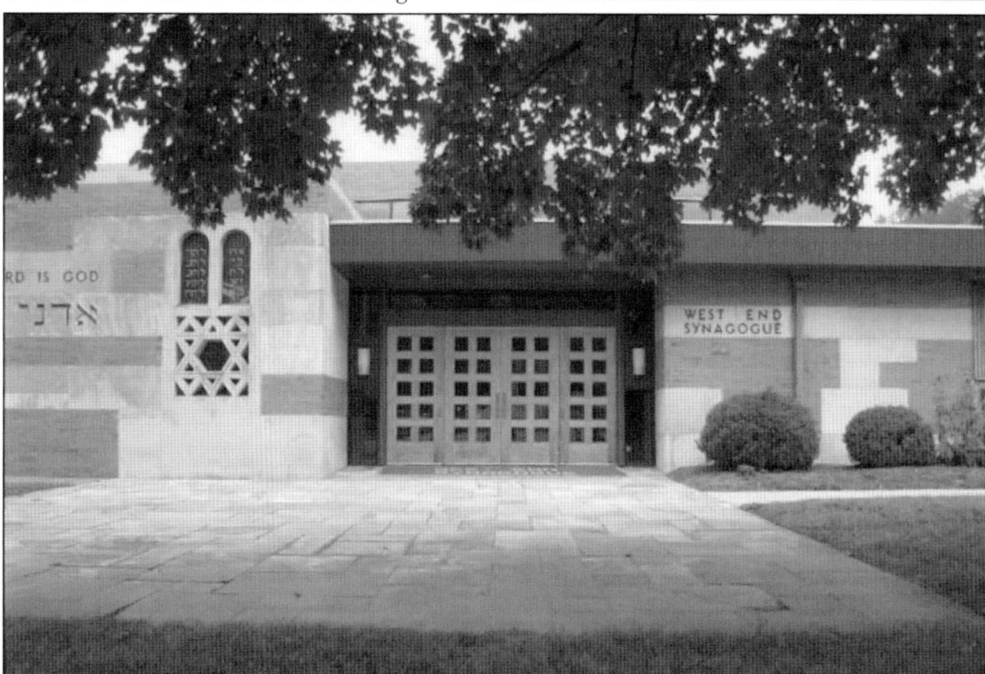

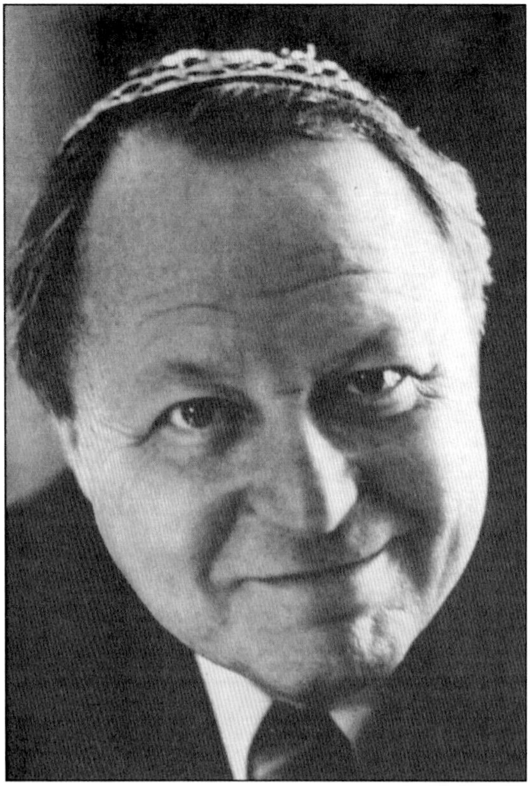

Arthur Hertzberg was rabbi at the West End Synagogue from 1947 to 1955 (with a leave of absence from 1951 to 1953, when he served as an Air Force chaplain). From Nashville he went to Englewood, New Jersey, where he remained until his retirement in 1986. In addition to writing numerous articles and editorial pieces for *Commentary* and *Atlantic Monthly* magazines, he participated in the 1963 March on Washington with Rev. Martin Luther King Jr. According to a biographer, Hertzberg "played a major role in some of the most significant issues the world Jewish community faced in the decades following World War II . . . including Hertzberg's call for the creation of a Palestinian state following the 1967 Six Day War." He died in 2006 at the age of 85.

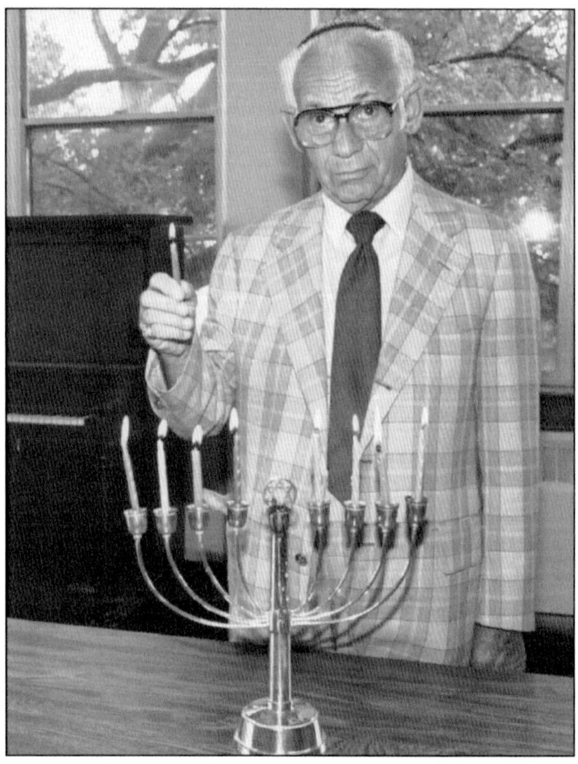

Bernard Glusman, cantor at the West End Synagogue from 1946 to 1979, was born in 1906 in Zurich, Switzerland. His first job as a cantor was in Giessen, Germany, in 1931. Six years later, amidst the turmoil in Europe, he and his wife, Anna, immigrated to the United States. He and Anna were the parents of two sons, Fred and Marvin, and a nephew, Robby Starkand, whom they reared as a son. Glusman died in 2000 at the age of 94.

The beginnings of today's Orthodox congregation in Nashville began with a request from the Hungarian Benevolent Society for a state charter in 1871. After meeting in rented halls for more than 15 years, the society joined forces with the Knights of Joseph, giving it a place to worship. In 1905, Sherith Israel (Remnants of Israel) was born when a private residence at 116 Fifth Avenue North was purchased, remodeled, and converted into a synagogue. In 1920, the home was demolished and a new structure built adjacent to the Ryman Auditorium, home of the *Grand Ole Opry*.

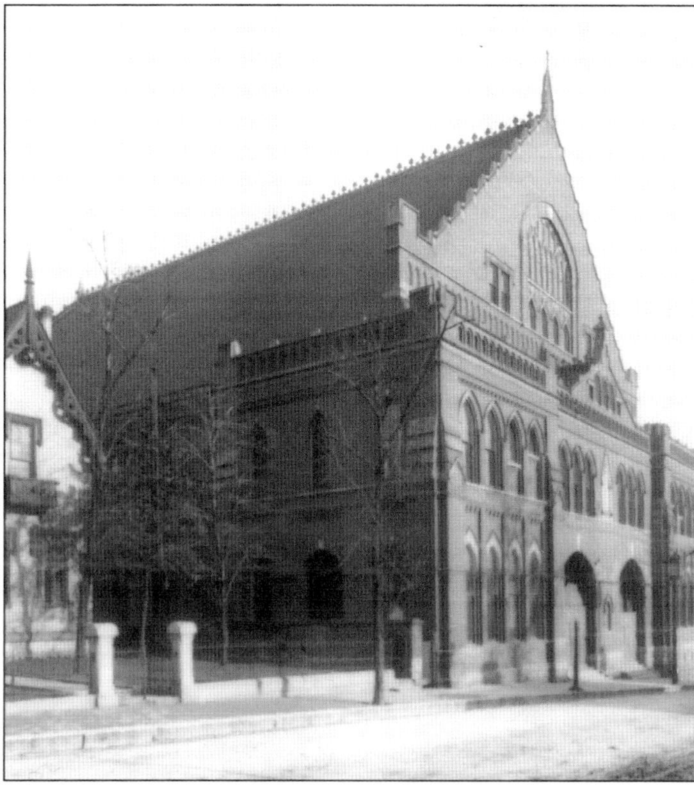

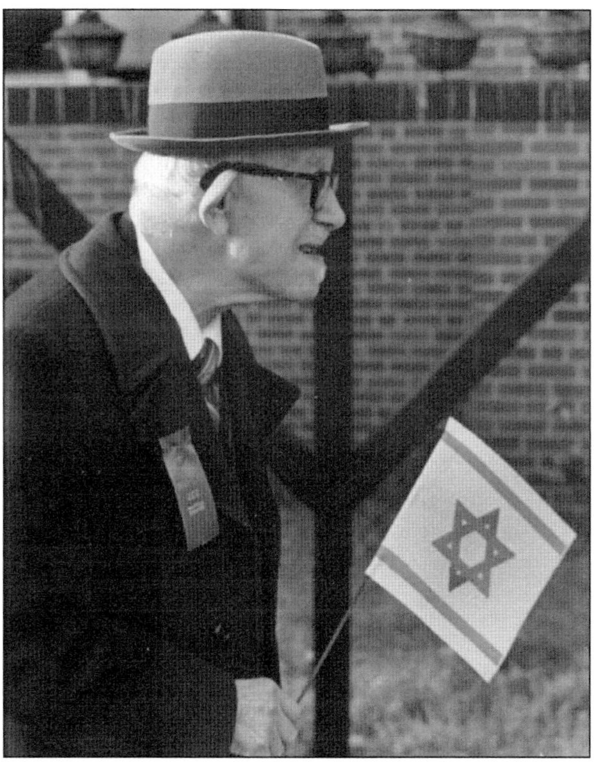

Rev. Aaron Abramson served longer in one position for a Jewish congregation in Nashville than anyone else. After moving here from Lithuania in 1913, he opened a watchmaking and jewelry store but became frustrated when he realized his customers expected him to be open on Shabbos. In 1918, he became cantor at Sherith Israel, and he remained there for the next 65 years until his death in 1983.

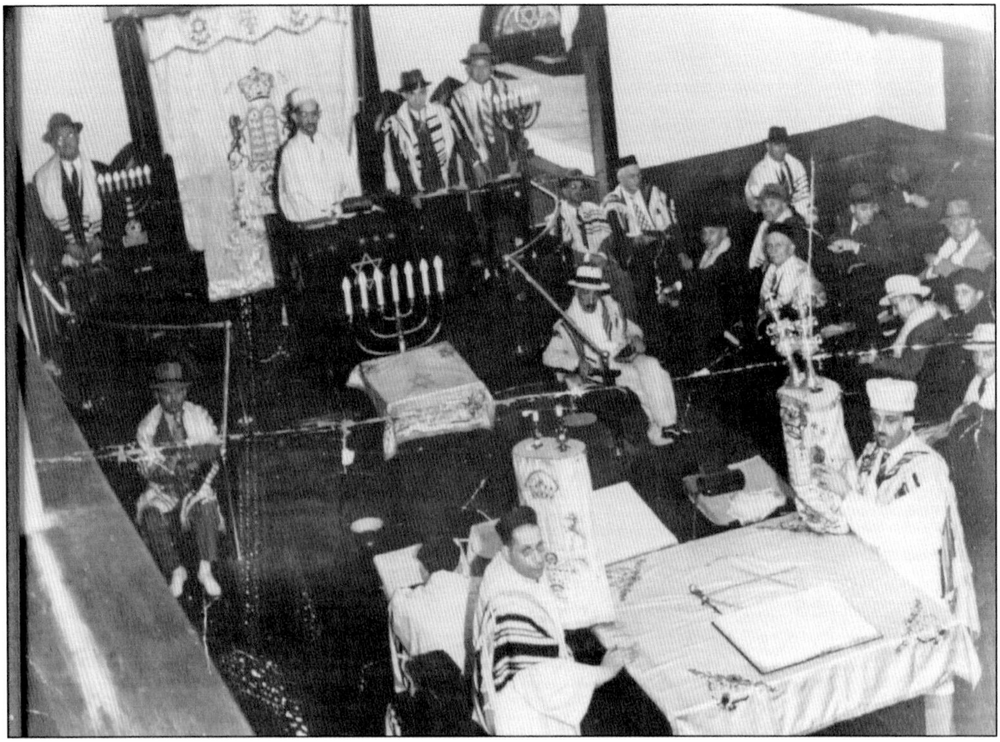

Isaac Yellin was rabbi and Reverend Abramson cantor at the Fifth Avenue Synagogue during these services in 1934.

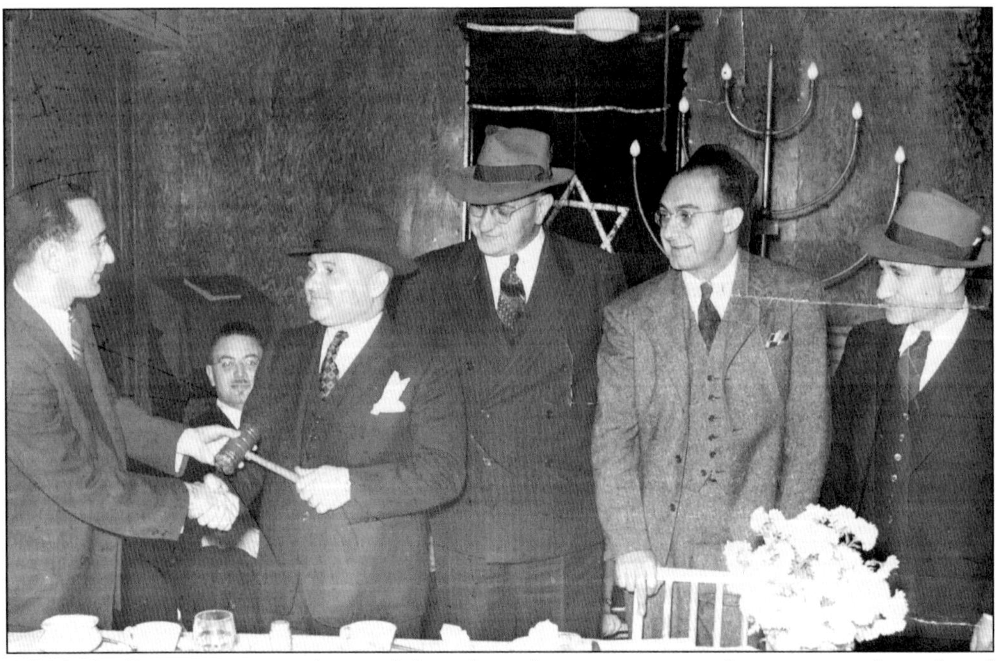

All Nashville congregations have adult and youth groups to provide a variety of social and cultural activities for their members. This photograph shows the men's club from the Fifth Avenue Synagogue in 1939.

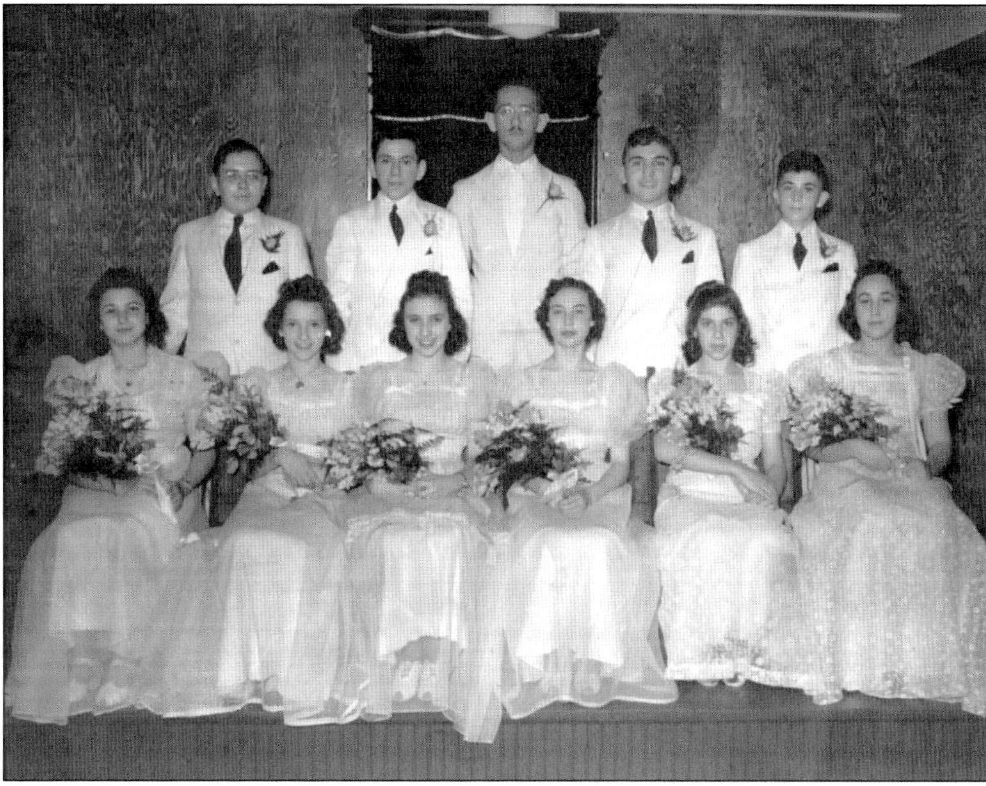

All three Nashville congregations had confirmation classes in 1938. Shown here are the students enrolled in the educational program at the Fifth Avenue Synagogue who were completing their religious education that year.

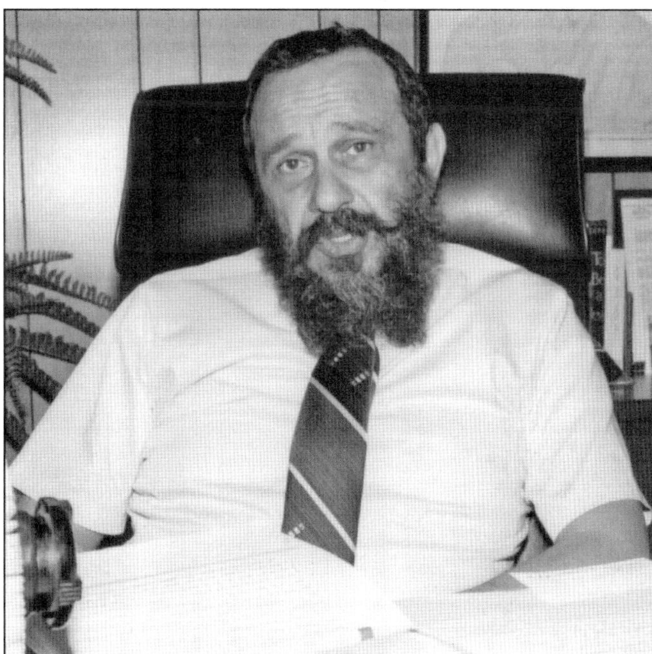

For 53 years, Rabbi Zalman Posner's name was synonymous with Orthodox Judaism in Nashville. He first became rabbi there in 1949, and—except for a one-year period from 1958 to 1959—continued to lead the congregation until his retirement in 2002. An important Hasidic scholar, Rabbi Posner has been widely recognized for his many contributions to Jewish thought and is credited with being the driving force behind the creation in 1954 of Nashville's Akiva School. His wife, Rita, was a kindergarten teacher at the Akiva School for many years.

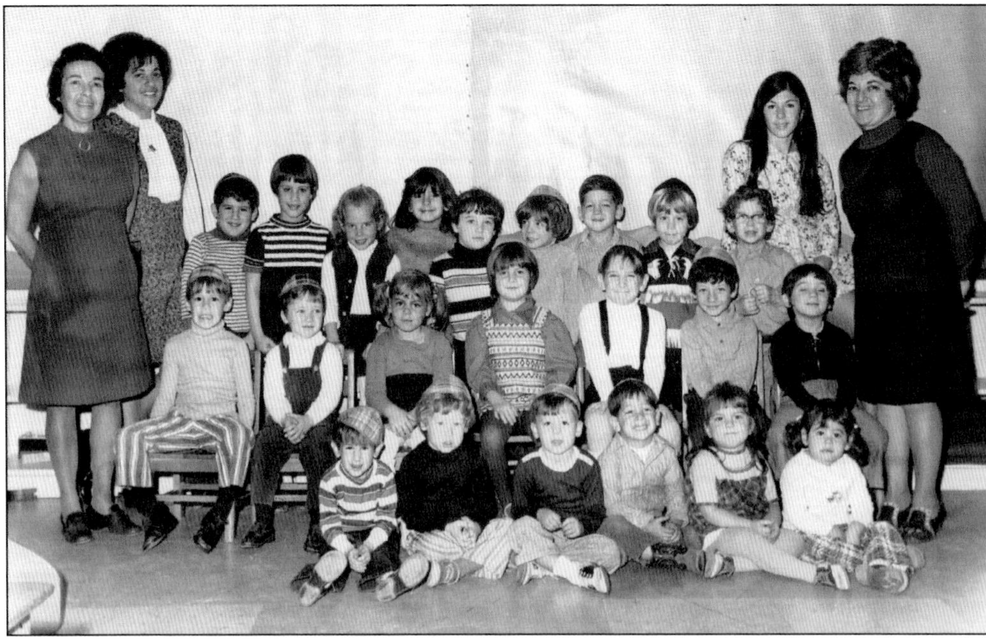

Akiva School was founded in 1954 as a small traditional day school affiliated with Sherith Israel. In 1999, Akiva moved to a new facility adjacent to the Gordon Jewish Community Center on Percy Warner Boulevard. In the 1990s, the board of directors decided to integrate general academic and Judaic studies programs, making Akiva an academic institution competitive with Nashville's other high-level private grade schools.

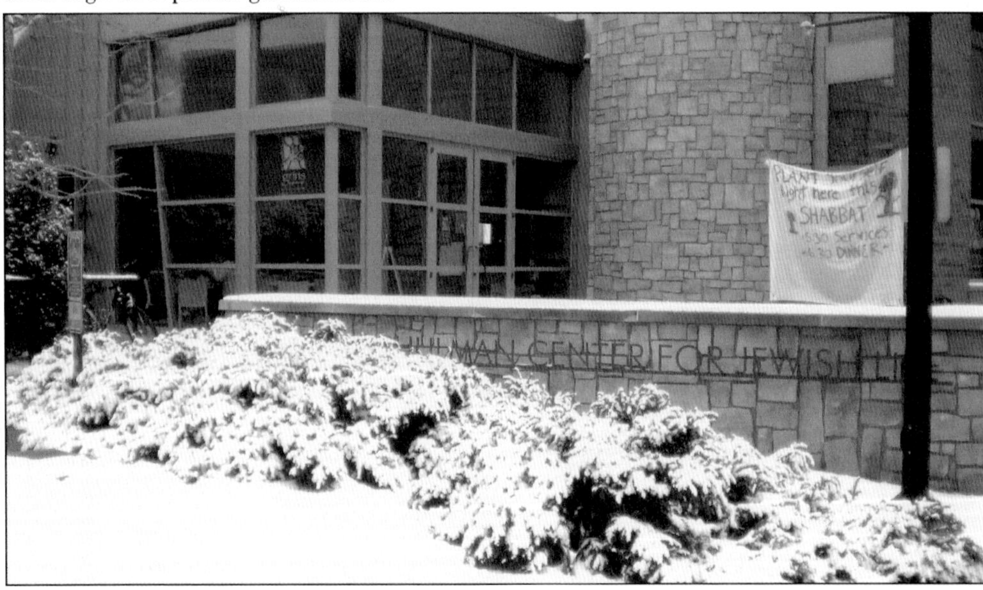

There has been a Jewish presence on the Vanderbilt University campus for more than 100 years. A Hillel group was officially organized in 1963, and there were already two Jewish fraternities (Alpha Epsilon Pi, still active, and Zeta Beta Tau, no longer exclusively Jewish) and one sorority (Alpha Epsilon Phi, no longer on campus). In 2002, the Ben Schulman Center for Jewish Living was built, offering, according to its director, "the most modern recreational and social services for Jewish students available on any American campus." (Author's collection.)

Three

The People and the Families of Jewish Nashville

The strength of every community is its people. Nashville's Jewish community has never been as large as that of Memphis, Louisville, or Atlanta. Throughout the 1940s and 1950s, the population was always estimated at around 3,000, perhaps lower than it really was. The numbers grew, slowly but consistently, as people moved here for new jobs and as students who came to Nashville to attend Vanderbilt University decided to stay after graduation. By the 1960s and 1970s, the estimates were up to around 5,000, and by 1980, that number had climbed to 6,000. Today, as Nashville has grown, so has the city's Jewish population. Current estimates are 7,500. And while there are many recent arrivals and new residents and families, there are also many Jewish families who can trace their roots in the city back more than 100 years. The names of those families are easily recognizable to those who have lived here for a long time. Among them are Werthan, May, Frank, Small, Levy, Goldner, Zander, Loventhal, Kornman, Garfinkle, Kuhn, Weil, and Cohn. Then there are all the names of families that were here for generations but, because some had only daughters who changed their names when they married, are gone: some of these are Lebeck, Morse, Lowenheim, Bernheim, Bernstein, Shyer, and Jonas. This chapter will turn back the clock and remember them all, parents, grandparents, and great-grandparents—those who carried the torch and enriched the community. They met, married, started the businesses, and joined the organizations that made Nashville's Jewish community what it is today. This chapter contains both captivating photographs and fascinating stories—much like the people who make up the history of the Jewish community in Nashville.

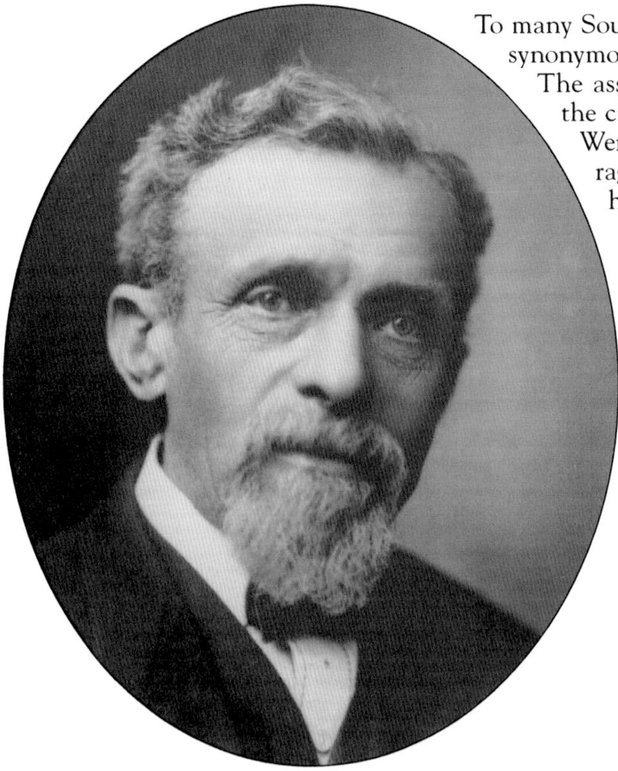

To many Southern Jews, the name Werthan is synonymous with Nashville's Jewish history. The association between the family and the city began with the arrival of Meier Werthan from Germany. Starting as a rag peddler in 1868, Werthan joined his brother-in-law, Sigmund Godhelp, in 1869 in opening a produce store. In the 1880s, they began selling reconditioned cotton and burlap bags, finally changing the name of the business to Werthan Bag and Burlap. Meier served as the secretary and treasurer of Vine Street Temple and president of B'nai B'rith.

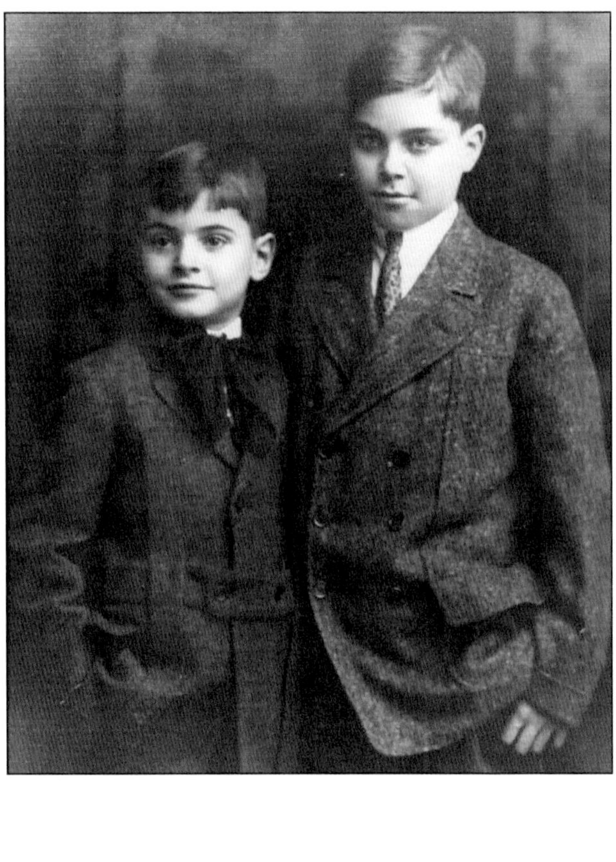

Meier Werthan had two sons, Morris and Joe. Morris, who joined the family business in 1895, had two sons, Albert (left) and Bernard, shown here in 1913. Both went to work for the company and also assumed leadership roles in Nashville's Jewish community.

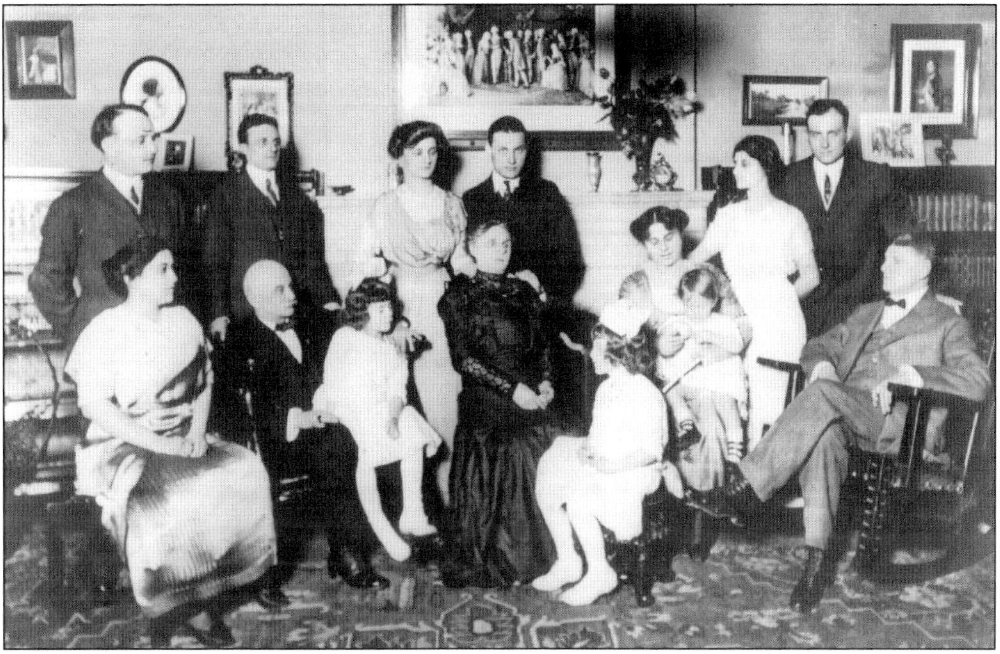

This 1912 photograph includes members of the Blum and Lowenheim families. David Lowenheim (far right, seated) was married to Tessie Blum, the daughter of Joseph Blum (first row second from left, with a child on his lap) and granddaughter of R. D. Blum. David Lowenheim's father, Joseph, was a Mason and claimed that this had saved his life in the days immediately following the Civil War. As the story went, Joseph was a peddler in West Tennessee, traveling through a rural backwoods area, when he was set upon by members of the Ku Klux Klan. Somehow determining that he was Jewish, they were about to slit his throat when he flashed the Mason's distress signal to prove that he was one of them. The men, recognizing the sign, decided that, Jewish or not, he was still a Mason, and they let him go.

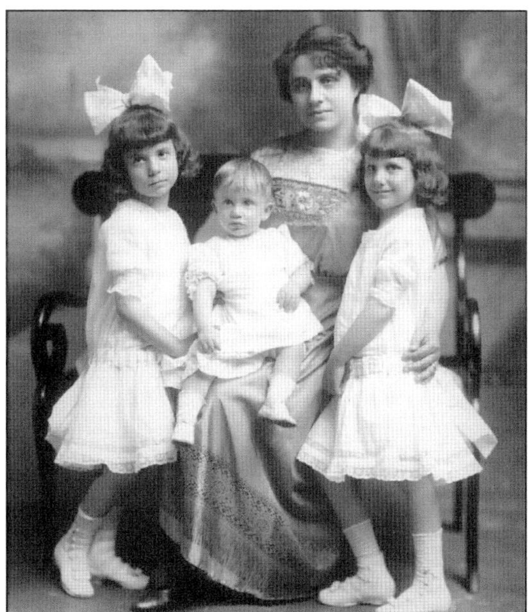

In this photograph from 1913, Tessie Blum Lowenheim is seated, surrounded by her three children, Elizabeth (left), Joe, and Mary Jane (who later married Albert Werthan). Tessie's husband, David Lowenheim, started in business with a dry goods store in Union City, Tennessee, with his brother Ben. After moving to Nashville, he opened D. Lowenheim Jewelry. Active in many local Jewish organizations, he was also a stockholder and director of the Nashville Baseball Club.

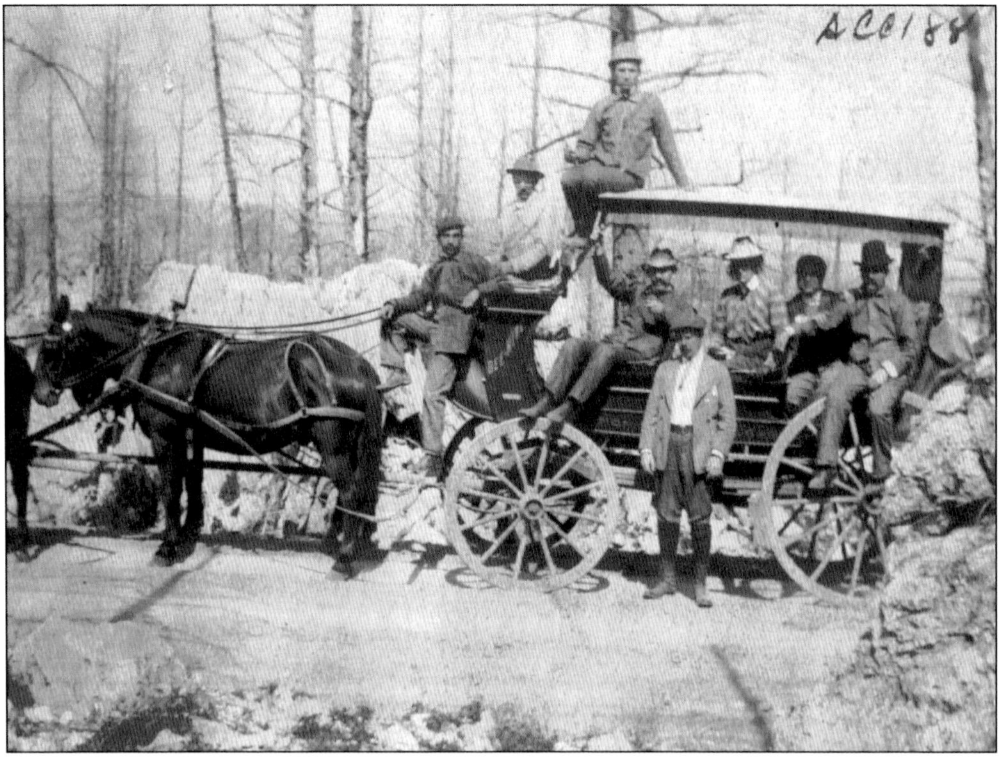

Clarence Bernstein, pictured atop this wagon in 1903, was the son of Phillip and Leah Frank Bernstein. Phillip and his brother Bernhard owned a dry goods store on Broad Street. Clarence was married to Daisy Bernstein, and they were the parents of Leah Rose Bernstein, who later married Bernard Werthan.

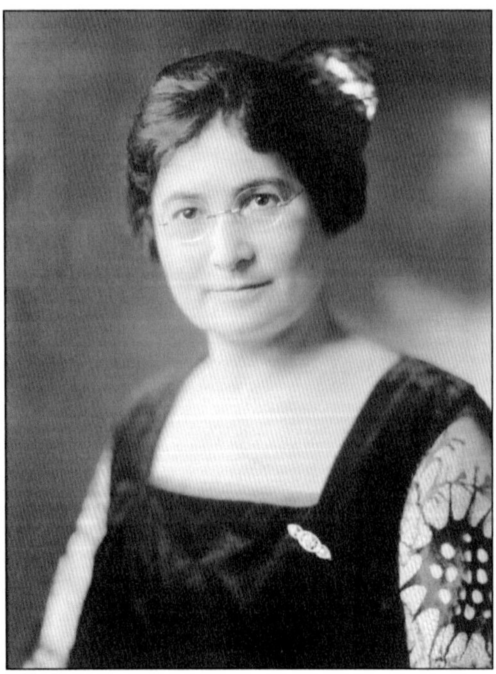

Daisy Marx Bernstein is said to have been the inspiration for the character of Daisy Werthan in Alfred Uhry's *Driving Miss Daisy*. Uhry said in an interview that his sister went to summer camp with May Werthan (Shayne) when the two were youngsters. Not wanting to use the name Uhry in his story as it was not autobiographical but desiring the name of a recognized Southern Jewish family, he remembered the Werthans from his sister's childhood and that a woman in May Werthan's family was named Daisy.

Leah Rose Bernstein, the daughter of Clarence and Daisy Bernstein, married Bernard Werthan. She is seen here with her son Bernard Jr. and daughter Joan.

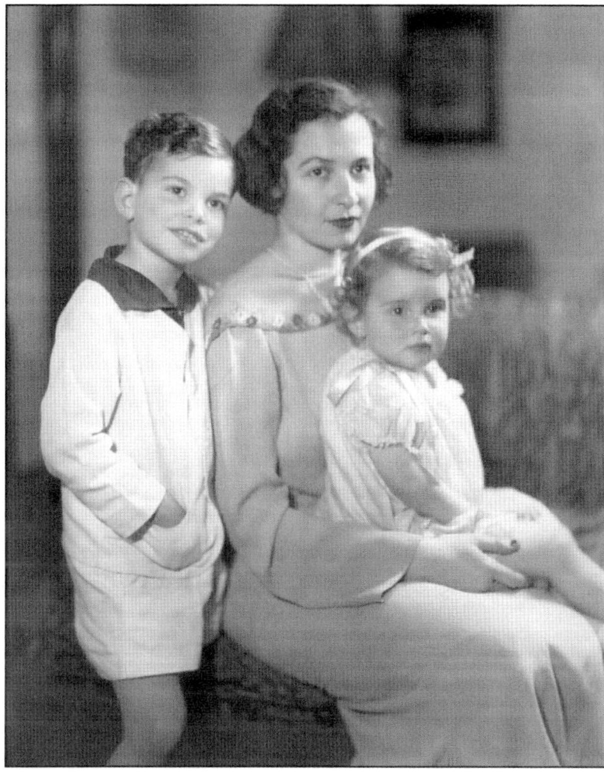

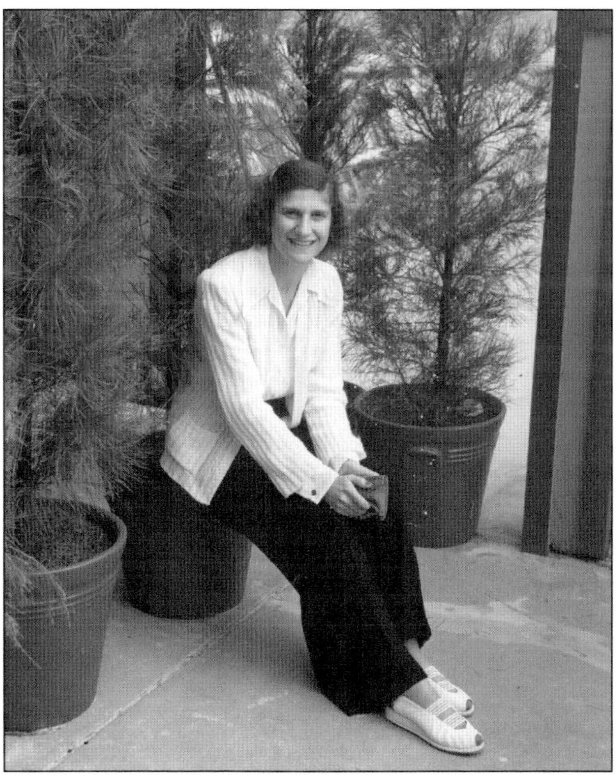

Mary Jane Lowenheim, the daughter of David and Tessie Blum Lowenheim, married Albert Werthan, Bernard's brother.

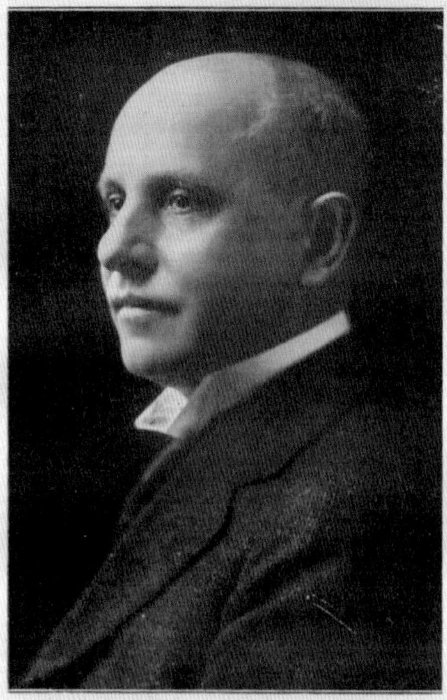

SAM LEVY
Chairman of Board

Sam Levy immigrated to the United States from Poland and after moving to Nashville became immersed not only in the Jewish community but in civic causes as well. He was a member of Nashville's Housing Administration, and one of the city's newly built housing projects was named the Sam Levy Homes in his honor. He was also a president of the YMHA.

Joe Fensterwald was the founder of Burk and Company, a downtown Nashville department store. His wife, Bertha, was the first president of the Nashville section of the National Council of Jewish Women, and it was in her honor (she died in childbirth in 1903) that the Bertha Fensterwald Settlement House, later known as the Bertha Fensterwald Social Center, was started in 1909. About 300 people per week took advantage of the center, which included a kindergarten, baby clinic, nutrition clinic, dental clinic, and sewing and embroidery classes for girls.

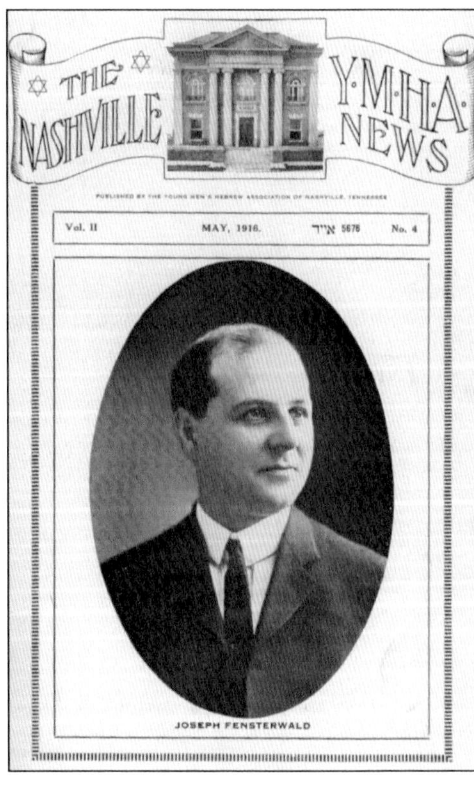

Sol Sawyer settled in Shelbyville, Tennessee, in the late 1800s, operating a store there before moving to Nashville. His daughter, Beulah, married Harry Blum Sr.

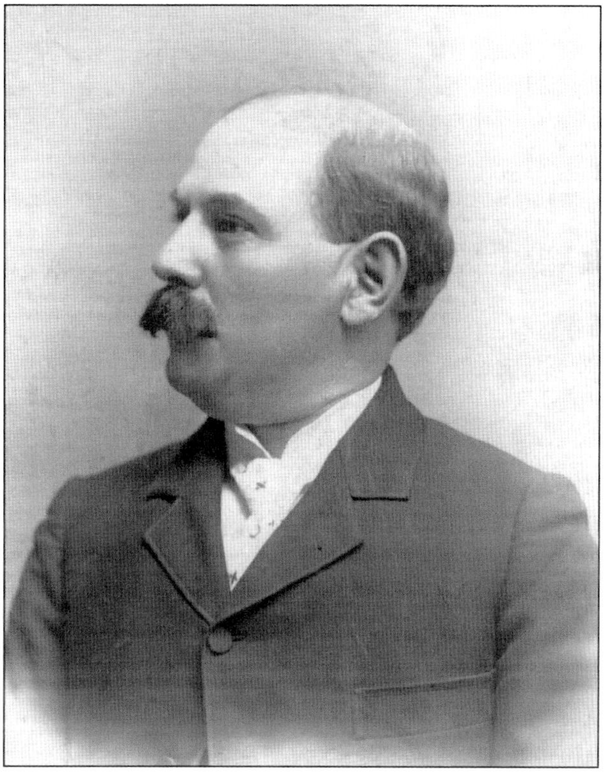

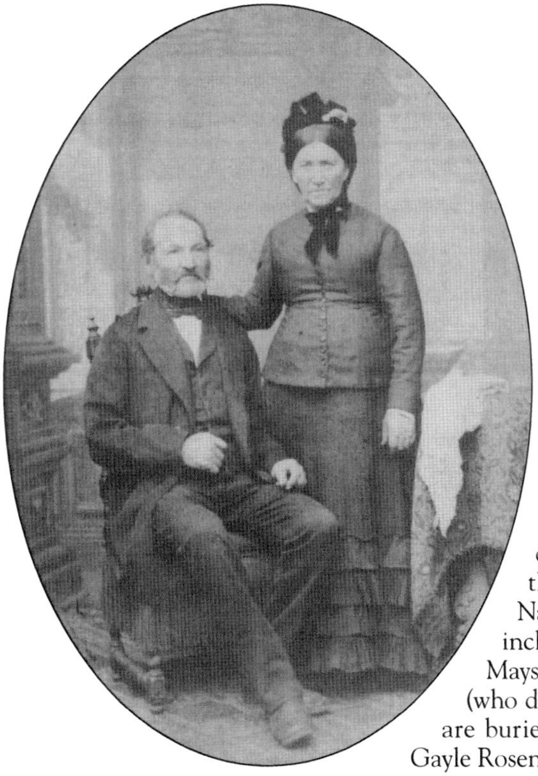

Lehman and Esther Kornman, born in Freisenheim, Germany, moved to Nashville in the 1880s to join their eight sons and daughters who were already living there. From those children came a number of well-known Nashville families over the next two generations, including Kornmans, Wises, Dembskys, Blochs, Mays, Biglers, Carrs, and Werthans. Both Lehman (who died in 1904) and Esther (who died in 1902) are buried in The Temple cemetery. (Courtesy of Gayle Rosen.)

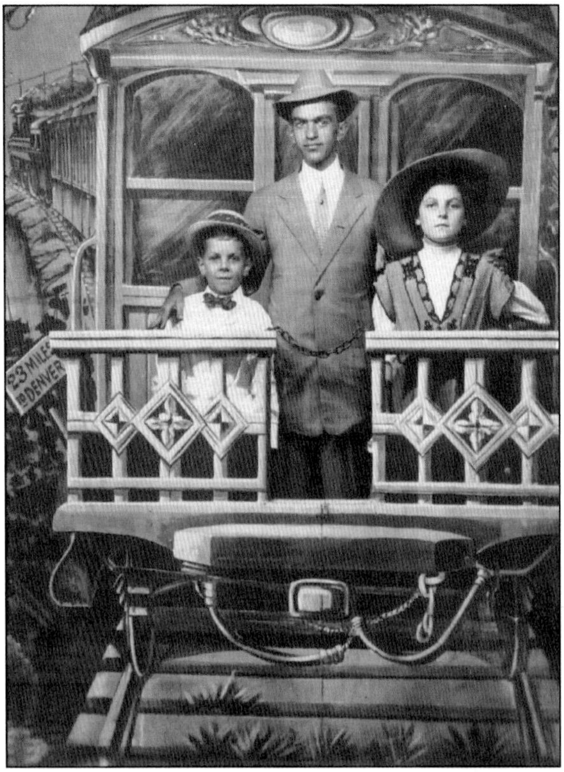

Leonard (left) and Beulah (right) Sawyer were the children of Sol Sawyer. Alvin Kornman (center) was their first cousin, the son of Sol Sawyer's sister-in-law. Beulah later married Harry Blum Sr., the son of Joseph Blum and grandson of R. D. Blum.

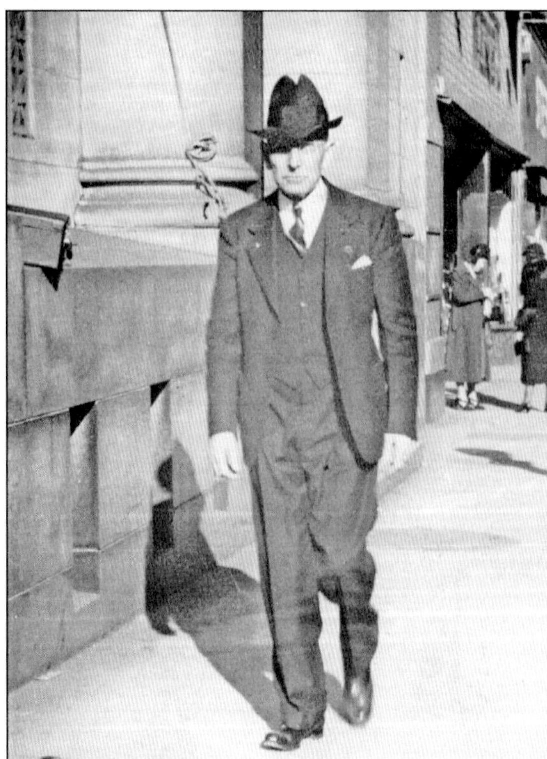

Herman Zander emigrated from Germany to the United States, meeting Rachel Henning in Montgomery, Alabama. She was originally from Nashville, so when they married, they moved here. Herman founded the Zander Insurance Company, which was later run by his son, Julian; Julian's son, Julian Jr. (Bud); and Bud's son, Jeff. The agency continues as one of the top insurance companies in Nashville nearly 100 years after it was started. Herman was an active member of Congregation Adath Israel, serving as its president in 1902–1903, and was president of B'nai B'rith.

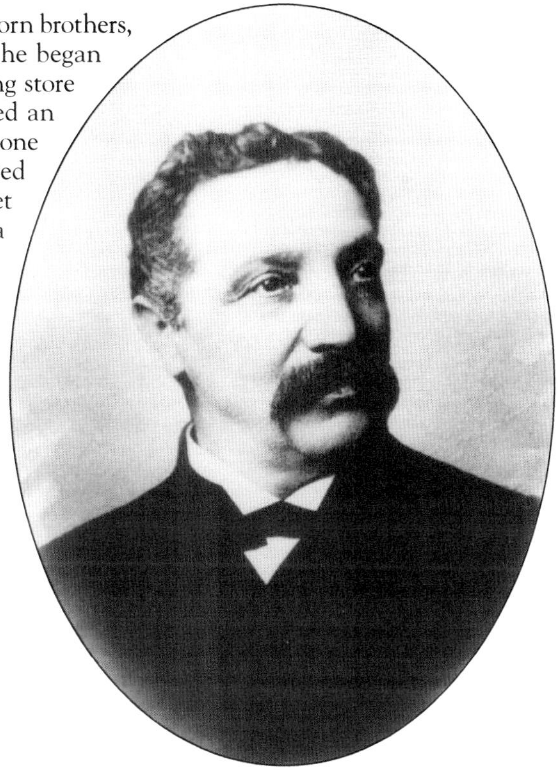

Leopold Loventhal, one of four Prussian-born brothers, arrived in Nashville in 1861. Although he began his business career by operating a clothing store with his brother Ben, in 1889, he opened an insurance agency that eventually became one of Nashville's largest. Loventhal, who died in 1895, served as president of Vine Street Temple and the Standard Club and was a member of the board of directors of B'nai B'rith. He was married to Mary Sulzbacher, one of three children of Martin and Dorothy Sulzbacher.

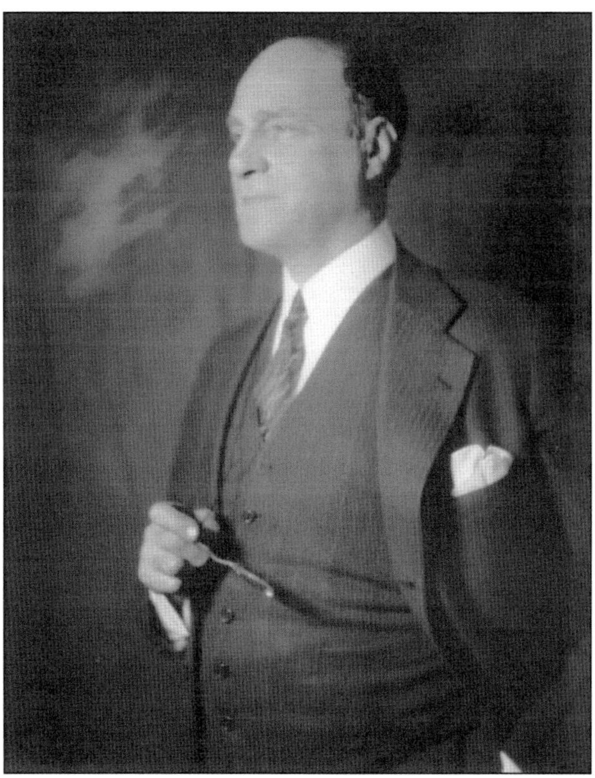

Lee Loventhal, Leopold's son, was born in Nashville in 1875. After attending public schools and Vanderbilt, he joined his father's insurance business. He was the first president of the YMHA as well as secretary of the Standard Club.

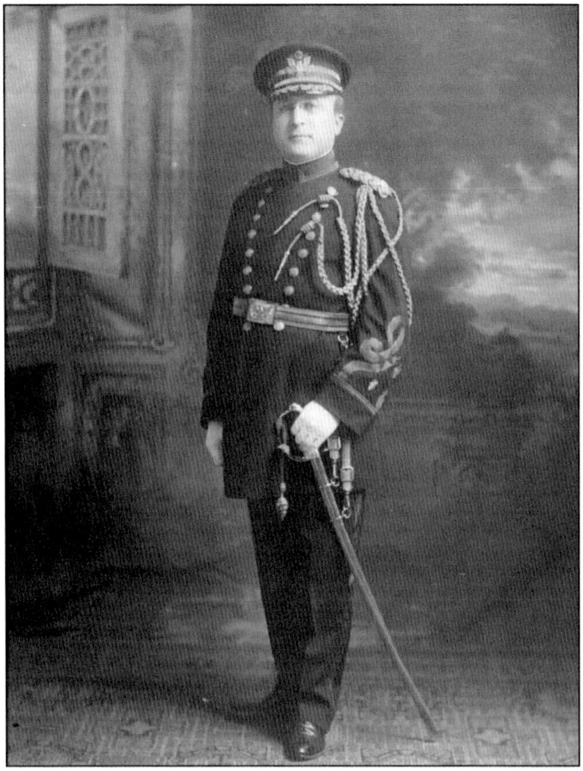

Aaron Bergeda (left) and his brother David (below) owned and operated a watch repair and jewelry store. An honorary colonel on the staff of Gov. Thomas C. Rye, Bergeda was also a member of the board of education and found himself embroiled in controversy in 1912 when he introduced a motion calling for Nashville public schools to discontinue the reading of the Bible. When the ensuing uproar threatened to become a full-blown religious war, he backed down, saying he was not personally opposed to reading the Bible in school, but had introduced the measure as a "gesture of courtesy" to Annie Garfinkle. He was president of the Gay Street Synagogue and the first Jewish member of the Knights of Pythias.

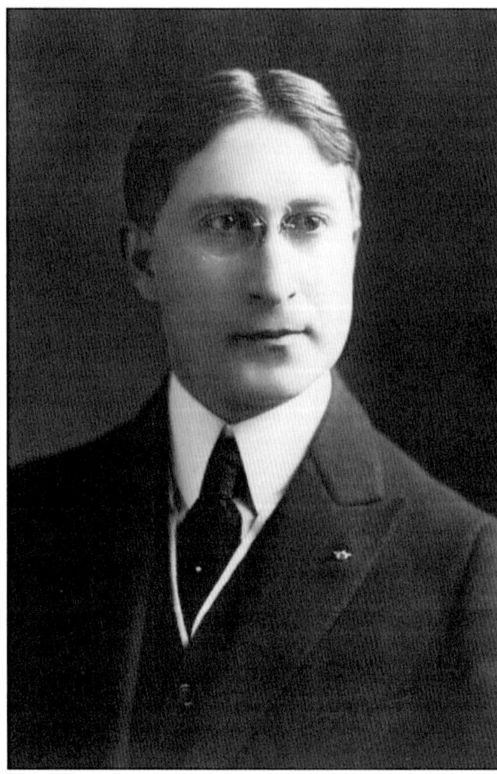

Harris Solinsky, at one time president of Vine Street Temple, was another honorary colonel on the governor's staff. Born in Russia, he operated a store in Pulaski, Tennessee, for 33 years before moving to Nashville and opening Harris Solinsky and Sons on the Public Square.

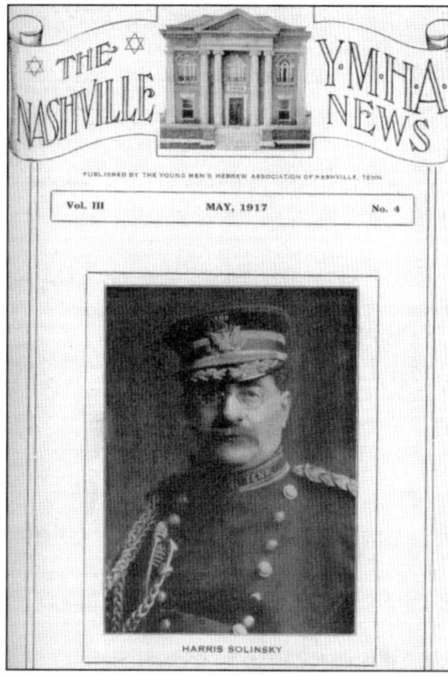
THE NASHVILLE Y·M·H·A· NEWS

PUBLISHED BY THE YOUNG MEN'S HEBREW ASSOCIATION OF NASHVILLE, TENN.

Vol. III MAY, 1917 No. 4

HARRIS SOLINSKY

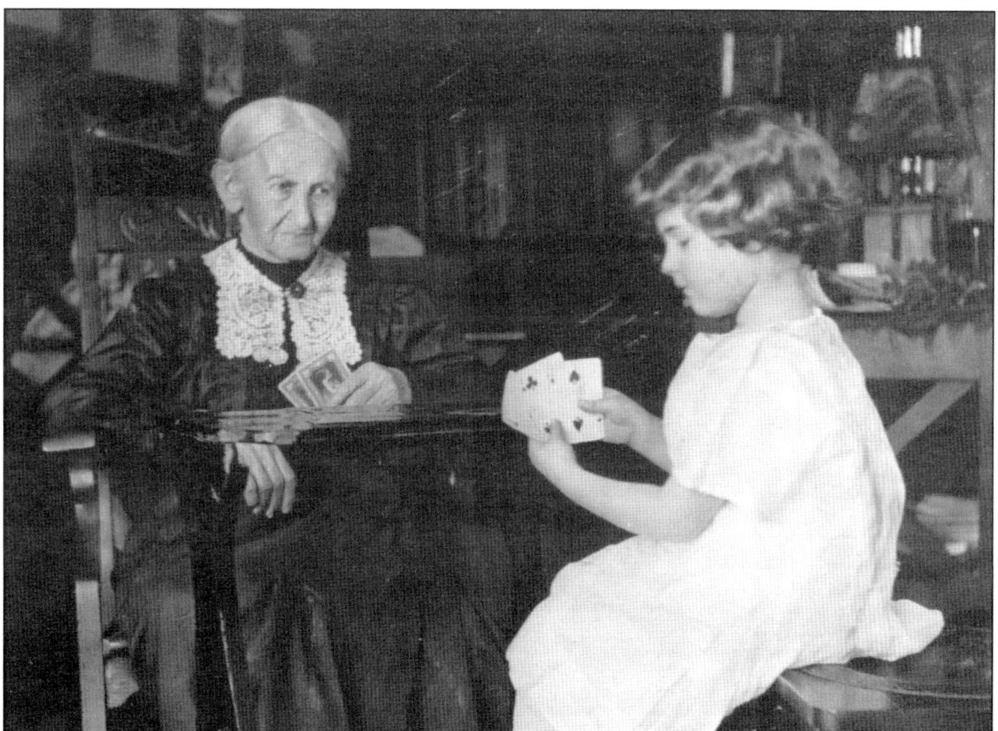

In 1912, a young Helen Solinsky (Harris's granddaughter) is playing cards with Minna Schiff Iser, the wife of Rabbi Alexander Iser. Minna, the sister of Caroline Schiff Cohen, had three daughters who operated a millinery store in Nashville for many years. Her other daughter, Sarah, taught in Nashville's public schools for 20 years and was superintendant of the religious school at Vine Street Temple.

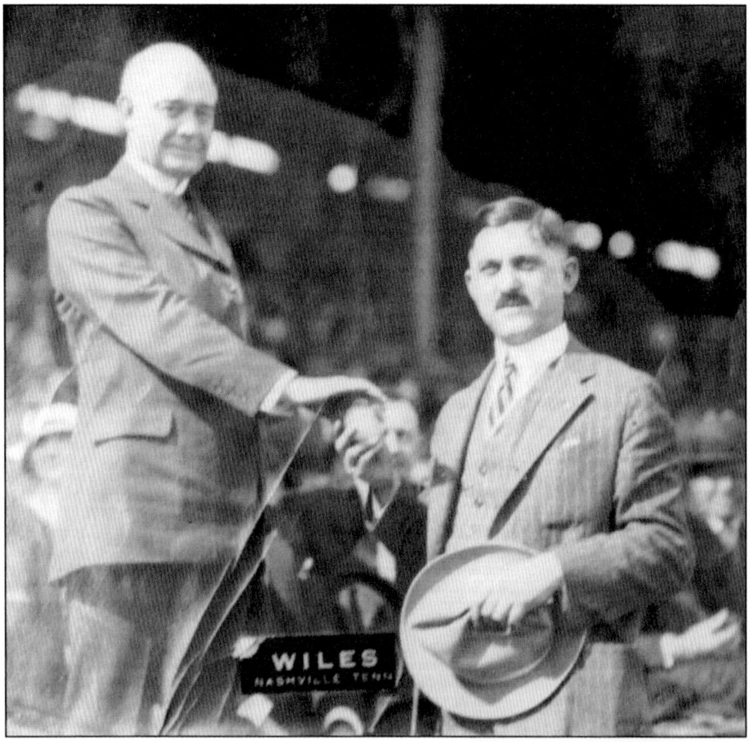

Jesse Albert was Sydney Albert's brother (see page 76). He is seen here with Tennessee governor Austin Peay, ready to throw out the first pitch at Sulphur Dell.

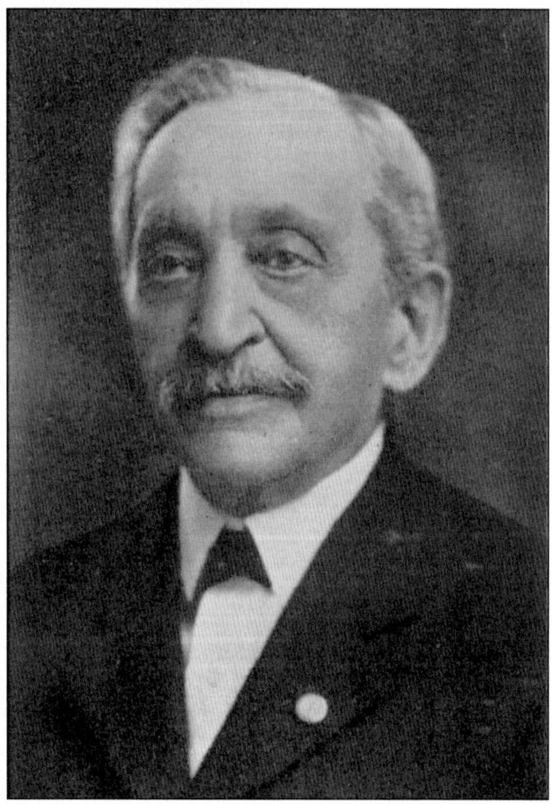

Jacob (Jake) Levine began his business career in Nashville working at a clothing store. Born in Germany in 1844, he settled in Pulaski in the 1860s and moved to Nashville in the 1870s. He started a tobacco manufacturing business here, along with a liquor store, but is best known as a justice of the peace. On one occasion, two men appeared in his courtroom, both claiming to own the same dog. "Squire" Jake Levine listened to the men's stories, and then told them to leave the courtroom while he thought over his decision. He made it a point to tell each man to leave by a different door. As they exited the courtroom, he motioned to a deputy to release the dog. When it jumped out of the deputy's arms and scampered after one of the two men, Levine's decision was made: he gave the dog to the man it followed. He was a member of B'nai B'rith and the Sons of Israel and died in 1934.

In the 1880s, 16-year-old Joseph Lightman came with his family to the United States from Hungary. He opened his first business, a fruit stand in the downtown area, in 1887. This was followed by a confectioner's booth, a saloon, a dry goods store, and a construction company. Joe, who was one of the founders of the Nashville YMHA, was the subject of a wonderful article written by his great-grandson, physicist and author Alan Lightman, in 1984. It was a tribute in which Alan recalled family stories and memories entitled "Time Travel and Papa Joe's Pipe."

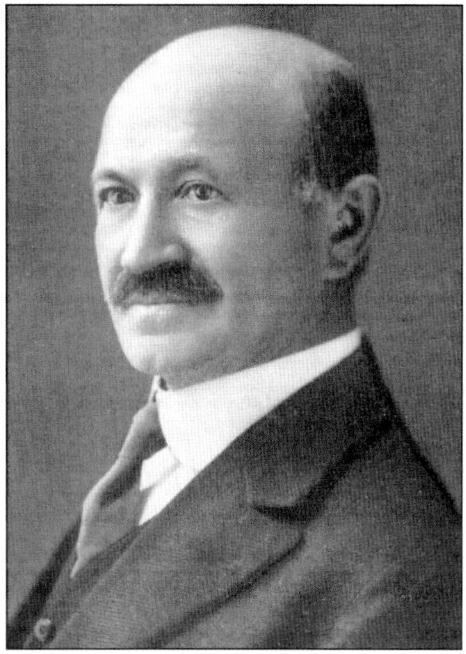

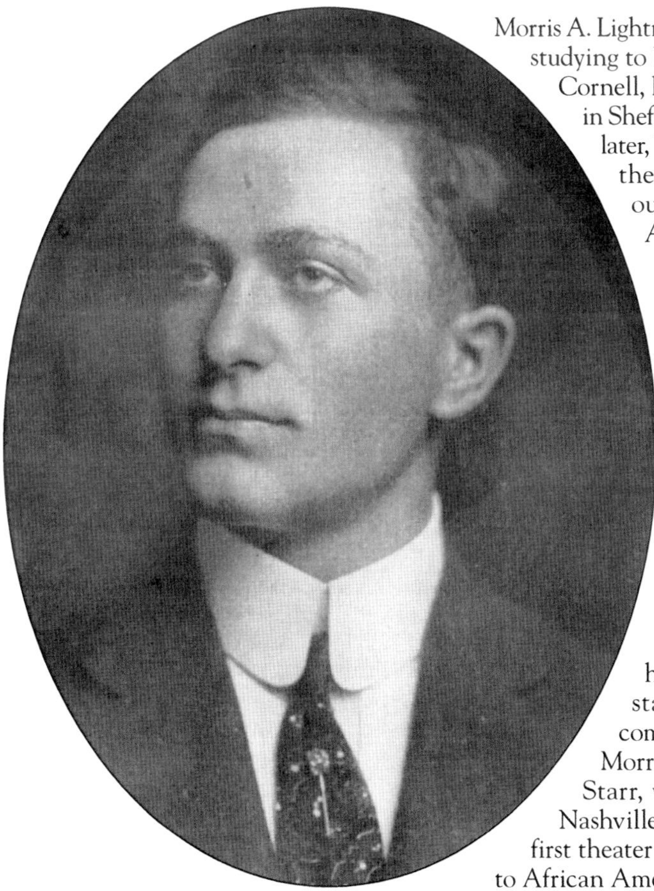

Morris A. Lightman was Joe Lightman's son. After studying to be an engineer at Vanderbilt and Cornell, he went into the theater business in Sheffield, Alabama, in 1915. Four years later, he was approached by a competing theater owner with a deal to trade out his theaters in northwestern Alabama for a partnership in a group of theaters in Arkansas, which he accepted. In 1925, he returned to Nashville and helped his father build and operate the Hillsboro Theater. Three months after it opened, Tony Sudekum built the competing Belmont Theater on the same block, determined, it is said, to run the Lightmans out of the theater business. It worked. Morris moved back to Arkansas and began building the MALCO chain, which today has more than 300 screens in five states. After Morris retired, the company was run by his son Richard. Morris's daughter Carrie married Jake Starr, whose brother Milton operated Nashville's Bijou Theater—said to be the first theater in the South to cater exclusively to African Americans.

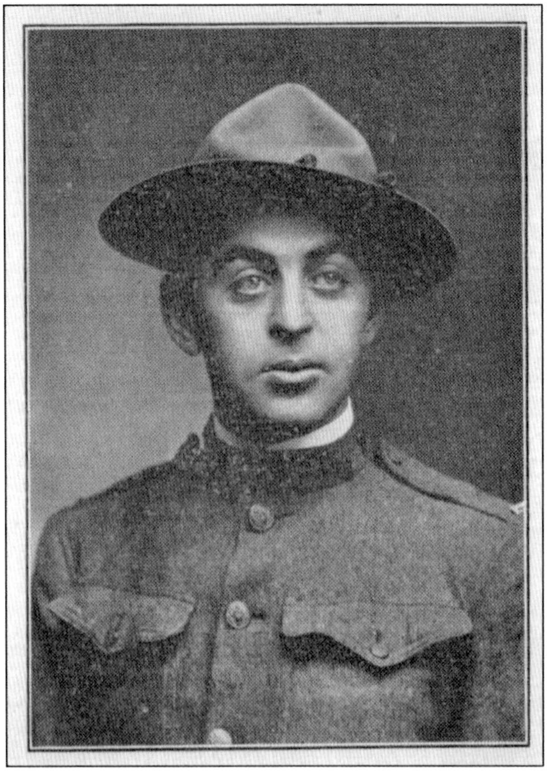

Morris Hartman was the son of Sam Hartman, who owned Hartman Hotel and later the Ideal Laundry. Sam was murdered by a former business partner in 1918 (see page 73). Morris served as a medic in World War I and became a Nashville pediatrician when the war was over. He was married to Helen Heilbron of Owensboro, Kentucky, who worked for Homer Jonas at Kay Jewelers for 20 years.

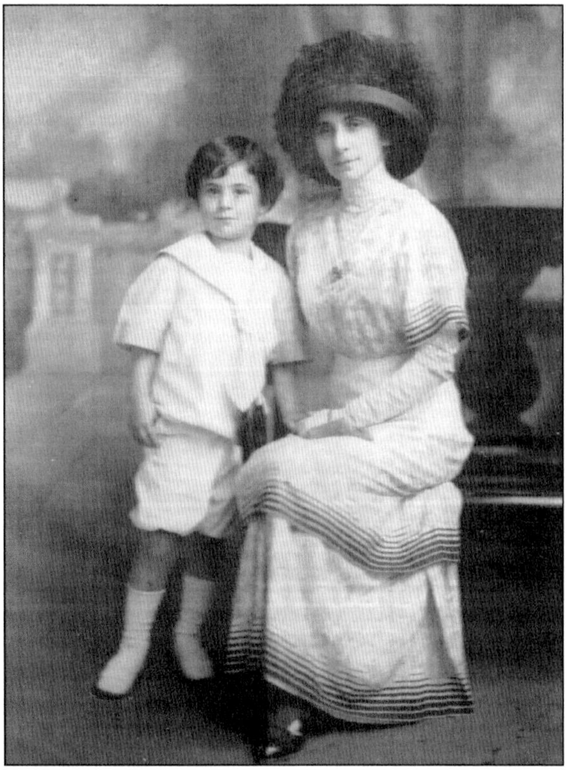

Adolph Jonas was a partner with his brother, Leopold, in the L. Jonas and Company wholesale and retail store (see pages 78 and 79). Mrs. Adolph Jonas is shown here with her son, Homer, who later married Elizabeth Lowenheim (their daughter is Betsy Chernau). Homer went into the jewelry business, opening the Kay Jewelry store in 1928. After Homer died in 1965, Elizabeth married Julius Jacobs. She died in 2007 at the age of 101.

Sam Shyer (standing) was one of the six children (three sons and three daughters) of Sol and Henrietta Shyer, a nephew of Michael Shyer, and a cousin of Harold L. Shyer (see page 80), whose father was Louis Shyer. Sam was married to Pauline Frieberg (seated), and his sister Hattie married Clarksville's Elias Glick.

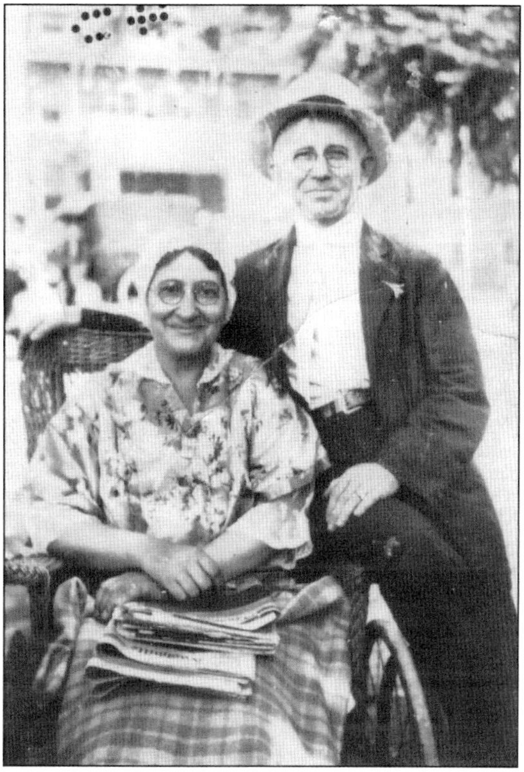

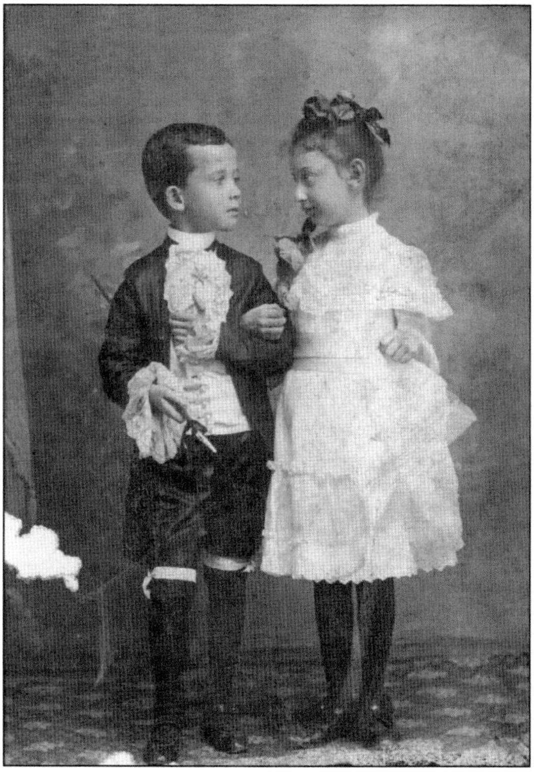

Louis Shyer and his brother, Abe (left, with their sister), married two sisters, Norah and Ruth Lazarus.

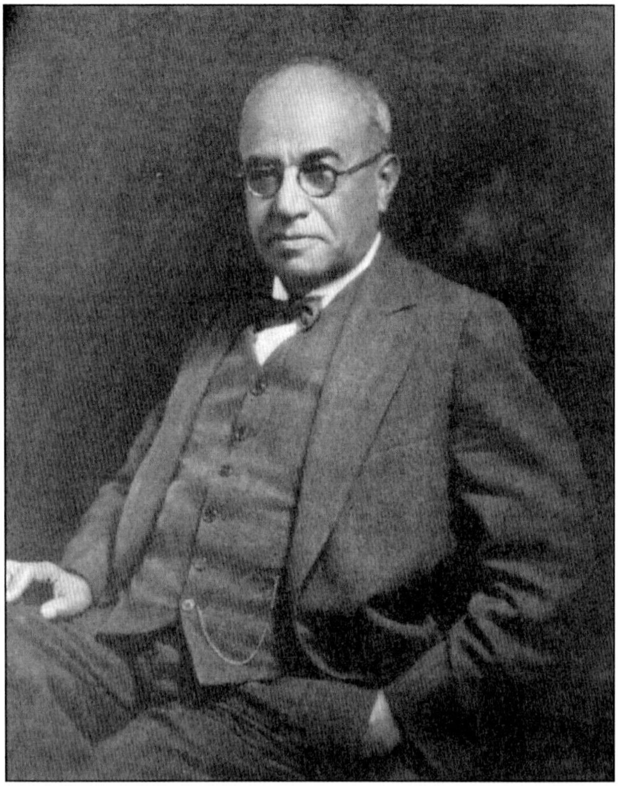

Jacob May was the patriarch of the May family and founder of May Hosiery Mills. He immigrated to New York from Germany, where he was born in 1861. He later worked as a peddler with a horse and wagon in New Hampshire, selling hosiery products throughout New England. After saving enough money, he opened a retail store in Laconia, New Hampshire, and sold the hosiery made in that city at its many mills. He and his wife, Rebecca Weingarten May, moved to Nashville in 1896 after he won a contract to provide labor at a Tennessee prison (see page 98). He was the father of Mortimer and Dan May and grandfather of Leon and Jack May. (Courtesy of Melanie Hirt.)

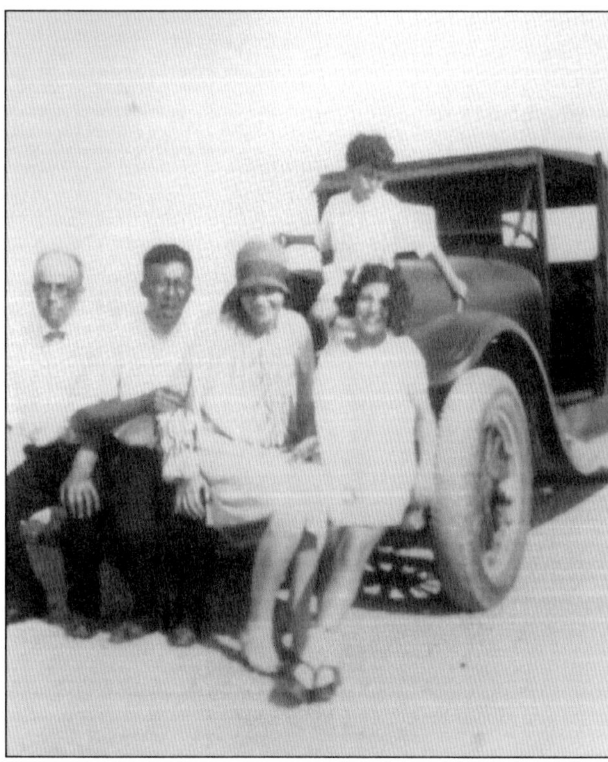

This photograph shows the May family in 1929. From left to right are Jacob, son Mortimer, daughter-in-law Gertrude Bloch May, granddaughter Reba, and grandson Leon. (Courtesy of Melanie Hirt.)

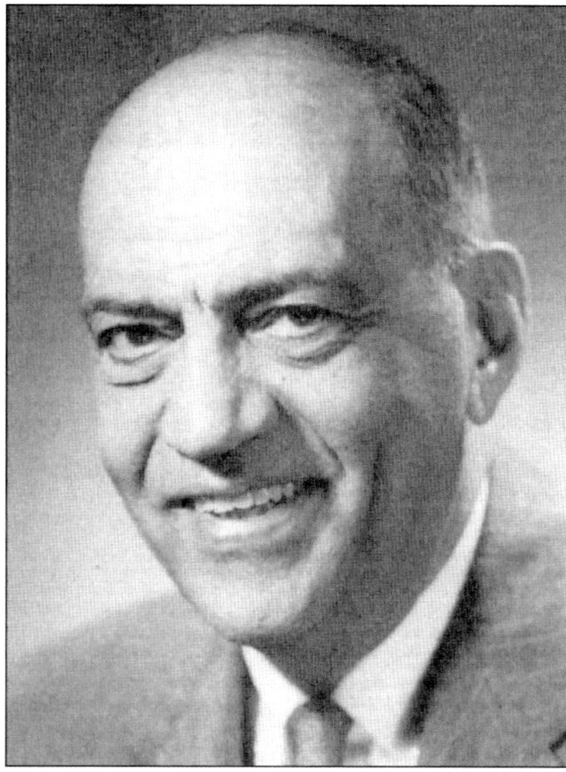

Dan May and his brother, Mortimer, were the sons of Jacob May. Dan, who died in 1982, was one of the founding fathers of Metropolitan Government of Nashville, an early Metro councilman, and chairman of the board of education. While many Nashvillians are aware of the May family's contributions to both the Jewish community and the greater Nashville community at large, they are not as familiar with the family's successful efforts to save hundreds of lives in the 1930s by sponsoring numerous Jewish emigrants trying to escape Hitler's Europe. Although they were successful in almost all of their efforts, they failed in one very sad case: Jacob May's oldest brother, Abraham, and Abraham's youngest daughter were killed in concentration camps. (Courtesy of Melanie Hirt.)

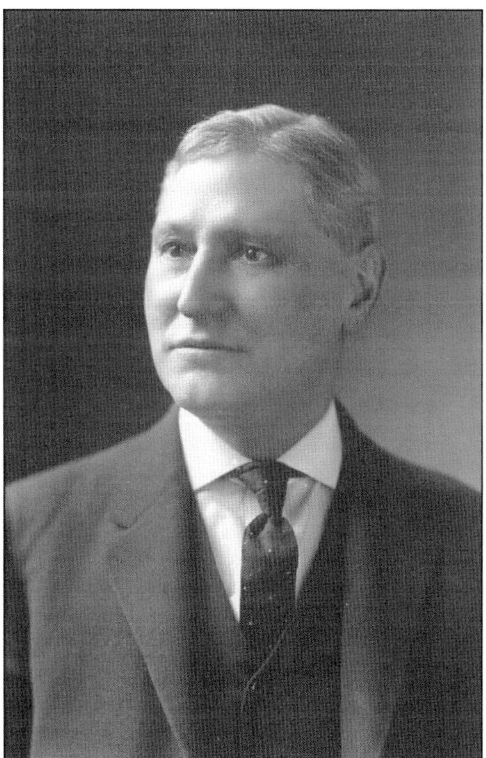

Abraham Frank, born in 1858, married Sarah Lowenheim, David Lowenheim's sister. In business, he operated a store selling wallpaper. He and Sarah were the parents of two daughters, Leah and Bernice, and one son, Irving.

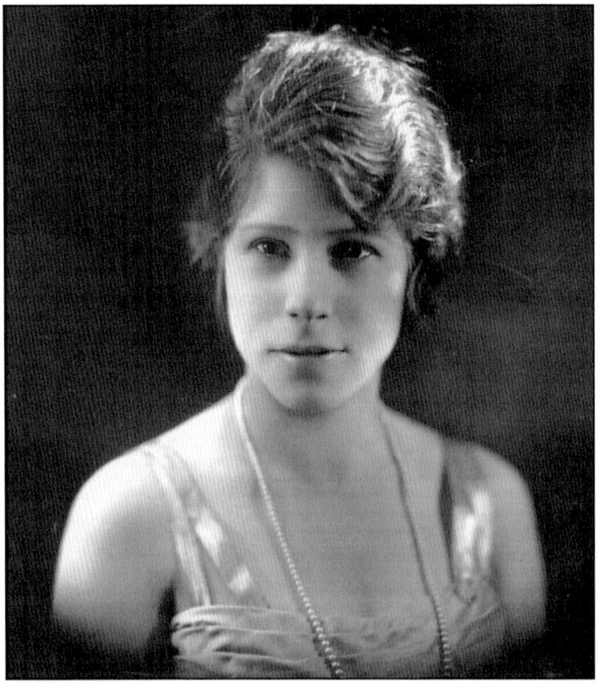

Bernice Frank, born in 1898, one of the two daughters of Abraham and Sarah Frank, is seen here at the age of 17 in 1915. She later married David Gross and died in 1955.

David Gross Jr. was the son of David and Bernice Frank Gross and the grandson of Abraham Frank. Joining the Army Air Corps as a pilot, he is said to have shot down the first German fighter over Germany in 1944. Not long after, he died when his P-47 Thunderbolt fighter was shot down over occupied France. Here he is relaxing with Doris Guttman. She later married Isadore Kaufman, a Nashville businessman who owned the Highway Pup restaurants.

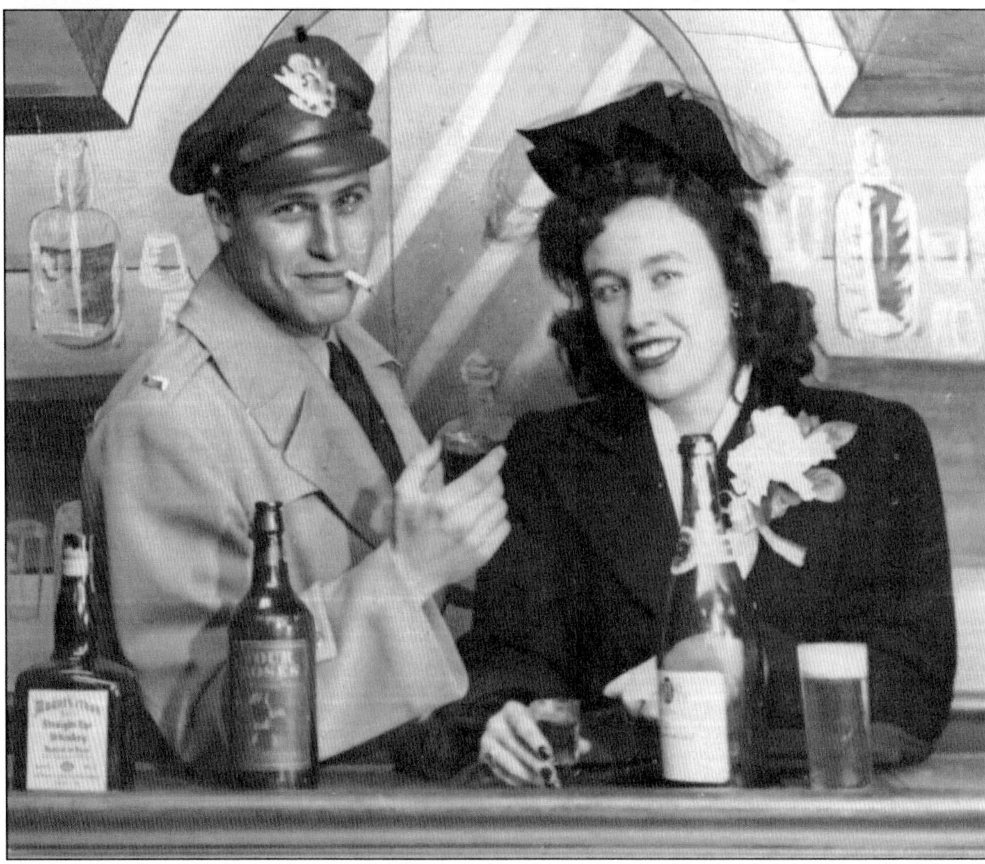

Mike Lebeck was one of three sons of Emanuel Lebeck, all of whom were partners in Lebeck Brothers Company. Mike served as a board member of Ohavai Sholom and vice president in 1898. He also was one of the founding members of the Standard Club (which would later become the Woodmont Country Club). He died in 1922.

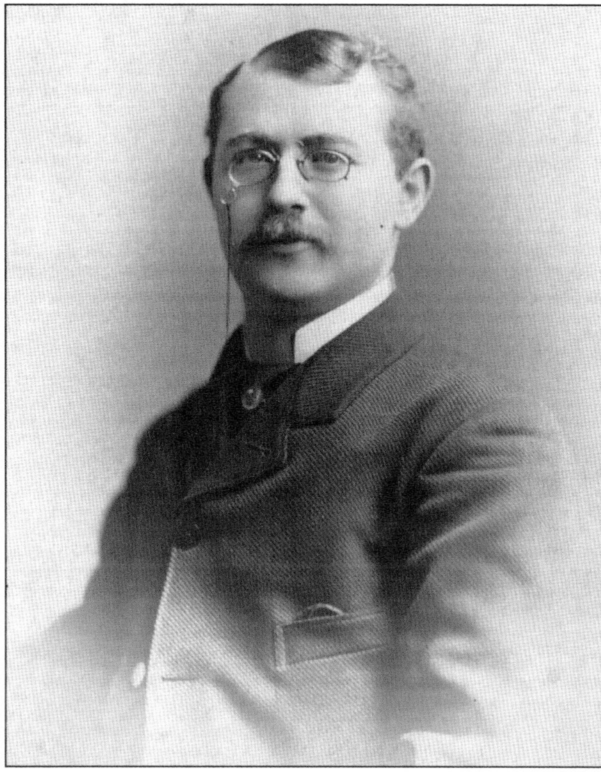

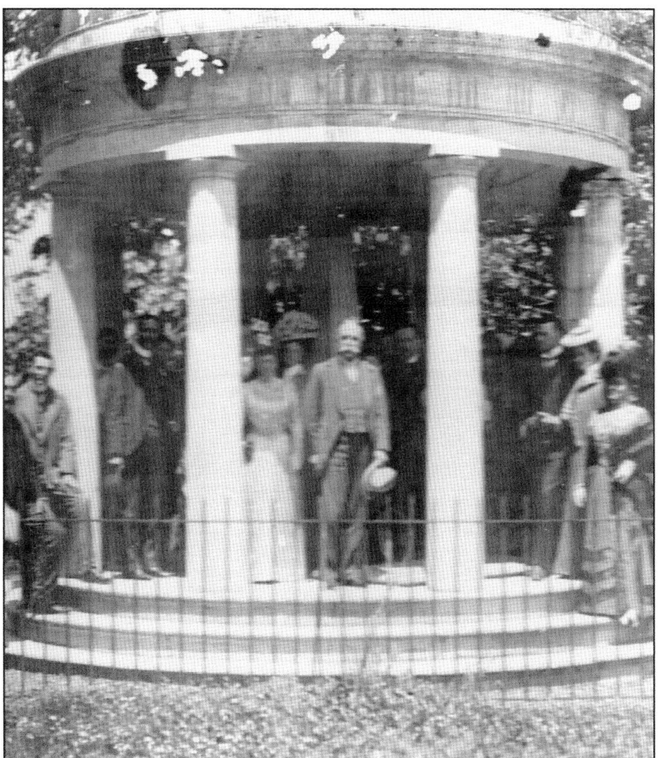

Annie Weil Lebeck is seen here during a visit to the Hermitage with Pres. William H. Taft in honor of former Pres. Andrew Jackson in 1911. A graduate of the Cincinnati Conservatory of Music, Annie was an accomplished singer well known in the community for her cultural, social, religious, and philanthropic service. She and her husband, Mike, had two sons, Clarence and Morton.

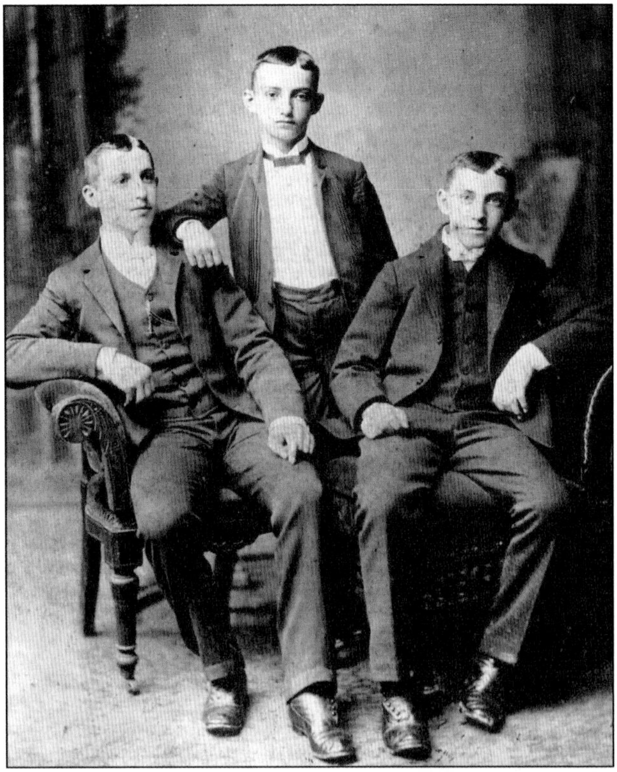

From left to right, Joe, Ike, and Isadore Morse were brothers, all of whom were born in Nashville and were involved in the operation of the family's store, Joe Morse and Company.

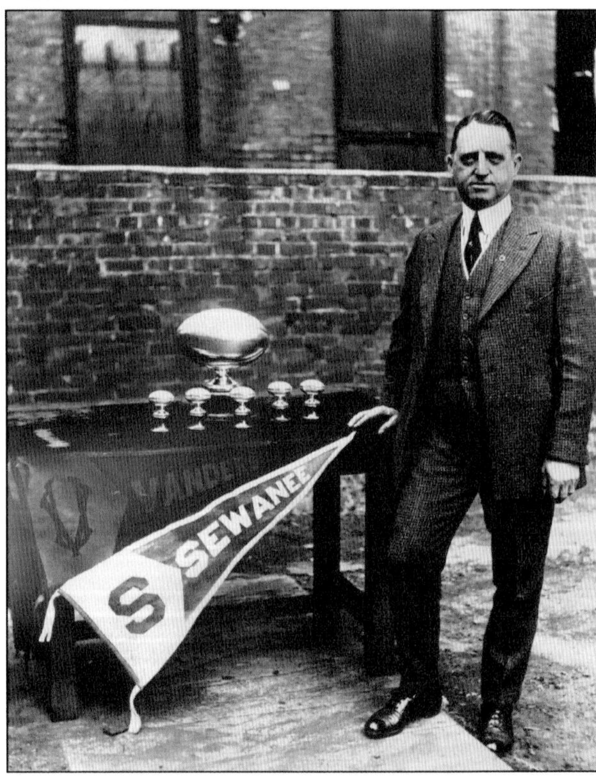

Joe Morse Sr. was born in Nashville in 1874 and worked for Bloomstein Brothers before founding Joe Morse and Company in 1897. He was married to Mae Sulzbacher, the daughter of Charles and Hannah Spitz Sulzbacher. Mae's sister, Jennie, married Lou Frank, and their son founded Joseph Frank and Son Men's Store. Another of Mae's sisters, Dorothy, married Sig Marks. Joe was president of Vine Street Temple, the YMHA, B'nai B'rith, and the Woodmont Country Club. He died in 1941.

Mae Sulzbacher Morse was Joe Morse Sr.'s wife and the mother of Joe Morse Jr. and his two sisters, Rosalyn and Corinne.

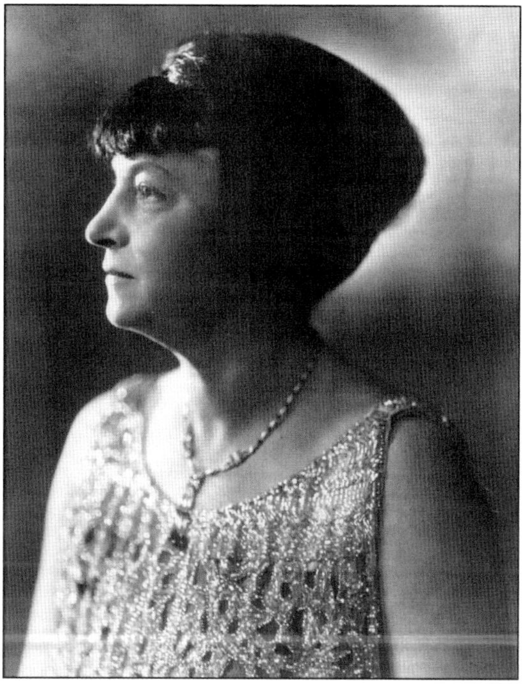

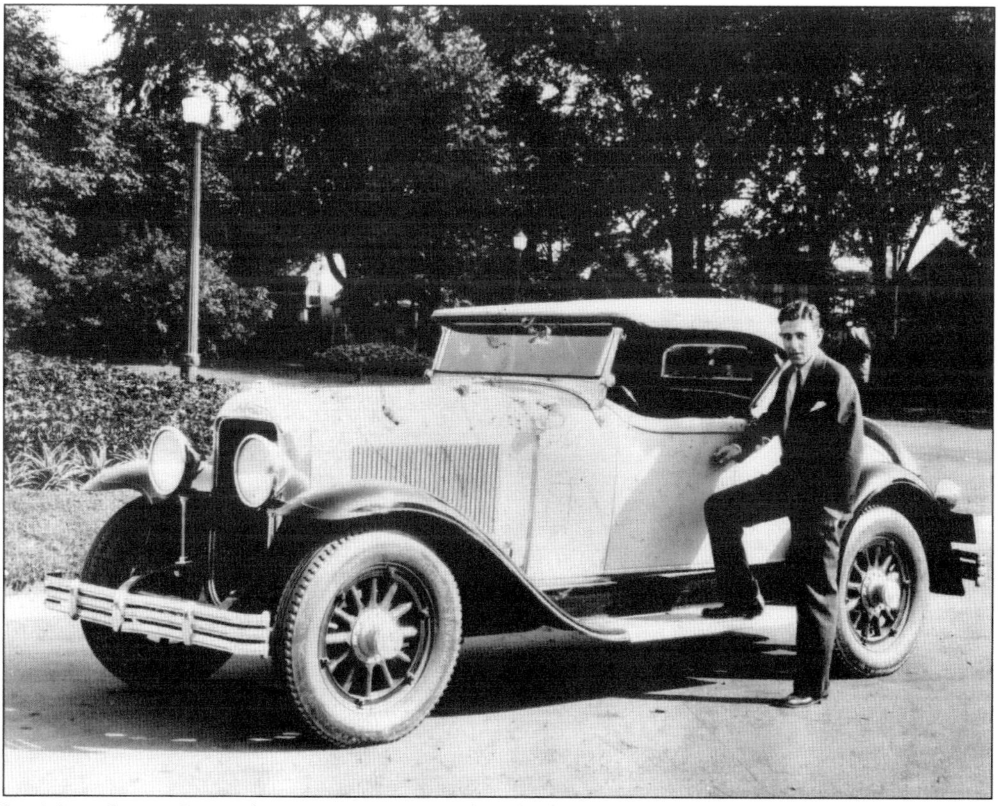

Joe Morse Jr. was Joe and Mae Morse's son and worked with his father at Joe Morse and Company until the store closed.

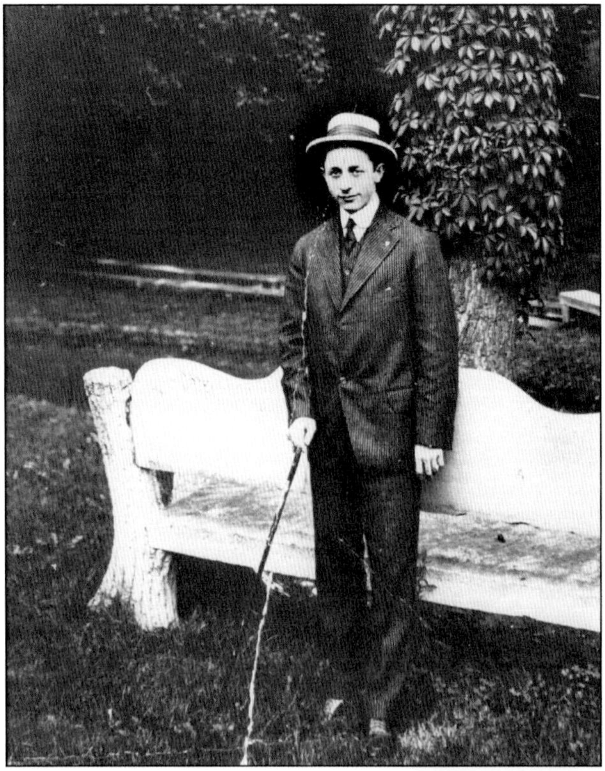

Leon (Lee) Goldner, founder of Goldner Jewelers, and his wife, Henrietta, were the parents of Fred Goldner Sr. (left). In the early 1950s, Fred Sr. decided to branch out into a new area when his son-in-law, Bill Neaderthal, pointed out that many of the items they sold, such as Cross pens, Zippo lighters, and similar products, had another potential market—specialty advertising. Fred and his wife, Ida (below), also had a son, Fred Goldner Jr. He became a prominent Nashville physician, and all members of the Goldner family have been involved in Jewish civic and community organizations.

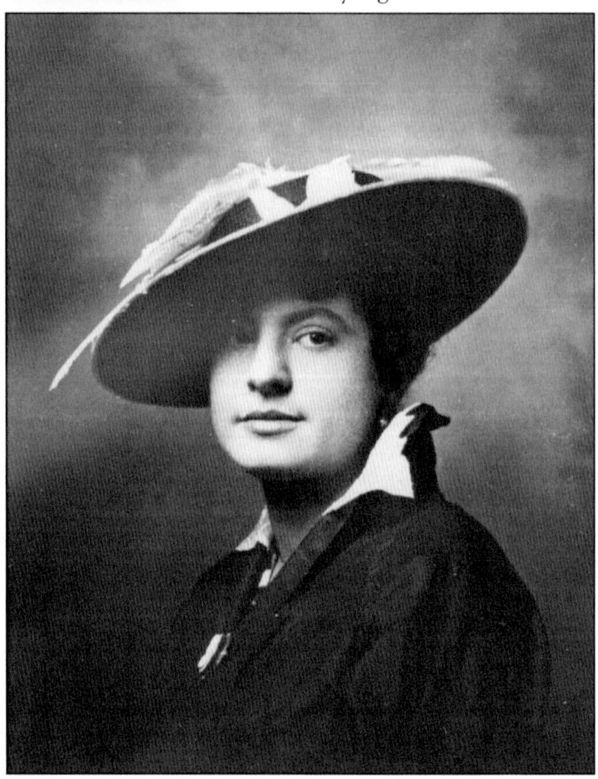

Corinne Lieberman (Mrs. Charles) Cohn was the daughter of Simon Lieberman. Her father had served for 16 years on the Nashville Board of Education, and she continued the family's commitment to education, also serving on the board. Because of her many contributions over the years to the local school system, Cohn High School in West Nashville was named in her honor. Her son, Paul Cohn, and his son, Paul Cohn Jr., picked up where Simon and Corinne left off, also serving on the school board for many years. Within the Jewish community, Corinne was president of Vine Street Temple Sisterhood for eight years and was vice president of the National Federation of Temple Sisterhoods at the time of her death.

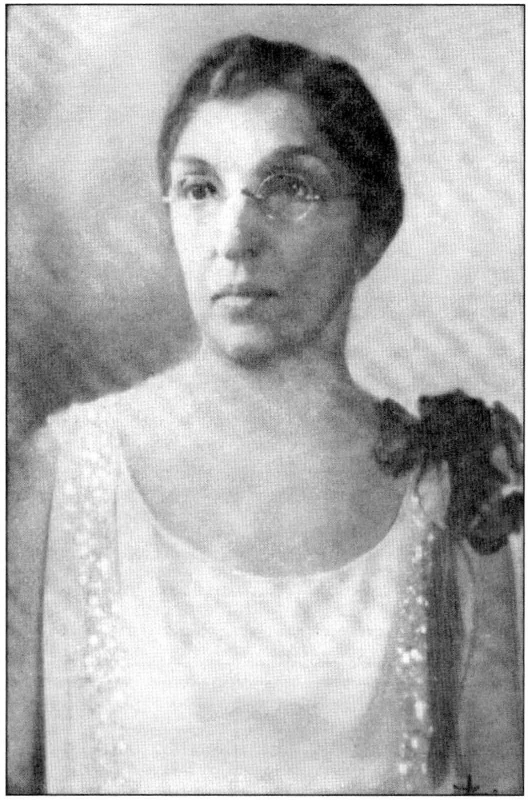

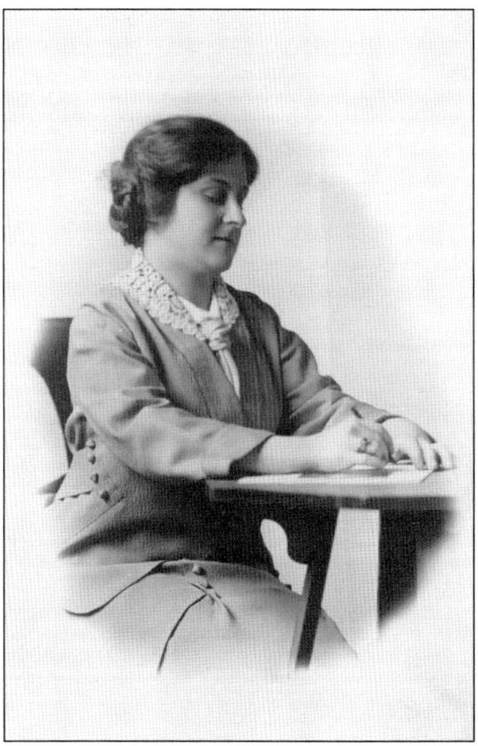

Annie Garfinkle was born in Nashville in 1891. She and her two brothers, Elkin and Dan, both attorneys, were all active in Nashville civic and community affairs. In 1912, Annie decided that a request by a group called the Daughters of America to place Bibles in Nashville's public schools was wrong and challenged the move in a letter to the city's newspaper editors. She then got board member Aaron Bergeda to introduce a measure that would prohibit reading the Bible in the city's grammar and high schools. When the Nashville Minister's Alliance and a number of churches protested, Bergeda and other board members backed down, referring the proposal to a committee for "further study." It was never brought up again. Garfinkle married Oscar Nochlin in 1919, and the couple had two children, Ellen (Mrs. Irwin Ross) and Perry. In 1913, Garfinkle founded the B'nai Zion Society, the forerunner to Nashville's Hadassah chapter, and she and her husband-to-be also started the Nashville District of the Zionist Organization of America. She died in 1968.

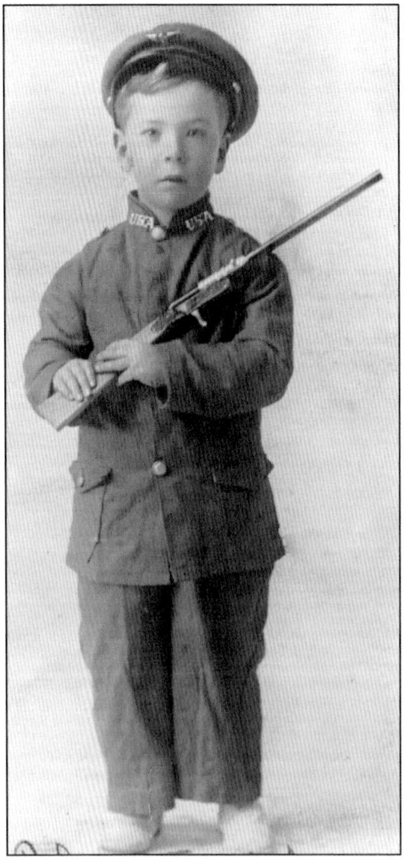

Robert Teitlebaum Sr. was just four years old in this 1915 photograph. After graduating from the Wharton School of Business at the University of Pennsylvania, he went into the women's ready-to-wear business and became a partner in Loveman, Berger, and Teitlebaum. As president of the company, he oversaw the move from downtown to include a suburban store in Belle Meade. He died in 1985 and is buried in The Temple cemetery. His son, Robert Jr., was a sportswriter for 30 years, including a stint at the *Tennessean*. He died in 2008.

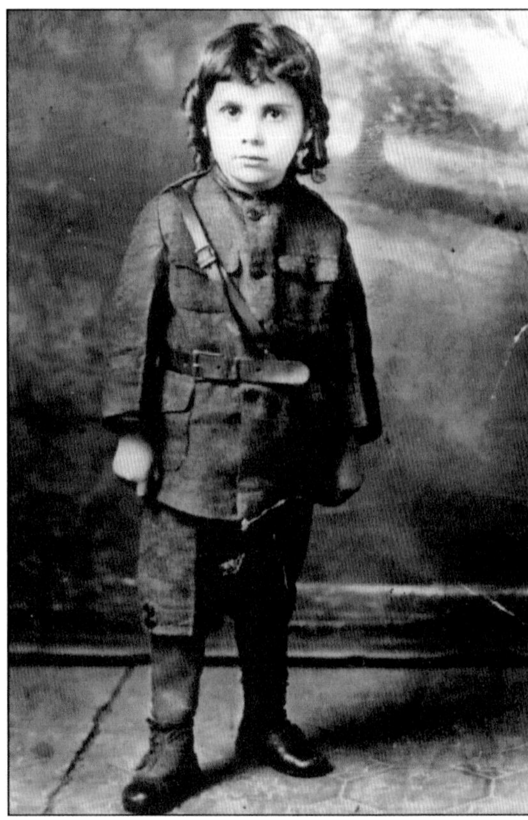

Herschel Katzman was four years old in this 1918 photograph. Born in Nashville to Russian immigrants Sam and Lottie Katzman, he attended Hume-Fogg High School and Vanderbilt University. While his father was a tailor with a shop on Twenty-first Avenue South, Herschel went into commercial real estate and is best known for Nashboro Village and the Iroquois and Valley Ridge Apartments. He died in 1997, but his wife, Louise Brooks Katzman, as of this writing, remains active in civic and community affairs and is still playing tennis regularly at 94. (Courtesy of Terry Rosenblum.)

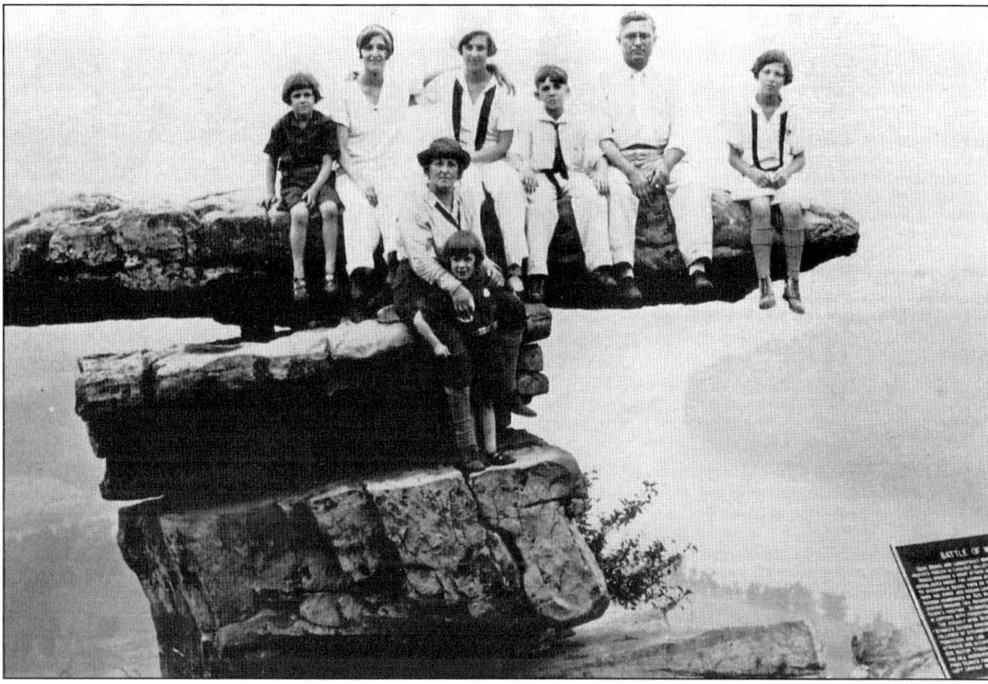

Louise Brooks Katzman and her family were sightseeing at Umbrella Rock on Chattanooga's Lookout Mountain when this photograph was taken in the 1920s. Pictured atop the rock from left to right are L. H. (Louis) Brooks Jr., Natalie Brooks Strauch, Elsie Brooks Kornman, Boris J. Brooks, L. H. Brooks Sr., and Louise; below in front are Rachel Weschler (left) and Joseph D. Brooks (right). (Courtesy of Terry Rosenblum.)

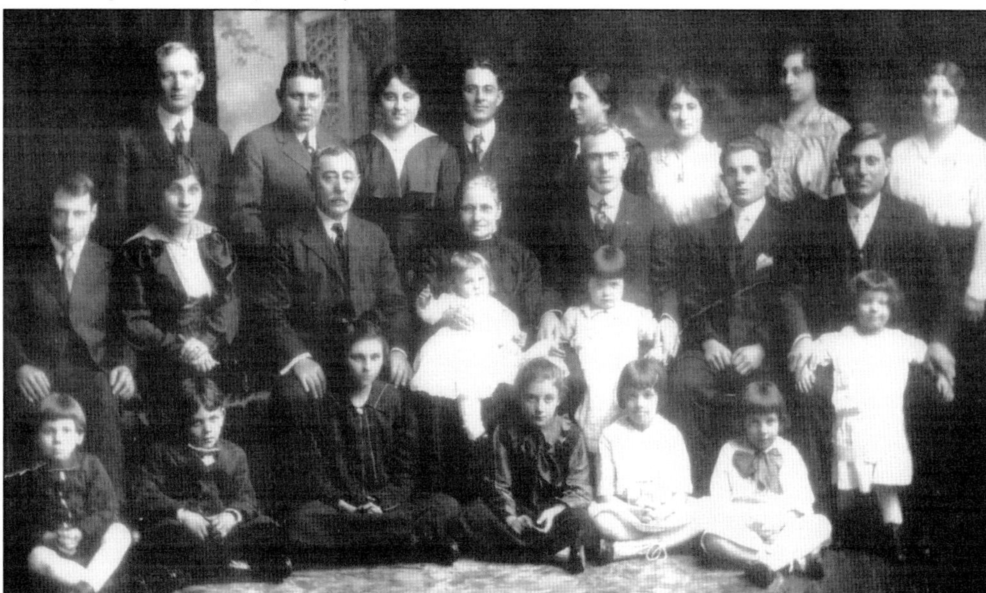

The members of the extended Brooks and Averbuch families, shown in this photograph from early 1900s, went on to form the branches of a number of Jewish family trees in Nashville over the next 50 years. (Courtesy of Terry Rosenblum.)

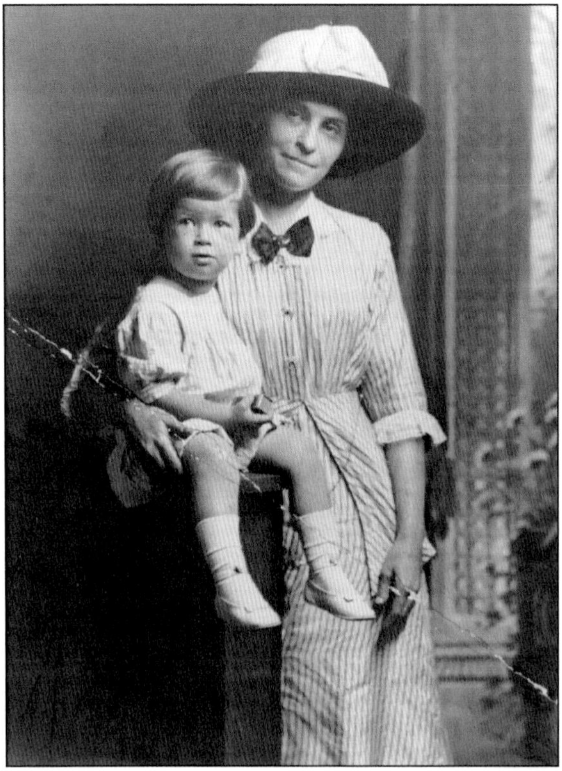

Lillie (Mrs. Sol) Frankland is shown here in 1912 with her grandson, Louis Leftwich Jr., the son of Louis Leftwich Sr. and Lillie's daughter Pearl. Leftwich Sr. was a graduate of Peabody and Vanderbilt Law School and served as attorney for the Nashville Credit Men's Association. His primary responsibility was to draw up bills favoring businessmen for introduction into the Tennessee legislature. He was a member of the YMHA, a Mason, and an Odd Fellow. Another one of Lillie's daughters, Celia, married Lee Zibart, who started the Nashville bookstore that bore his name.

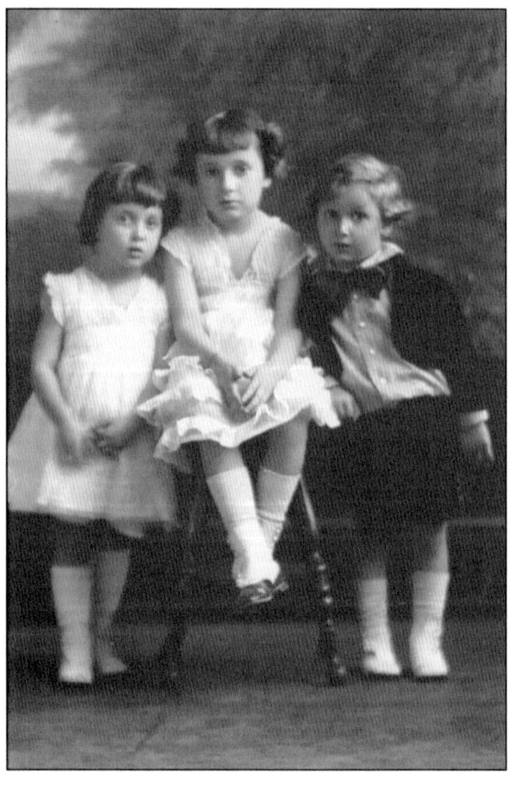

Alma Silverman (left) was the middle child of Ben and Lottie Belle Silverman of Nashville. She married Ray Koch, and they had three sons: Larry, Marvin and Carl. Rose Silverman (center) married Julius Cohen of Greenville, Kentucky. They had three daughters and a son. The youngest of the three children was Sam (right), who lived and worked in Nashville before moving to Memphis.

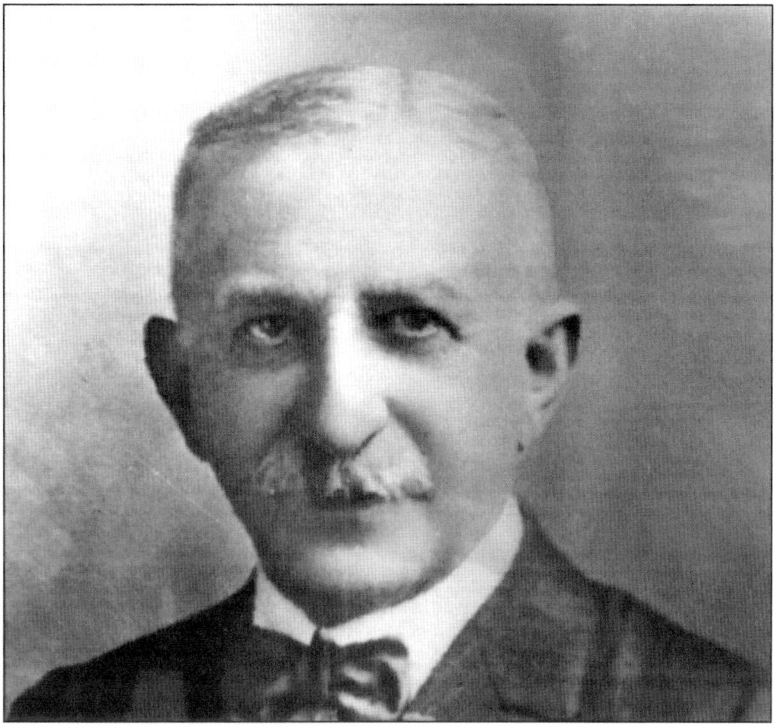

Raphael Zadoc Levy, born in 1854, was one of one Zadoc Levy's five sons. He married Ada Jaros, and they were the parents of two sons, Herbert and Alfred. Raphael joined the family-owned store as part of the second generation of Levys in 1874 along with brothers Solomon and Jacob. Raphael died in 1923.

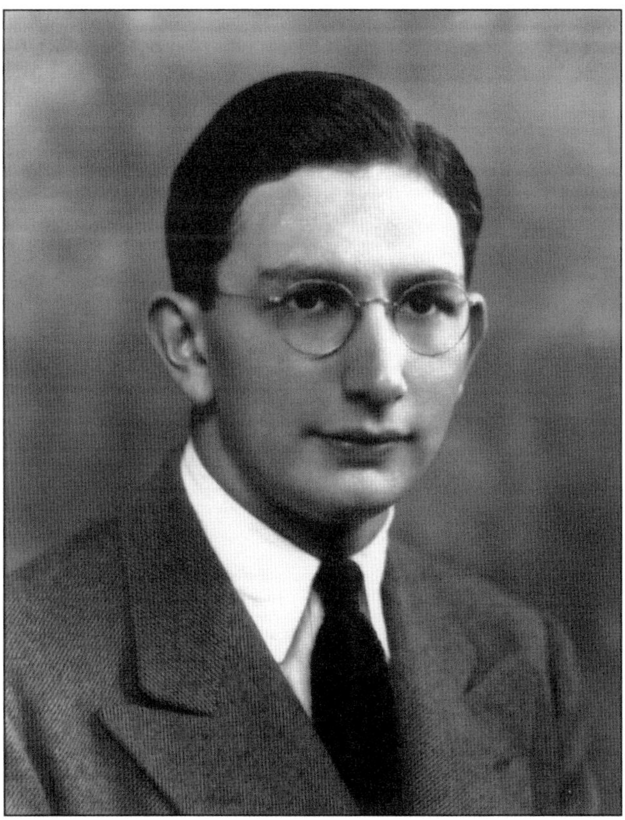

Ralph Levy Sr., the son of Herbert and Fannie Marx Levy, was the fourth generation of Levys to operate the store. He was born in 1920 and died in 1976 and was married to Annette Rose Levy, now Annette Levy Ratkin. They had two sons and a daughter: David, a past president of the JCC who still operates Levy's; Ralph, an officer of The Temple and an attorney; and Gail. In the 1970s, Nashville television viewers enjoyed watching Ralph and his cousin A. J. doing the Levy's television commercials, which his son David continued after he passed away. All of the Levys have been active in serving and working for The Temple and various Jewish organizations for five generations.

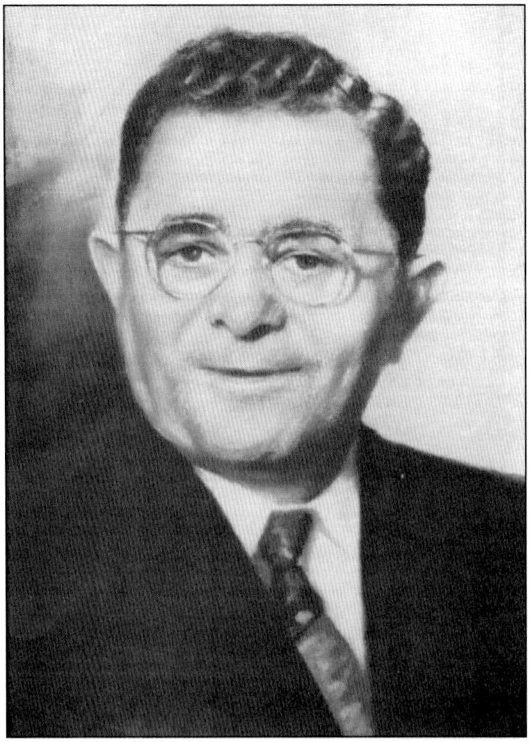

David Bubis, the founder of the American Tea and Coffee Company, was married to Hattye Raphael. He started in business as a peddler, as so many others did, but soon went into business for himself, building his business from the "grounds" up. David was active in the YMHA and many Jewish organizations over the years until his death in 1967.

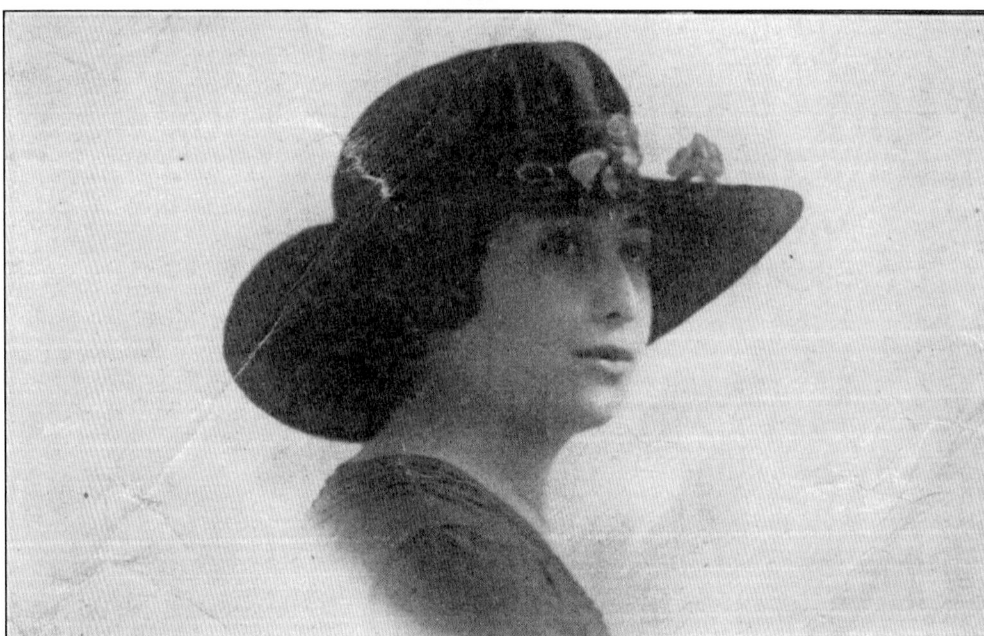

Hattye Raphael became David Bubis's wife and made significant contributions of her own to Nashville's Jewish community. She and David were married in 1920, and for more than 50 years, she was an important part of the YMHA, the YWHA, the Nashville section of the National Council of Jewish Women, and the Temple Sisterhood. She continued to do volunteer work into her 80s as a reader for WPLN's *Talking Library*.

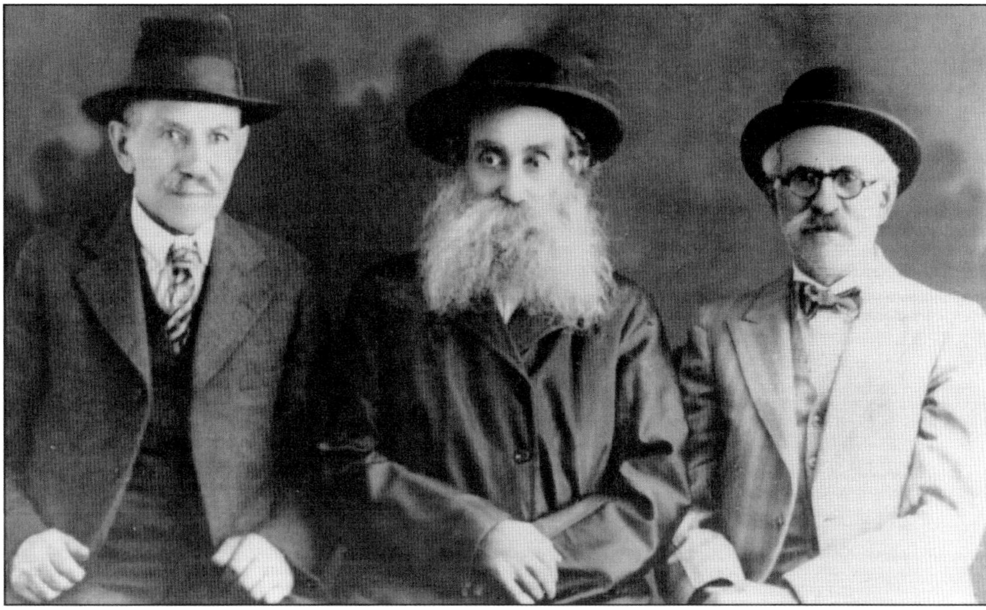

William (left) and Moses (right) Frank came to the United States from Hungary in their early 20s, William in 1880 and Moses a few years later. A third brother, Jacob (center), remained behind. William became a vegetable merchant in the Market House, while Moses opened a grocery store at Third Avenue North and Gay Street. Homesick and longing to visit Jacob in Hungary, they sailed from the United States to visit him in 1930.

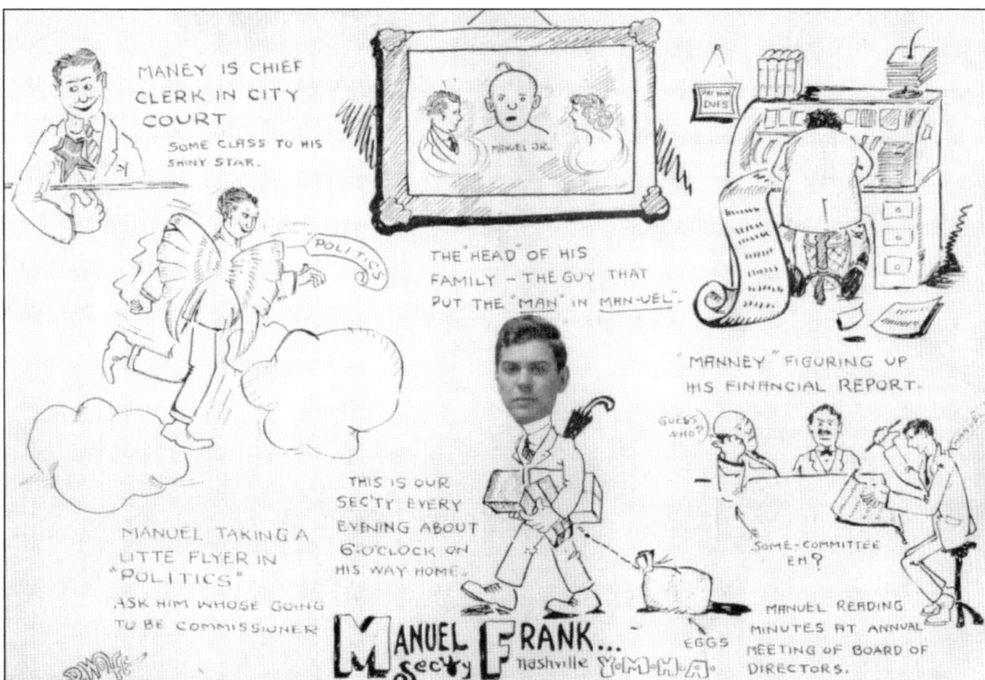

Manuel Frank was one of Moses Frank's two sons. When he began in business, he worked first as a railroad clerk, then a secretary to Nashville's City and Juvenile Courts. In 1918, he and his brother, Isadore, founded the Frank Fuel and Equipment Company.

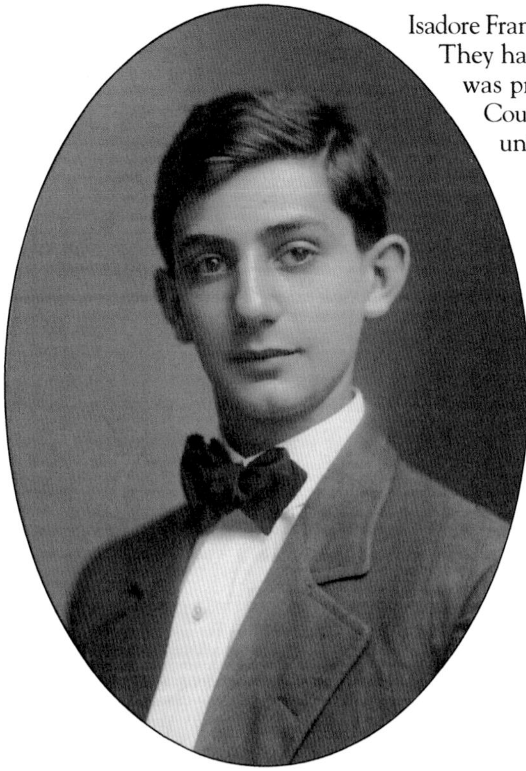

Isadore Frank, born in 1893, married Fedora Small in 1925. They had two children, Stanley and Patricia. Isadore was president of B'nai B'rith and the Woodmont Country Club and a member of Vine Street Temple until his death in 1970.

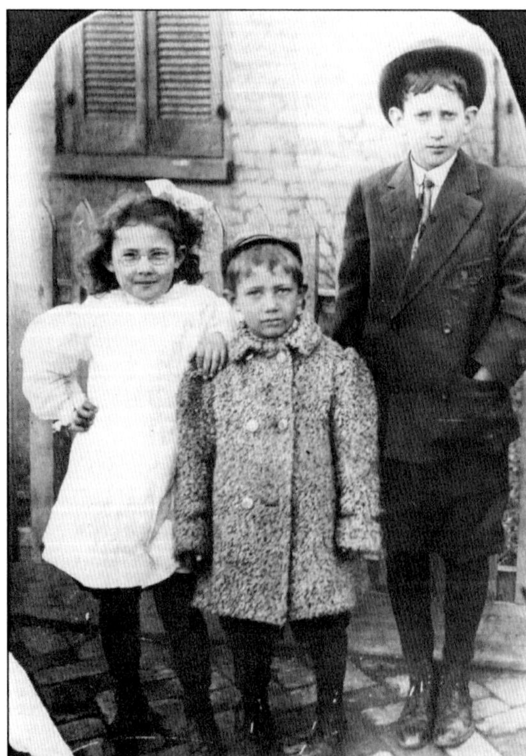

Fedora Small was the daughter of Louis H. and Rosa Small. She is pictured here with her two brothers, Irvin (who was killed in World War I) and Horace (right), in 1908. Fedora wrote two books about the history of Nashville's Jewish community, and Horace founded Horace Small Manufacturing, one of Nashville's leading specialty apparel companies for over 60 years.

Maud (Mrs. Joe) Kessler (left), Esther Schulman (right), and a friend enjoy a leisurely afternoon shopping in downtown Nashville in 1940. At that time, many of the stores the women would visit—Joe Morse and Company, Lebeck's, Burk's, Loveman's, Rich-Schwartz, Levy's, and others—were owned by local Jewish businessmen.

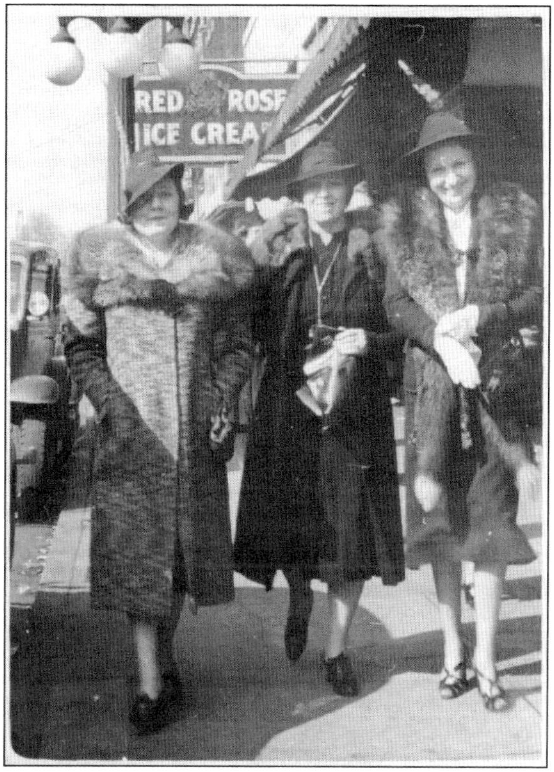

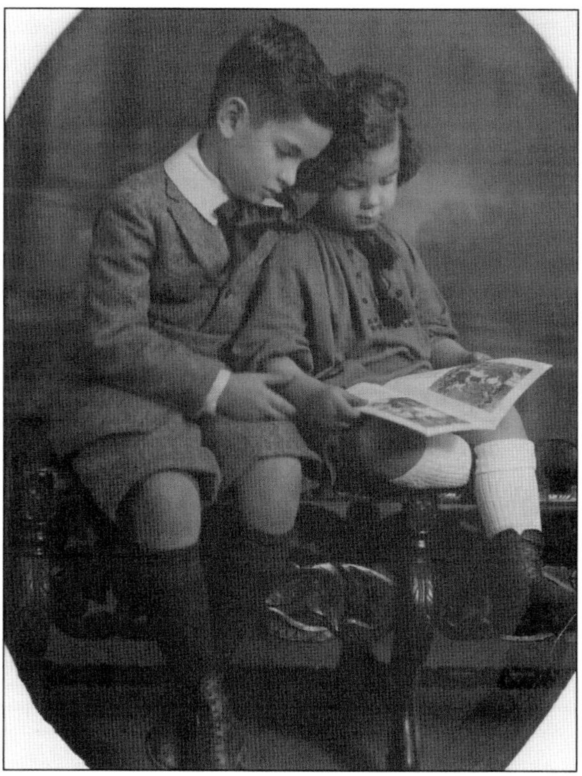

Maud and Joe Kessler had two children: a son, Julius, and a daughter, Fredrica. Julius died in 1968. Fredrica, better known as Freddie, never married, was a longtime salesperson for Rich, Schwartz, and Joseph, and for many years helped take care of her parents in their old age.

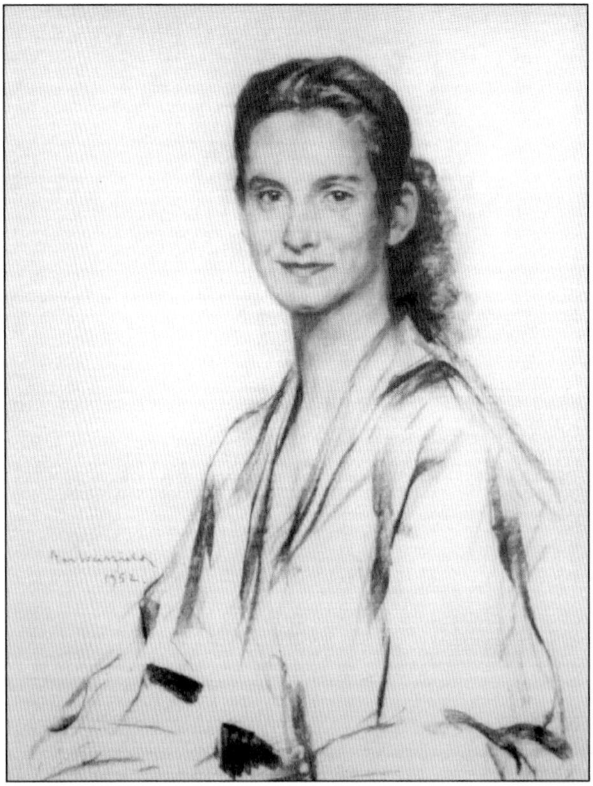

Mrs. Gus Kuhn Jr., the former Barbara Jacobs, was one of several prominent members of Nashville's Jewish community who were subjects of portraits by noted Nashville artist Max Westfield (see page 126). The original work from which this was reproduced was done in 1952.

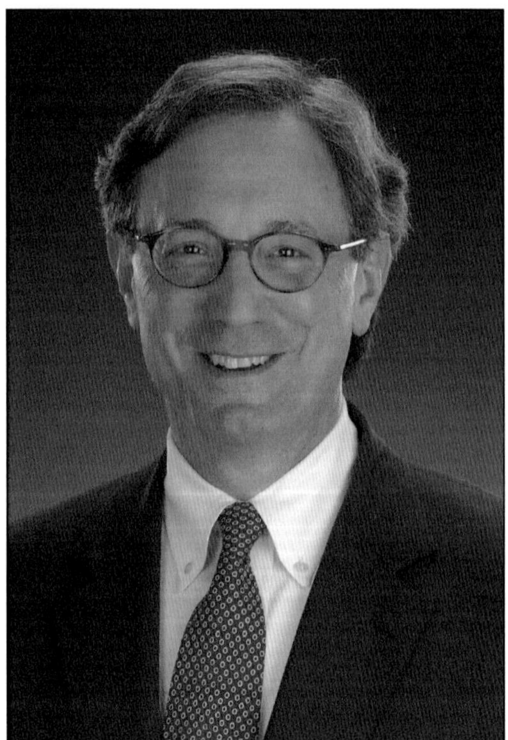

William Kuhn is a Nashville native, the son of Barbara and Gus Kuhn Jr. After graduating from the Wharton School of Business at the University of Pennsylvania, he attended Hebrew Union College for one year and then returned to Nashville to become vice president of the family-owned Kuhn's–Big K Stores. A member of The Temple, he served on the board and was chairman of the Social Action Committee, where in 1986 he was instrumental in starting The Temple's participation in the Room at the Inn program, housing the homeless during the winter. Near the end of the 1980s, he decided to make a career change and reenrolled at the Hebrew Union College–Jewish Institute of Religion. He was ordained as a rabbi in 1994. Today he is the senior rabbi at Congregation Rodeph Shalom in Philadelphia.

Four

Nashville's Jewish-Oriented Businesses

The earliest Jewish settlers came to Nashville for many different reasons, but one of the most common was to earn a living. In the 1840s and 1850s, the small number of Jews who came to Nashville were usually peddlers, salesmen, or traders. Many of those who came during the next two decades advertised themselves as doctors, dentists, or druggists, but most were pitchmen with a "medicinal product." It was not until after the Civil War that Nashville's Jewish residents began to own their own businesses. Some of the peddlers had saved up enough money to open their own stores, and as they did, the need for salesmen and clerks increased, giving more Jewish people jobs. Some of the men who had been peddlers were actually traders—people who followed the soldiers from camp to camp during the Civil War, picking up scrap metal or fabric the troops left behind, then selling it to scrap dealers in the North. Some of these did so well that they went into the scrap metal business when the war ended. In one instance, the company that became known as Cline, Bernheim grew and prospered, lasting more than 150 years. R. Z. Levy and Sons, which had its beginning in 1855 and officially opened as Levy's in 1874, is also going strong more than 150 years later as Levy's, Clothier for Men and Women and is still owned by the Levy family. Prejudice and anti-Semitism prevented many Jews from entering the professions for many years, forcing them into business or sales. Now diminishing prejudices and greater opportunities have opened new doors. With the growth of Vanderbilt University and the educational community at large, including Tennessee State, Belmont, Lipscomb, and other area universities, many Jewish men and women in the community are professors, teachers, and research scientists. There are many Jewish singers, songwriters, and artists in the music business, and a substantial number of Jewish men and women are active in building construction, real estate, medicine, and law. This chapter will look at some of the Jewish-owned businesses that have employed community leaders for the past 150 years.

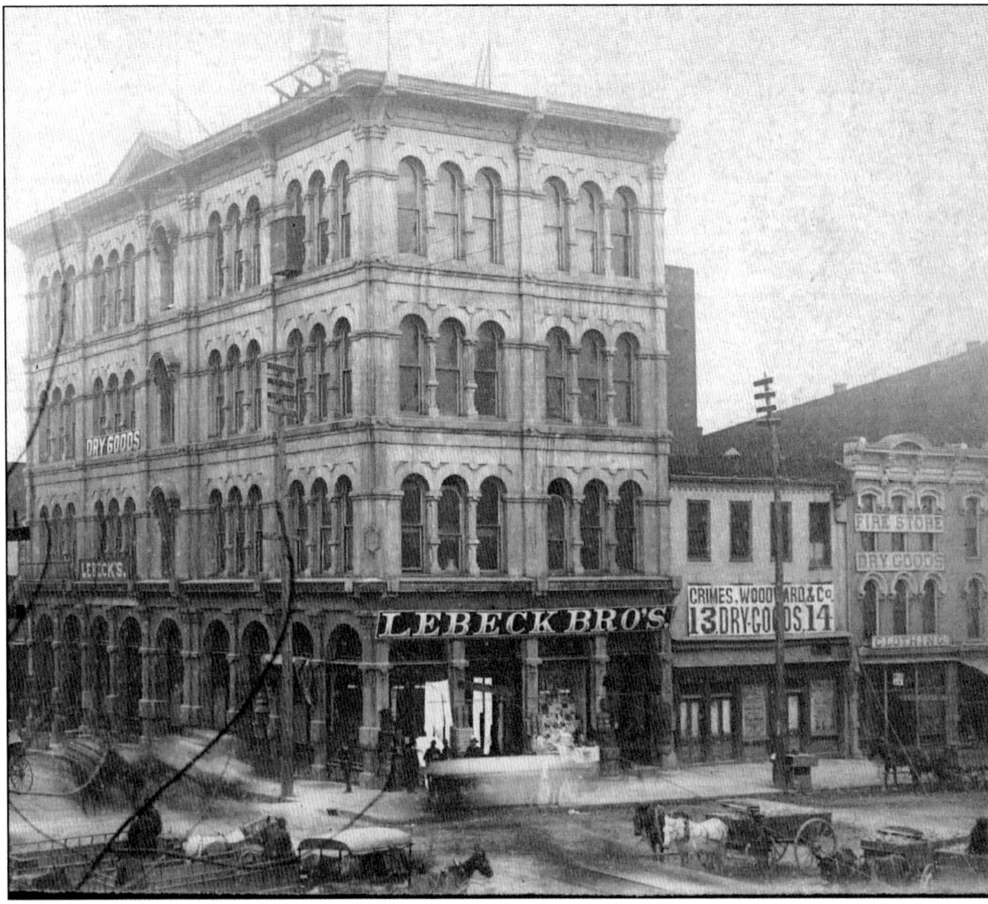

Lebeck Brothers Department Store was one of Nashville's most successful retail operations for nearly 75 years. This photograph shows the store much as it looked in 1874. Under the management of Michael, Louis, and Samuel Lebeck, it continued to grow and prosper before eventually being supplanted as the city's most popular store by Harvey's.

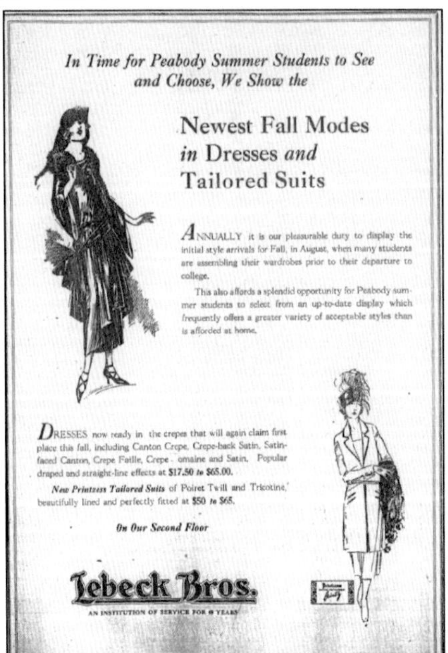

In an early advertisement in the *Tennessean* newspaper, Lebeck's touts its new fall line of women's clothing.

Before opening his own store, Mike Lebeck worked for his uncle, Solomon Frankland. Frankland had started in business as a peddler and then opened a store in Cottontown in Sumner County prior to the Civil War. After the war ended, he opened this store in downtown Nashville, where, as he points out in this advertisement, no one is really a stranger.

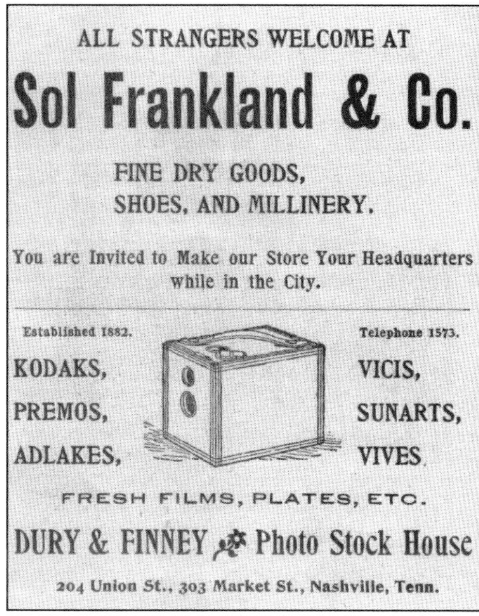

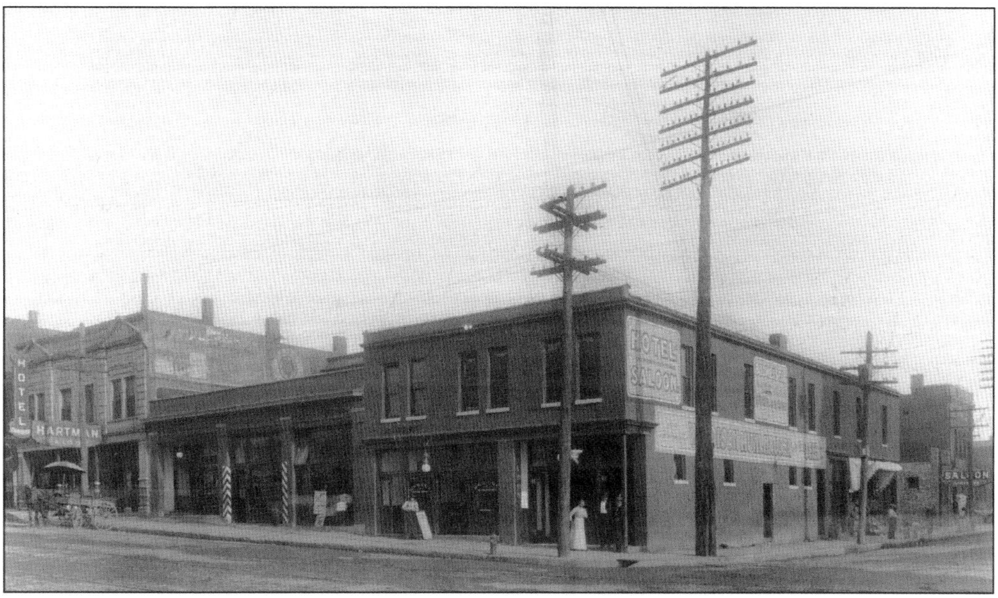

Samuel Hartman owned and operated the Hartman Hotel on Broad Street between Ninth and Tenth Avenues from 1901 and 1910. Located near Nashville's railway station, the hotel had a reputation for attracting traveling men looking for card games, gambling, and female companionship. An adjoining tavern added to its popularity. In 1910, Hartman sold the hotel, and in 1911, he opened the Ideal Laundry, which he continued to operate until he was murdered by a former business partner turned competitor in the laundry business, Leo D. Wege. According to a newspaper account of the incident, Wege walked into Hartman's office at the laundry and warned him not to involve Wege's son in a dispute between the two men. Wege claimed that after a brief argument, Hartman picked up a paperweight from his desk and threw it at him, just missing his head. Wege claimed that in self defense he then "reached into his pocket, took out his gun, and shot Hartman five times, fatally injuring him. He then walked out of the office, down the street, and into a nearby police station, where he reported what had just transpired."

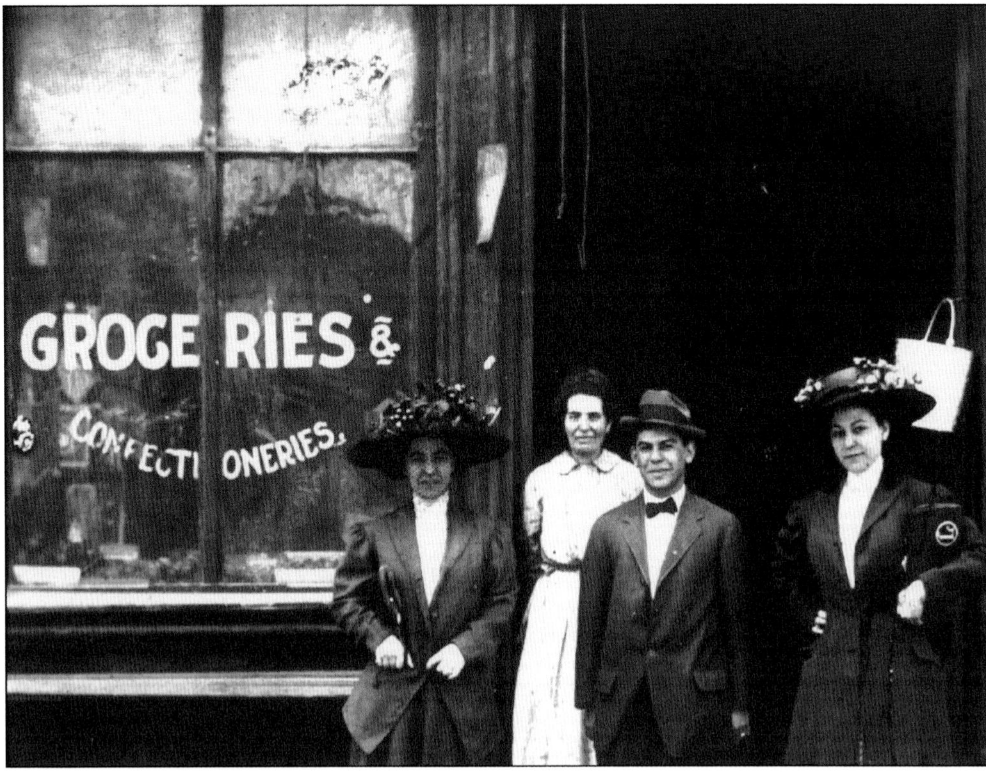

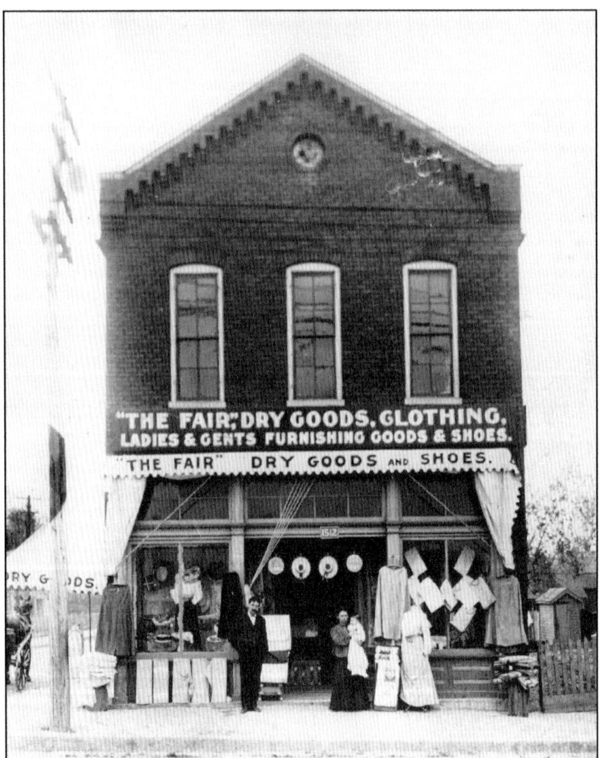

This store in downtown Nashville was known simply as Frank's Store, owned and operated by members of the Frank family (shown here). Like other similar stores in the downtown Nashville area owned by Jewish families, it was called a dry goods store, although it was probably closer to what would today be called a general store.

Pictured here is the Small family store as it looked in downtown Nashville in 1910. Owned and operated by Louis H. Small and his wife—the parents of Fedora, Horace and Irvin Small—the store was listed in business directories as a grocery and dry goods store at 1237 South College Street.

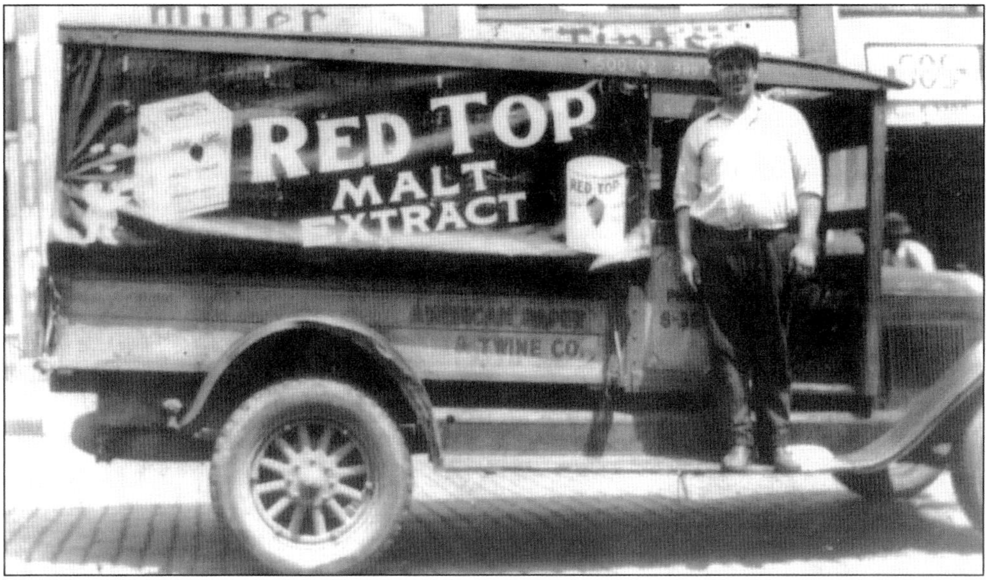

American Paper and Twine Company began in 1926, when two young men, Nathan Doochin and Milton Lockenbach, saw an opportunity to create a niche in Nashville's growing wholesale market. After 83 years, the company has become a leader in the wholesale distribution of office, packaging, janitorial, and food service products. What began in 1926 with a $500 investment, three employees, and one delivery truck (shown here) has grown over the years to encompass five distribution centers and a fleet of trucks delivering throughout the Southeast.

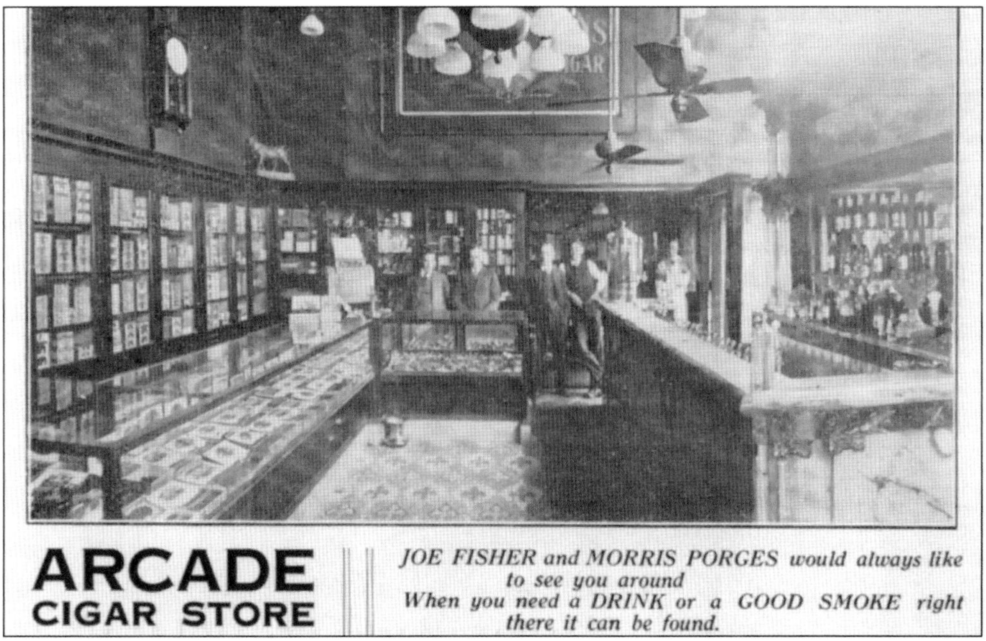

Nashville's downtown Arcade has often been called the city's first mall. Located between Church and Union Streets and Fourth and Fifth Avenues, it had more than 40 stores on two levels. One of the most popular in the early 1900s was the Arcade Cigar Store, shown here in 1915. It was owned and operated by two young Jewish men, Joe Fisher and Morris Porges, both of whom were described as active members of the YMHA.

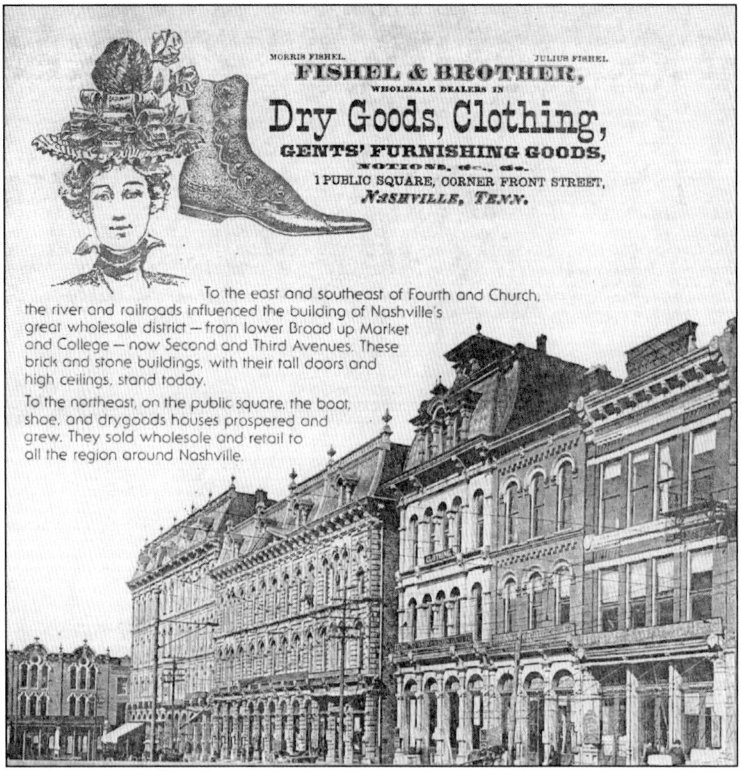

Morris Fishel moved to Nashville in 1865 and opened a dry goods store on North Market Street, joined by his brother Julius in 1867. Morris served as the first president of Congregation B'nai Yeshurun, the vice president of B'nai B'rith, and was later on the board of Vine Street Temple. Julius was a charter member of the Standard (Country) Club and also was one of the founders of the Nashville Hebrew Relief Society, a forerunner of Jewish Family Services.

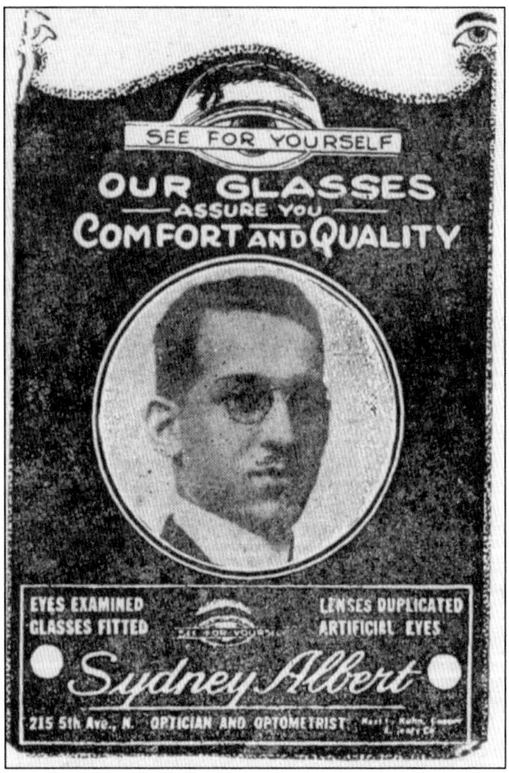

Sydney Albert, brother of Jesse Albert, was an optometrist in the early 1900s. Before going into business for himself, he worked at D. Lowenheim, advertising in early editions of the *YMHA News*. After setting up shop for himself, he promoted the services he offered at his store, which included, as this advertisement indicates, "artificial eyes."

Leo Schwartz (right), along with Julius Rich and Arthur Joseph, founded one of Nashville's finest upscale women's clothing stores, Rich and Schwartz (later Rich, Schwartz, and Joseph), in 1902. Leo was born in Atlanta in 1873 but grew up in Chattanooga. Married to Selma Harris Frank of Nashville, Leo was the first president of Big Brothers in Nashville.

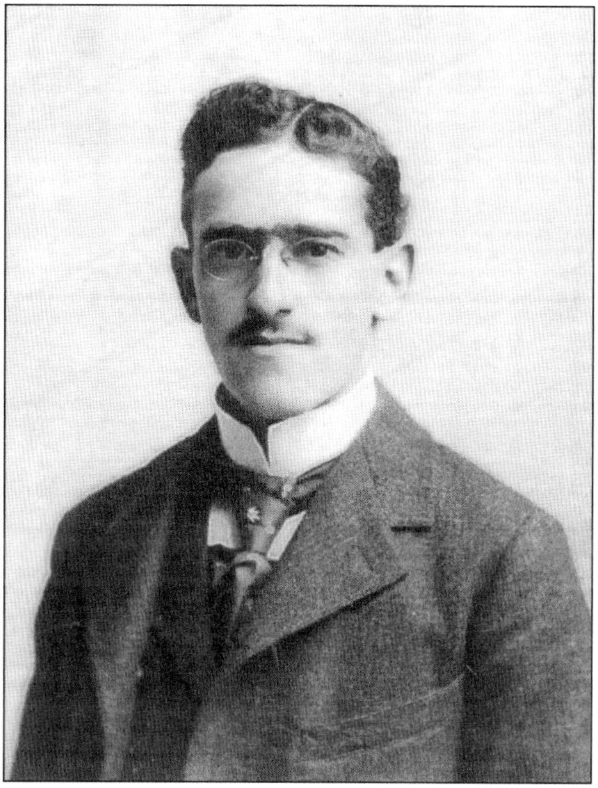

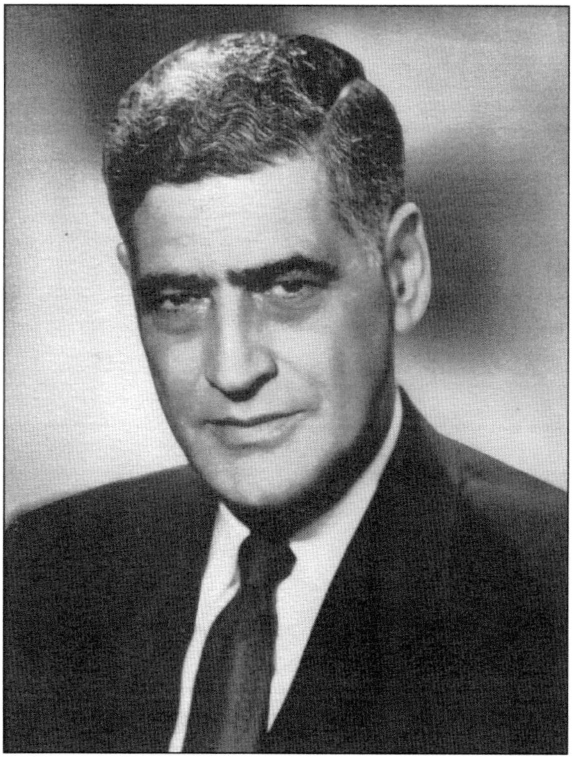

Leo's son, Morris Frank Schwartz, went to work at Rich, Schwartz after graduating from Vanderbilt. He took over operation of the store, becoming president of the company when his father died in 1952, shortly after the store's 50th anniversary. He continued the tradition of fine merchandise and personal service for nearly 40 more years, including expansion to the Belle Meade area.

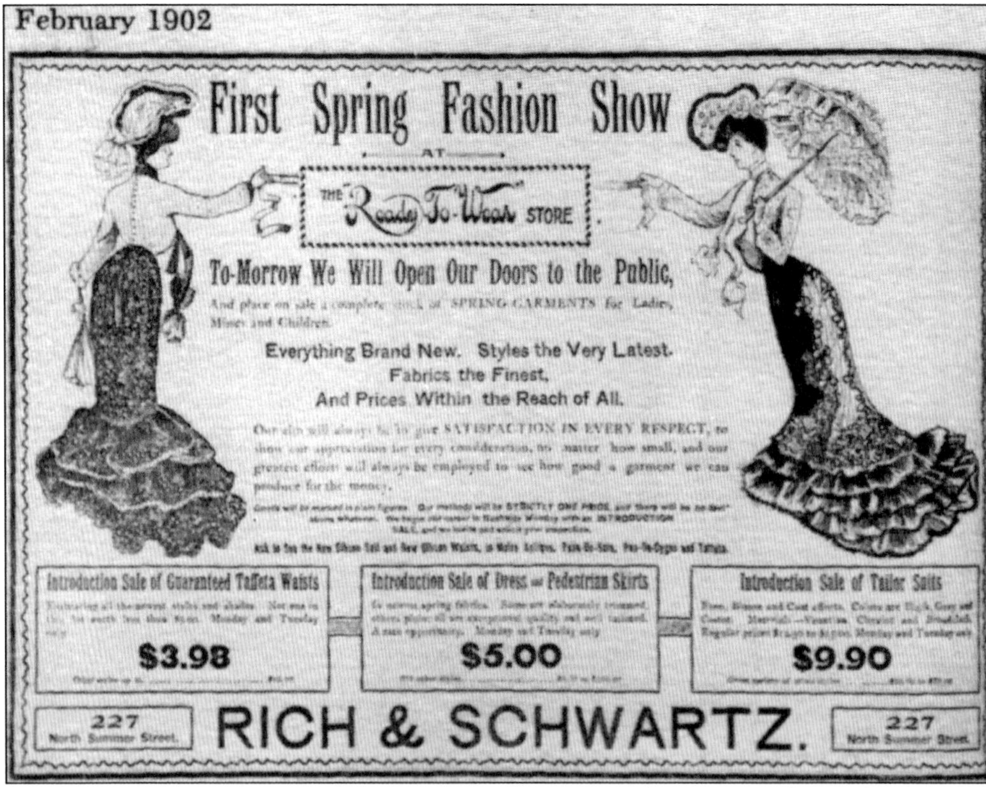

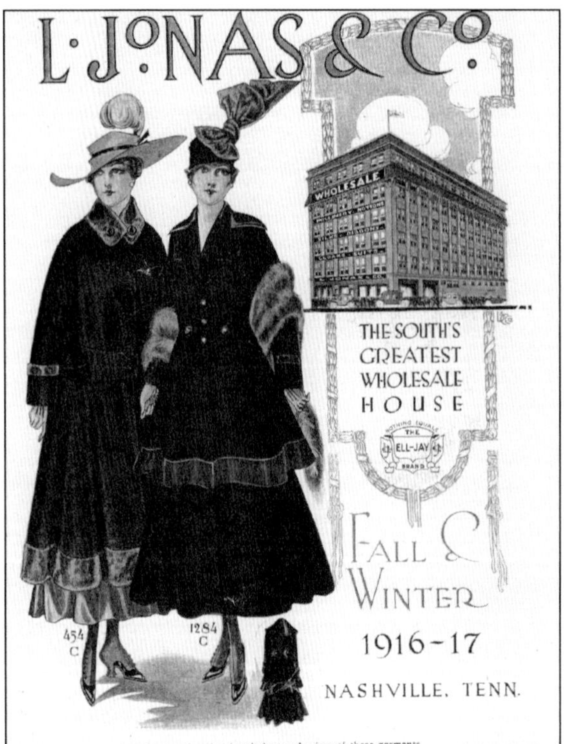

On the occasion of its 25th anniversary in 1927, *Nugents–The Garment Weekly* gives Rich and Schwartz credit for coining the term "ready-to-wear." That phrase was born, the article says, on March 16, 1902, when the store used it to describe what it sold to "a highly discriminating clientele demanding the best in women's apparel." The use of the term in the small box in the center of this advertisement is believed to be the first time it appeared anywhere.

Leopold Jonas, with his brother Adolph, founded one of Nashville's most prestigious apparel businesses, L. Jonas and Company, which billed itself as "the South's greatest wholesale house."

The Jonas brothers emigrated from Germany to the United States when Leopold was 16. They moved first to Maryland, then to Columbia, Tennessee, finally arriving in Nashville in 1885. Leopold was married to Rickie Hirsch, one of seven children of Nathan and Rosalie Hirsch. One of Rickie's sisters, Regina, married Sam Lowenstein, and their son, Milton, was one of the 101 people killed in the train wreck at Dutchman's Curve in Nashville in 1918. Leopold was a director of the chamber of commerce, the board of trade, and the Retail Merchants Association and was vice president of Cumberland Valley National Bank. Within the Jewish community, he was a trustee of Vine Street Temple and a member of the YMHA and B'nai B'rith.

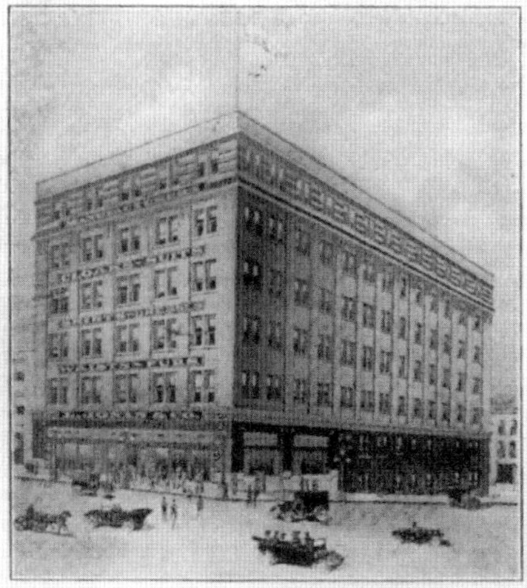

L. JONAS & COMPANY

Corner Eighth Avenue, Ninth Avenue and Commerce Street

NASHVILLE, TENN.

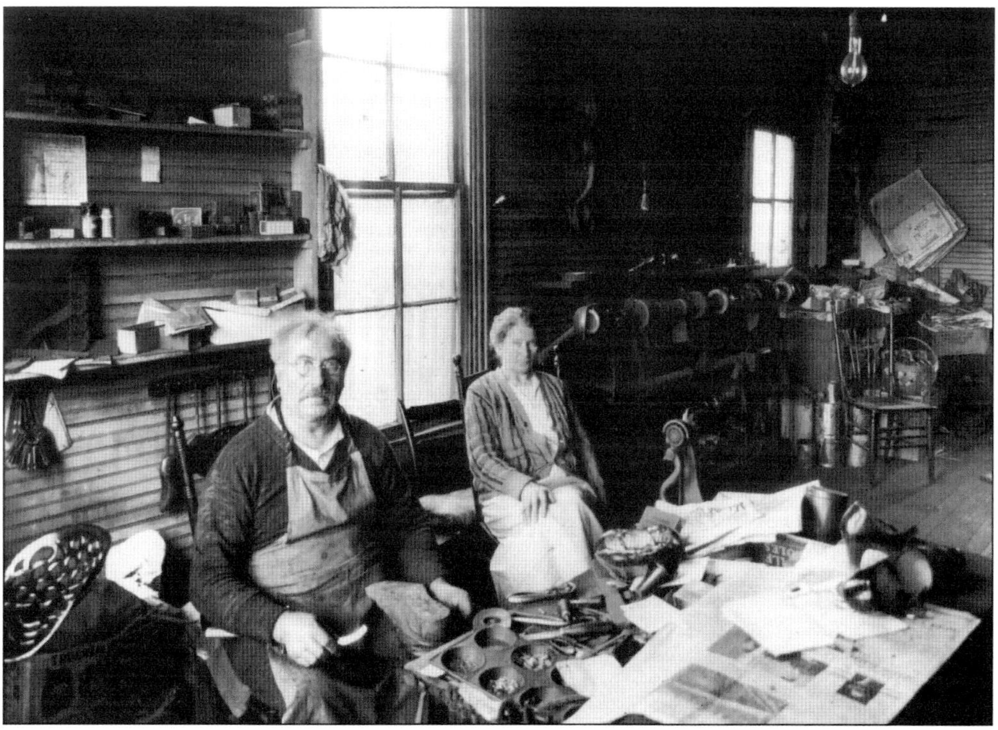

Ben and Elizabeth Wasserman immigrated to Nashville from Europe and owned and operated the New York Shoe Shop, seen here in 1928, on North First Street in East Nashville. They had two sons, Aaron and Isadore, and two daughters, Gertrude and Bessie. Isadore, whose daughter Barbara (Schwartz) now lives in Murfreesboro, worked at American Paper and Twine for more than 70 years, starting there while still in his teens. Bessie married Joe Zeitlin.

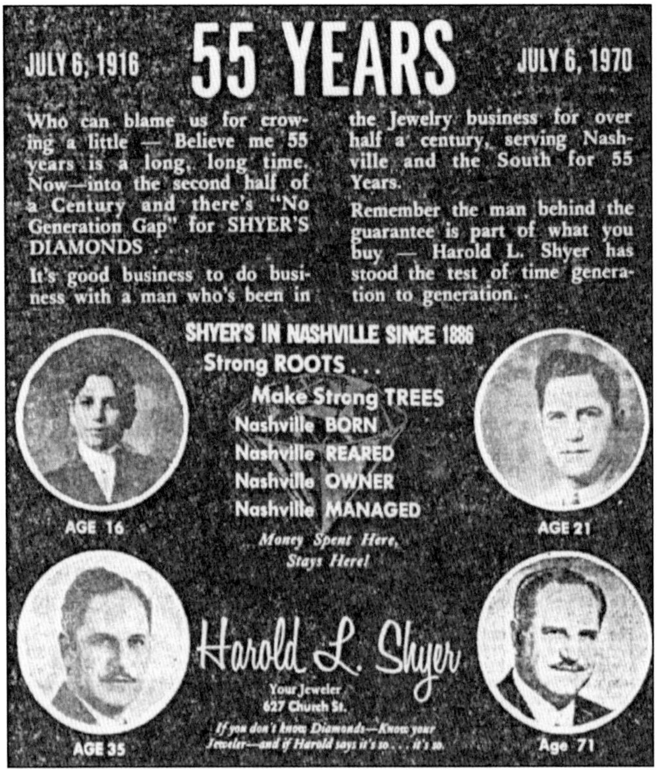

Harold L. Shyer's was one of Nashville's best-known jewelry stores, advertising heavily in the newspaper and on radio and television. The central figure in its ad campaigns was Harold himself, who ended every ad the same way: "If you don't know diamonds, know your jeweler . . . and if Harold says it's so, it's so."

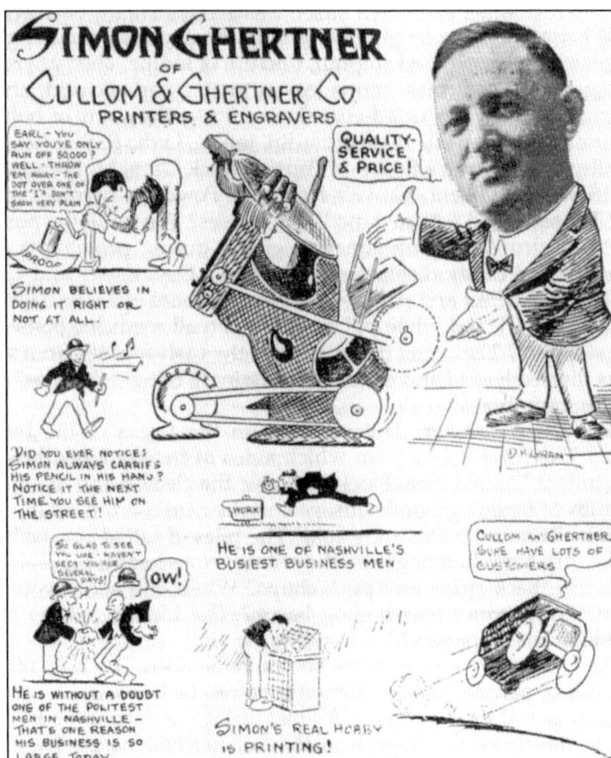

Simon Ghertner came to the United States from Romania around 1900, moving to Nashville shortly after that. By the 1920s, he had become a partner in Cullom and Ghertner printers. Because Ghertner served as chairman of the Religious School Committee at the Gay Street Synagogue, the Simon Ghertner Award is given in his memory each year to the seventh-grade student who is most proficient in Hebrew.

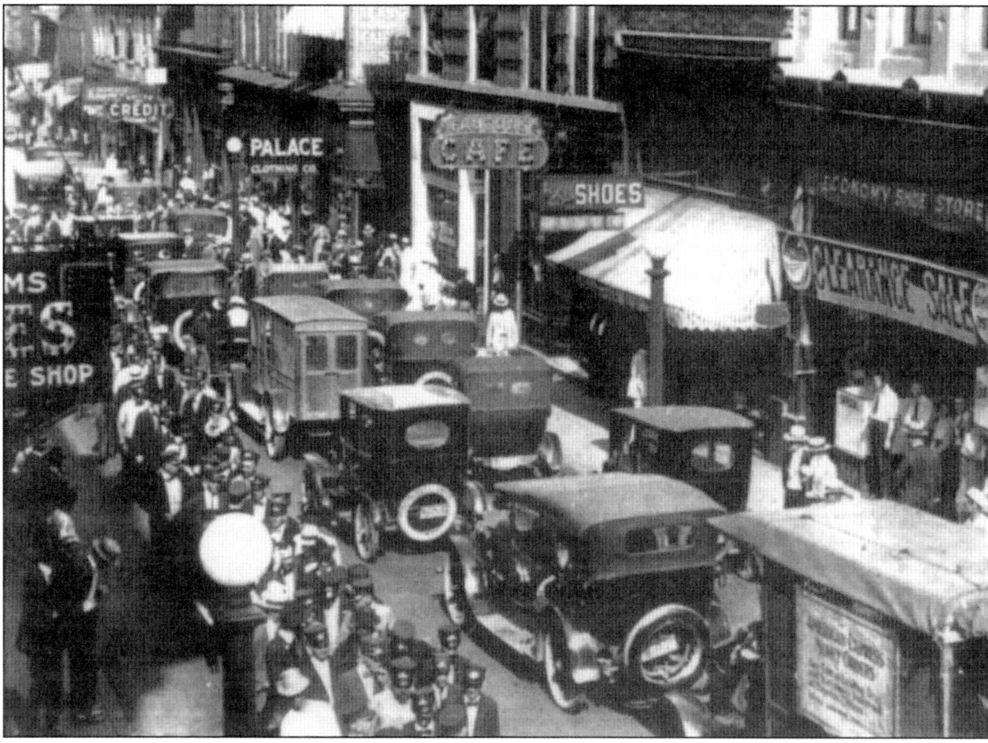

Fourth Avenue North in downtown Nashville was home to a number of Jewish-owned businesses in the early 1900s. In this photograph, one can see Abraham's Shoes, Economy Shoes, United Credit Clothing Company, Loventhal Brothers, Hirshberg's, and the Palace.

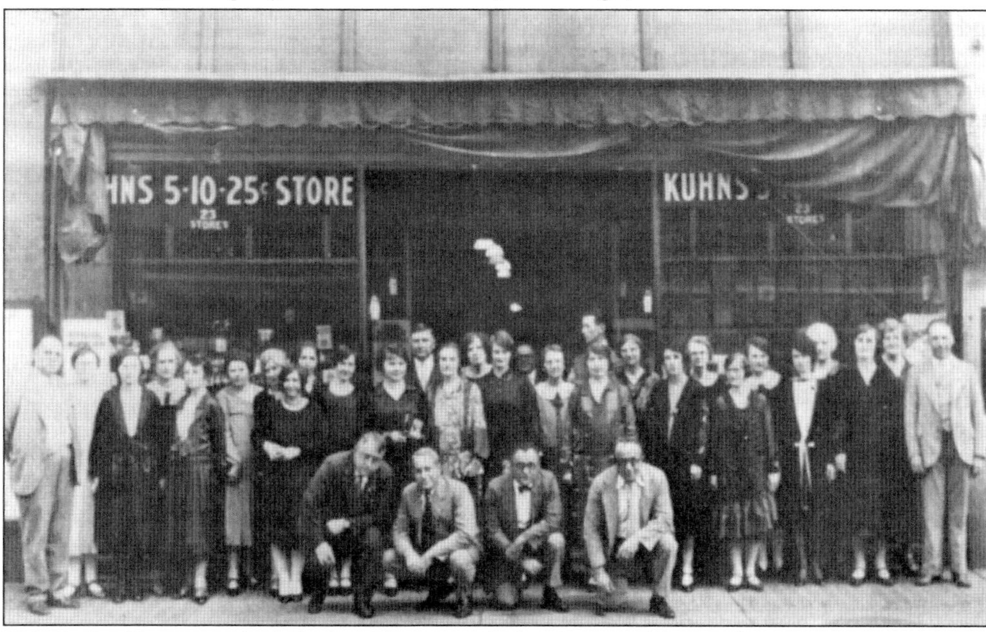

Kuhn's–Big K stores, which had 106 locations before being sold to Wal-Mart in 1981, started as Kuhn's 5 and 10 ¢ Store in the 1920s. This photograph from 1929 shows the staff of the downtown Nashville store and office.

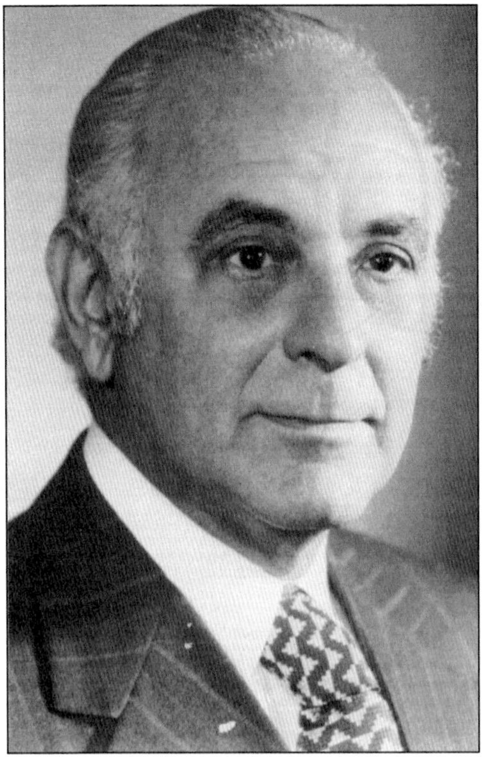

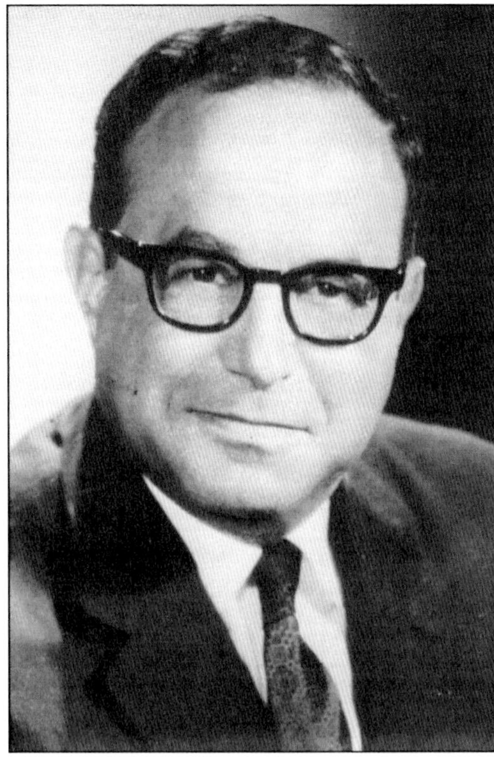

The second generation of the Kuhn family that headed up the company included brothers Jack (above left) and Gus Jr. (above right) It was under their leadership that the Big K stores were launched in 1962. Kuhn's employed a strategy similar to Wal-Mart, opening Big K stores, like the one pictured below in 1972, in small-to-medium sized towns in Alabama, Kentucky, Tennessee, and Georgia. Like Wal-Mart, they avoided the larger markets, which were likely to be heavily populated with Kmart stores. The success story continued throughout the 1970s, but, facing stiff competition from every direction, the Kuhns decided to sell out to Wal-Mart in 1981.

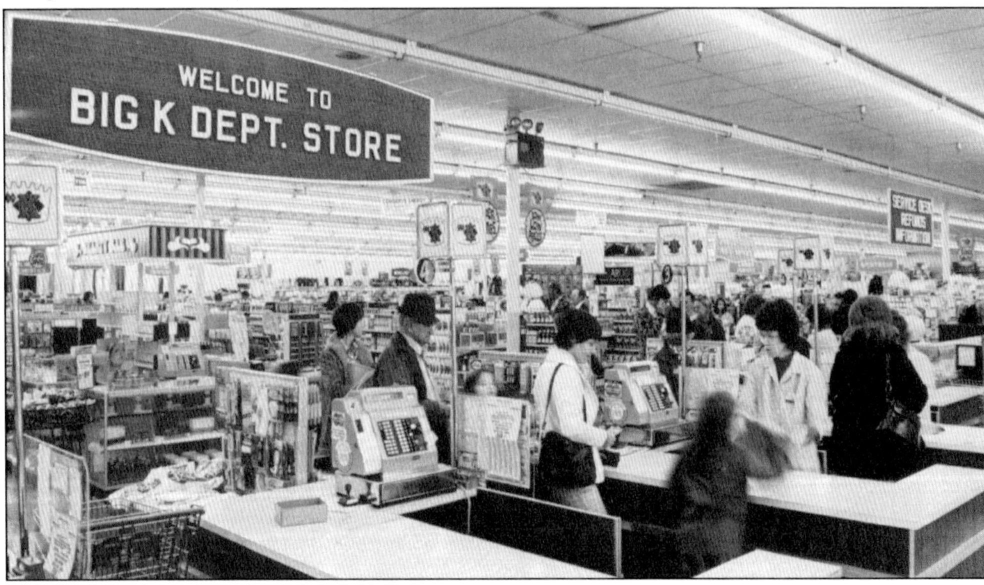

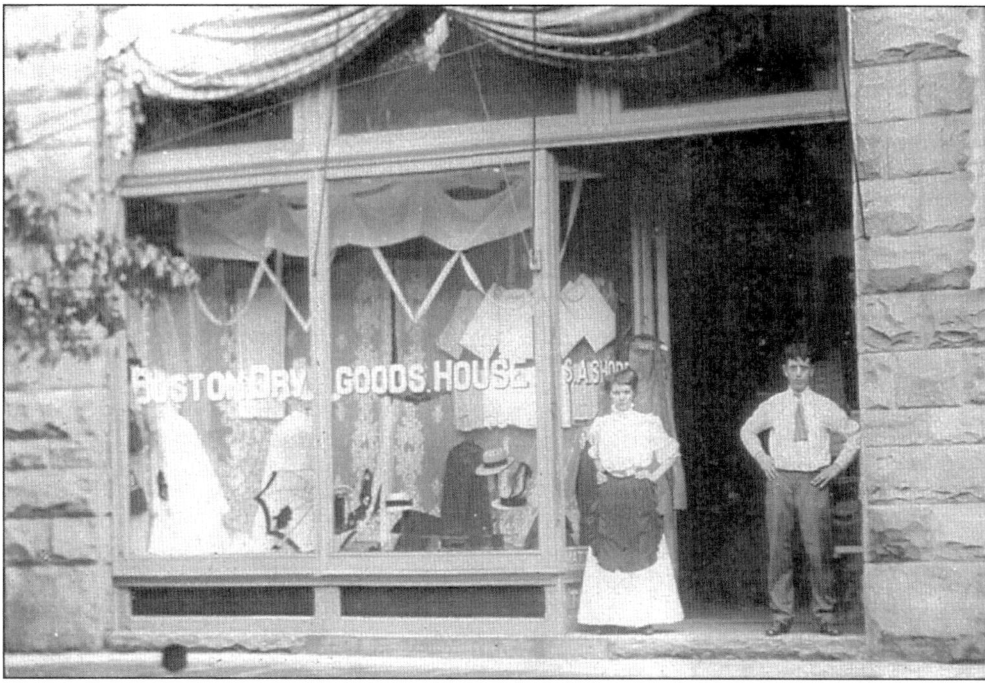

Sol Shore, father of famous entertainer Dinah Shore, was one of several Jewish men who chose to live and have businesses in small towns in Tennessee. His first store, in 1908, was 90 miles southeast of Nashville in Winchester. He later moved his family to Nashville, where Dinah attended Hume-Fogg High School and the family belonged to Vine Street Temple.

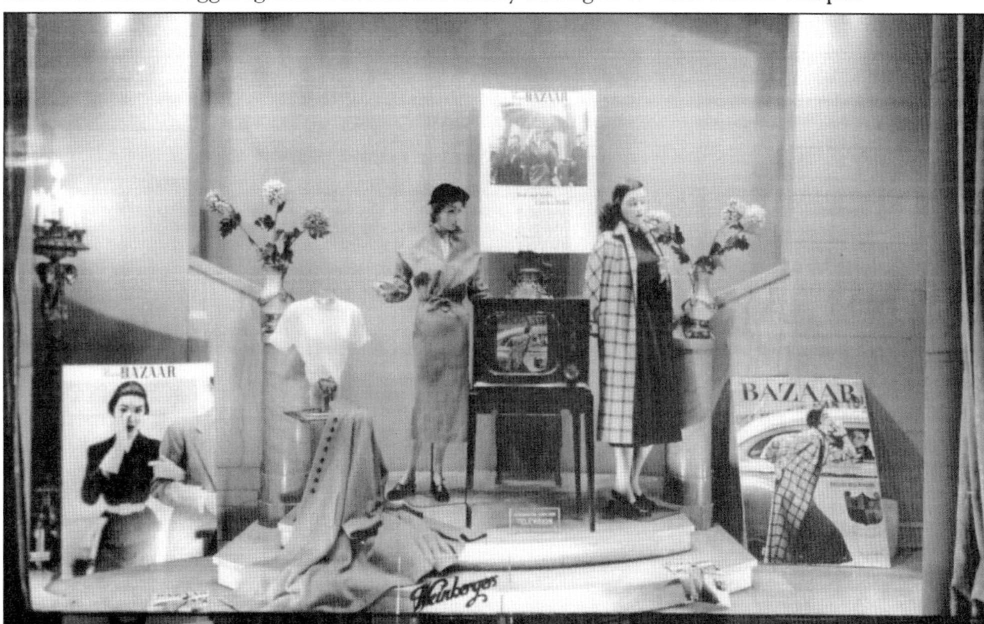

Weinberger's was an upscale women's clothing store owned by Maurice and Jennie Weinberger located in the lobby of the Tulane Hotel. While not as large as Rich, Schwartz and some other stores, it enjoyed a reputation for fine quality.

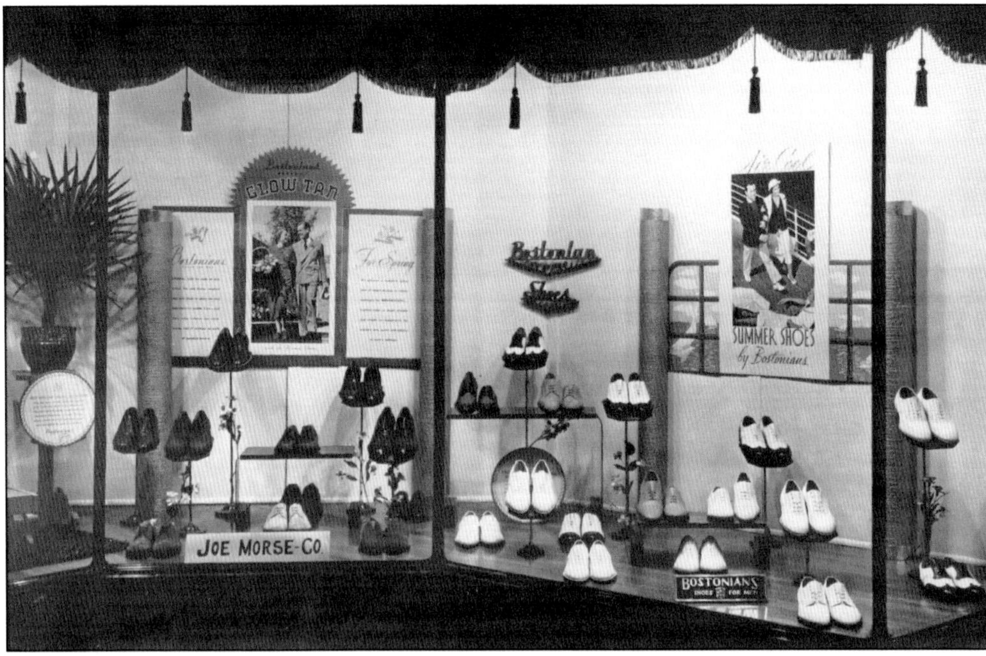

Joe Morse and Company was another of Nashville's downtown department stores that rose to prominence during the first half of the 20th century. Attractive window displays (above) showcasing famous brand-name merchandise brought customers into the store, where the bright, well-lighted, spacious departments and professional sales people (below) made them feel at home.

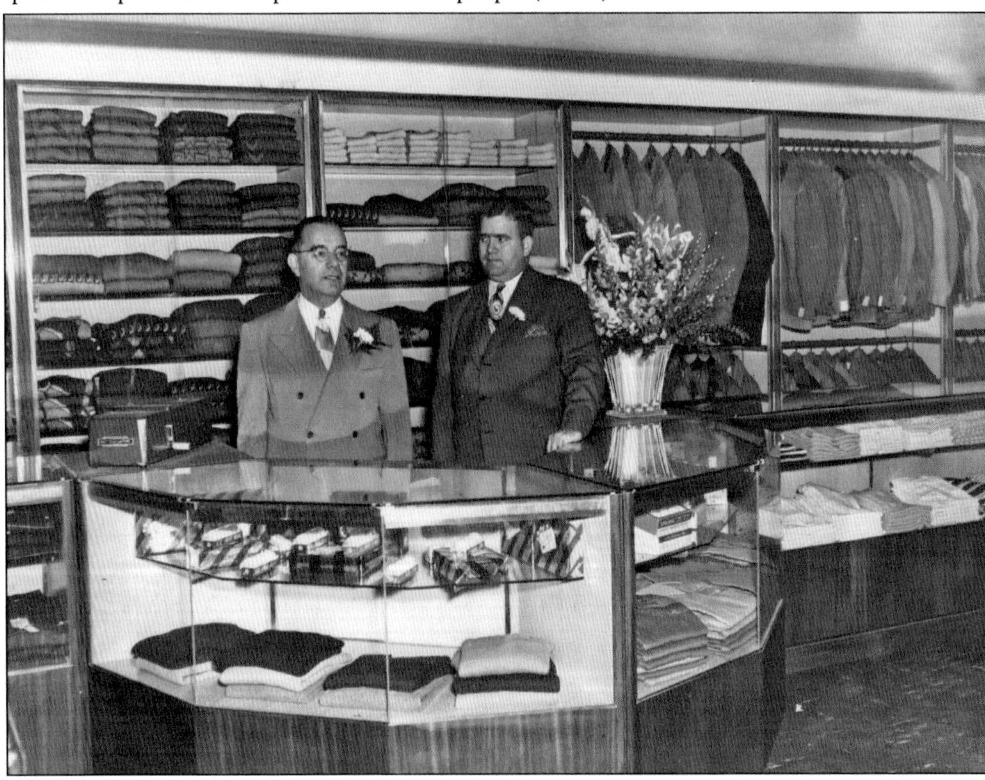

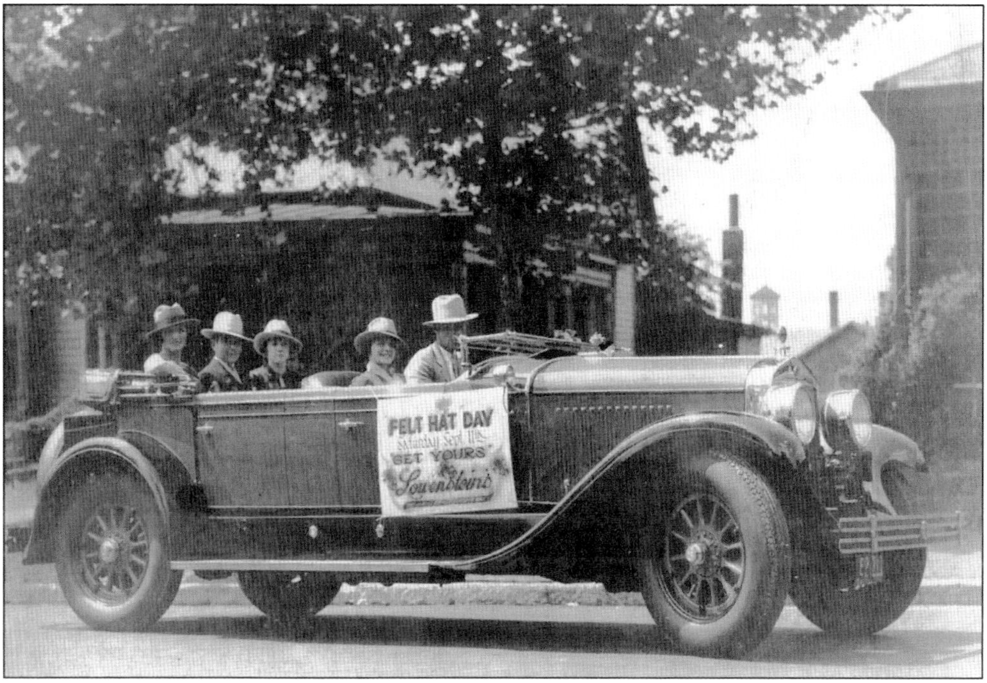

So that they could better promote Felt Hat Day at Lowenstein's, located on Deaderick Street in downtown Nashville, these people drove around town wearing the hats, inviting passersby to visit the store.

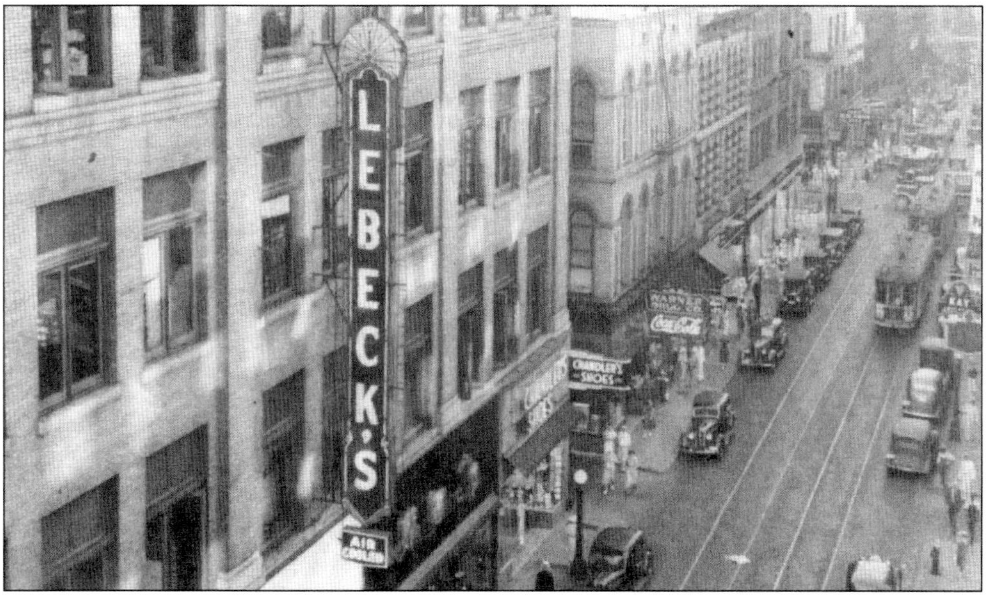

On page 72, Lebeck Brothers Department Store is shown as it looked in the late 1800s. Here it is again in the 1930s, on Church Street between Fifth and Sixth Avenues, where it moved in 1885. The original location in 1874 was 38 South Union Street, between College and Market Streets. In 1922, it expanded, occupying most of the block it occupied on Church Street. After more than 60 years of successful operation, the store closed in 1940, with the property eventually becoming home to Harvey's.

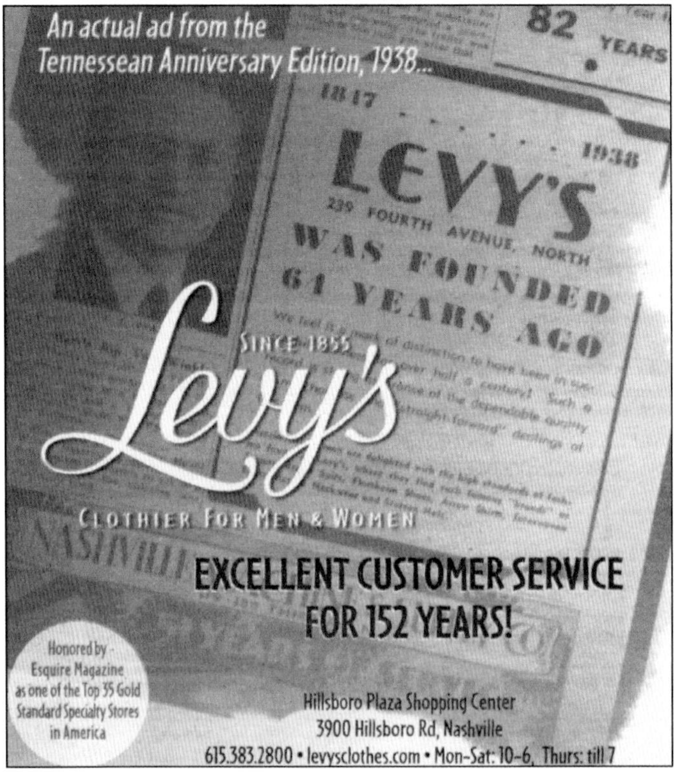

Levy's is Nashville's oldest retail store under original ownership. As this advertisement at left points out, the store, which opened in 1855, was still going strong in 1938 and 2007, five generations of Levys later. With just one location now, in Green Hills, the store expanded from men's fashions to include women's clothing about 30 years ago. Below, cousins A. J. (left) and David Levy (right) continued to do the store's television commercials for several years, with David replacing his father, Ralph Levy Sr., as one of the two spokesmen.

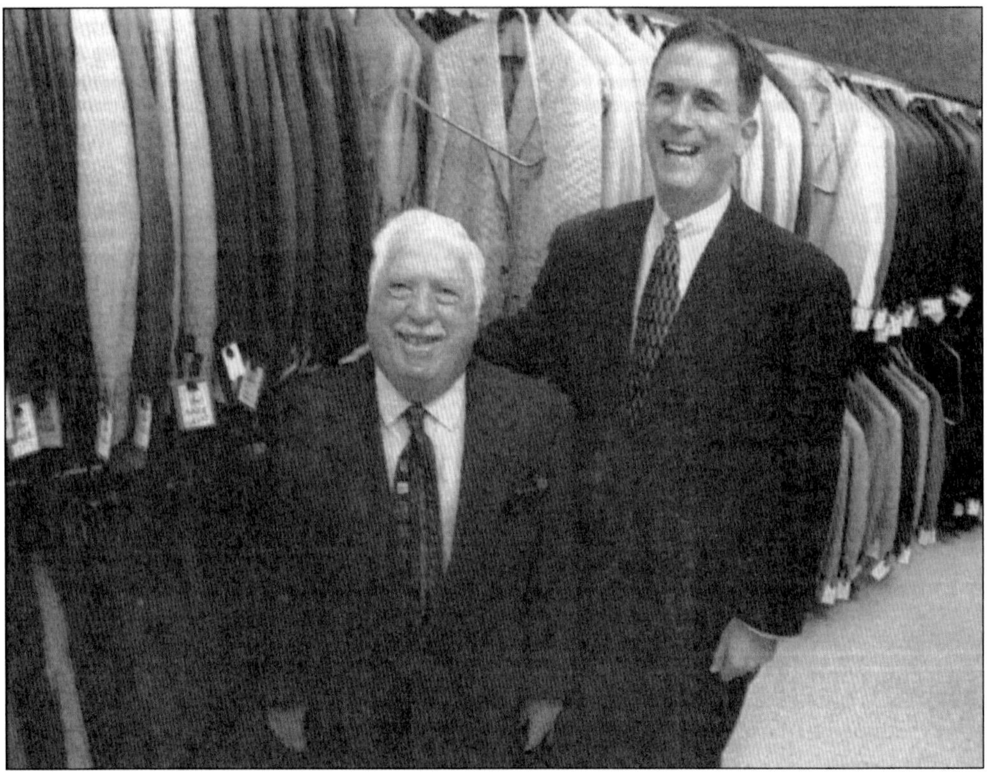

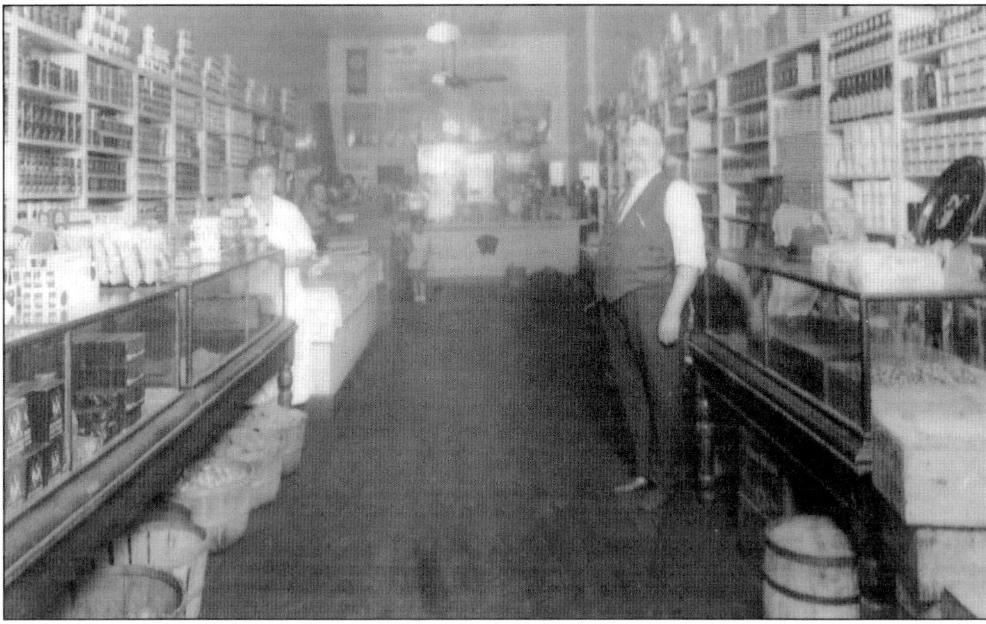

Hyman Zager and his wife, Sarah, came to the United States from Russia. Starting the same way so many European emigrants did, Hyman worked as a peddler before opening this store downtown on the Public Square. Two of his sons, Morris and Jake, later opened their own delicatessens, one on Fourth Avenue and the other on West End Avenue, just a block from the Jewish Community Center. Both delis did well and were Nashville institutions into the 1960s.

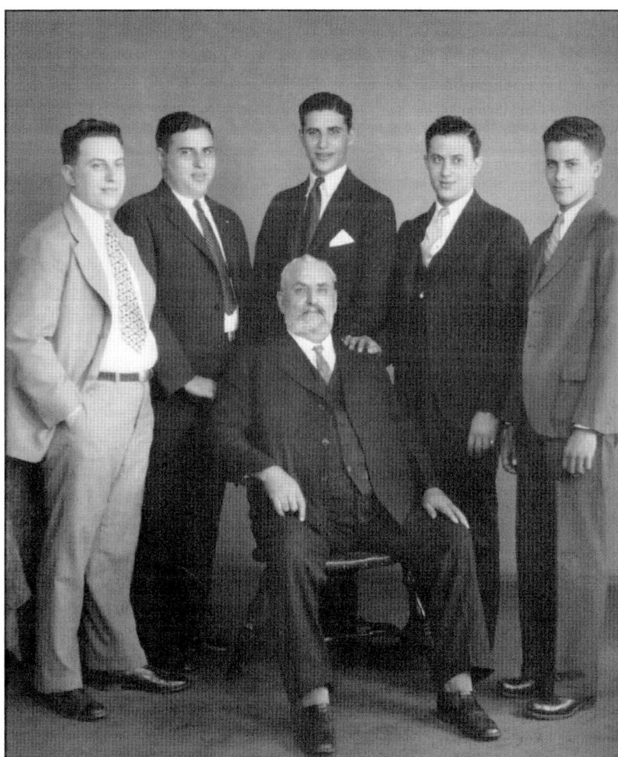

Hyman Zager (seated) had five sons and two daughters, who are not pictured. The five sons are, from left to right, Morris, Abe, Jake, Mike, and Perry. His daughter Jennie married Abe Cohen of Cohen and Sons Plumbing Supply. His daughter Rose, who never married, served in the WACS and moved to Chicago. Morris and Jake owned the delicatessens; Abe owned and operated a wholesale sporting goods business; Mike moved to Greensboro, North Carolina, where he owned several movie theaters; and Perry owned and operated his own service station in the West End/Vanderbilt area.

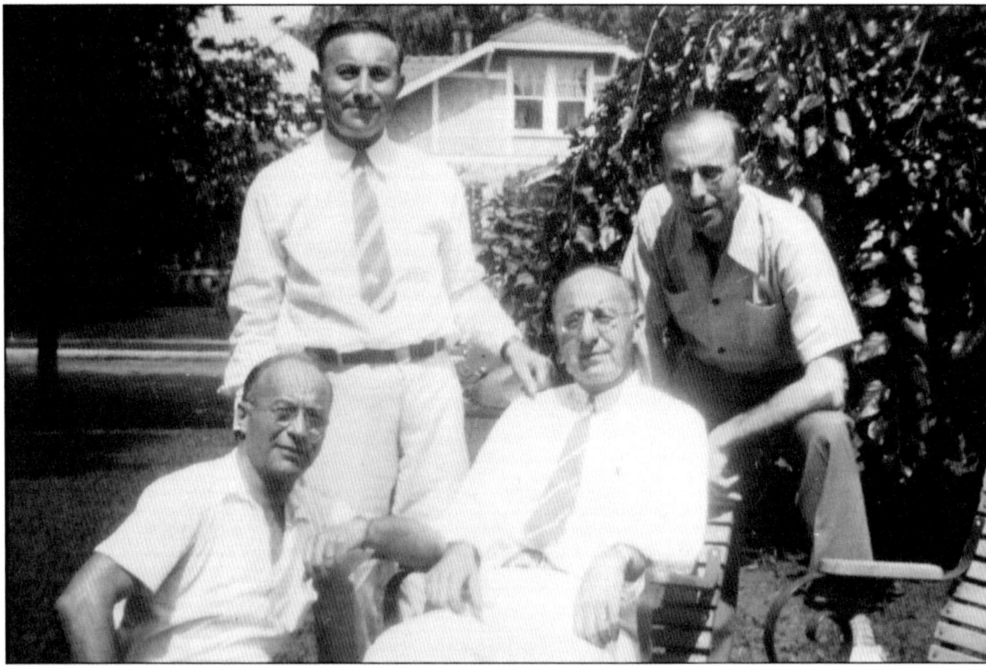

The Block brothers, from left to right above, were Aaron, Sam, A. J., and George. They were good businessmen who found a niche and took advantage of it, building a successful wholesale company that continued for more than 50 years. Block Brothers, below, was Nashville's leading buyer of hides, furs, pelts, and sheep and goat skins, as well as roots, herbs, walnuts, and pecans.

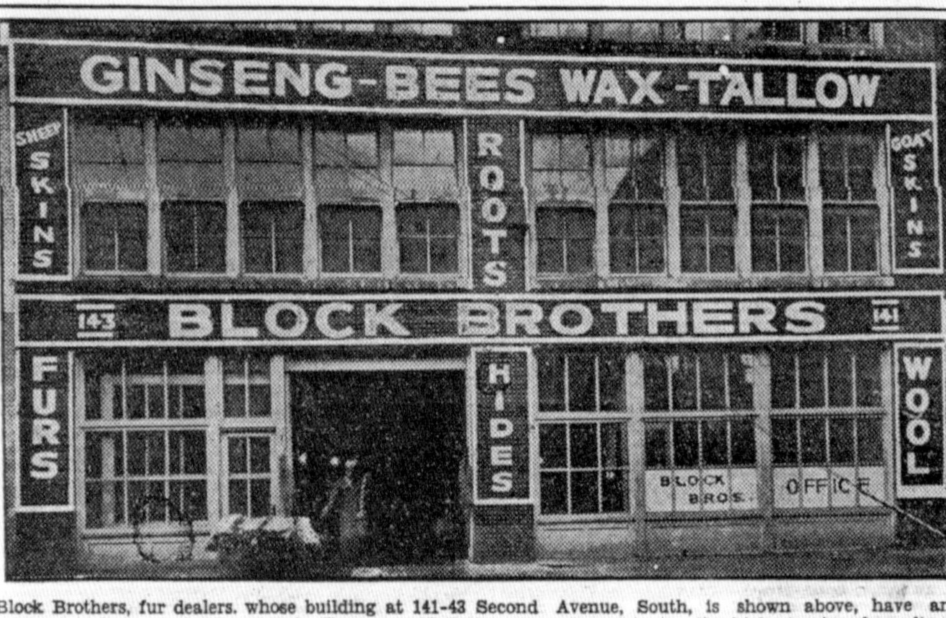

HOME OF LARGE FUR DEALERS

Block Brothers, fur dealers, whose building at 141-43 Second Avenue, South, is shown above, have announced to hunters and trappers in Tennessee that they are prepared to pay the highest prices for pelts of all kinds. The firm is one of the largest of its kind in the South.

Across America, the Hassenfeld brothers are best known for Hasbro (for HASsenfeld BROthers) toys. But one of the brothers, Harold Hassenfeld (right) went in another direction, founding the Empire Pencil Company in nearby Shelbyville, Tennessee. In 1951, Harold and his brother, Merrell, also opened a pencil factory (Jerusalem Pencil, Ltd.) in the three-year-old state of Israel, helping to create jobs and strengthen the young nation's economy.

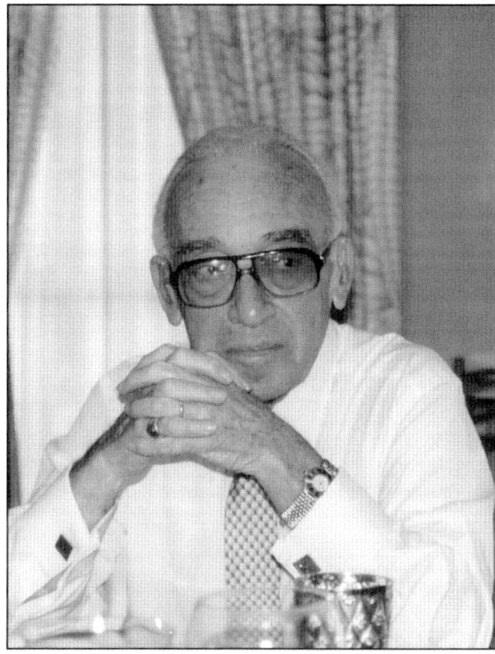

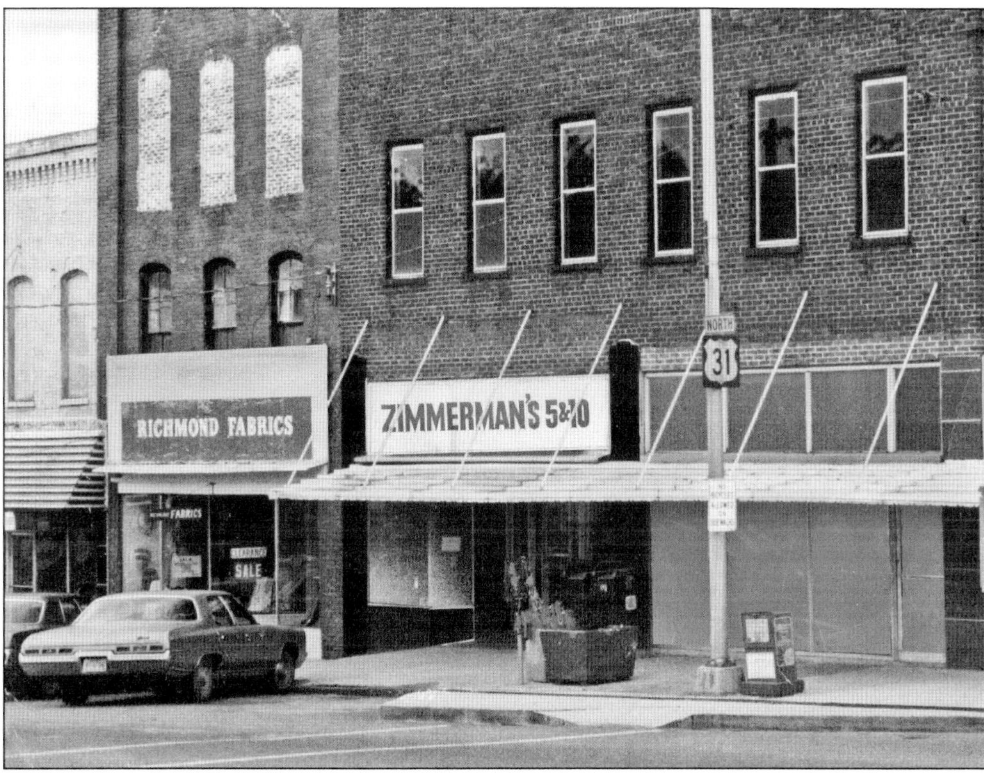

Harry Zimmerman opened the first of 10 variety stores in Nashville in 1934. This, one of the earliest, was in the heart of Nashville's downtown shopping district. By 1956, all of the retail outlets had been closed, sold, or converted to a wholesale operation that became known as Service Merchandise and would eventually include 140 catalog showrooms across the country.

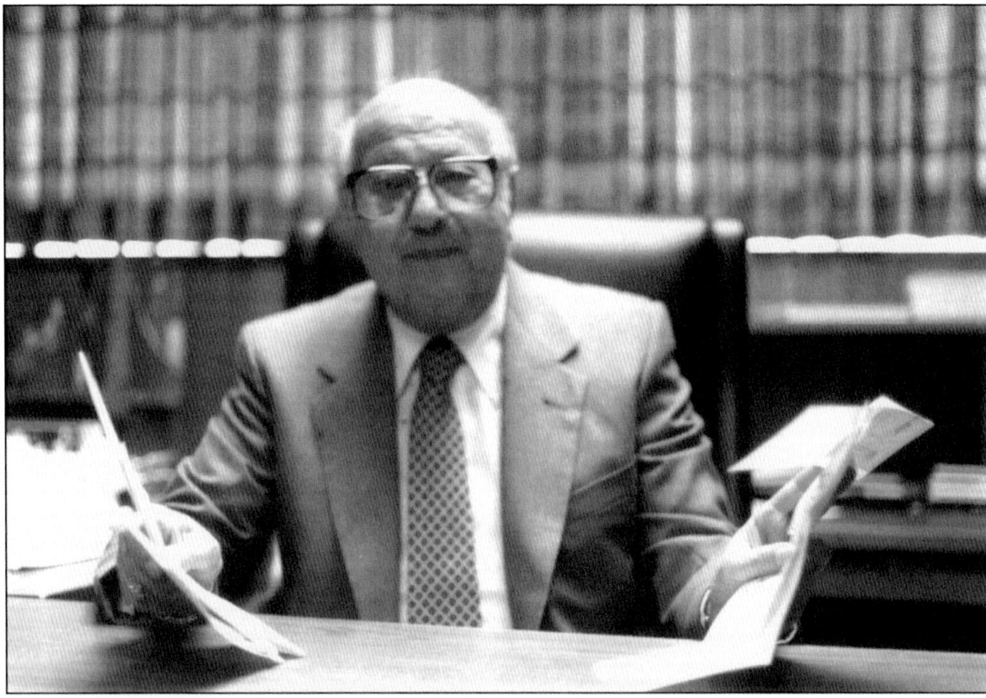

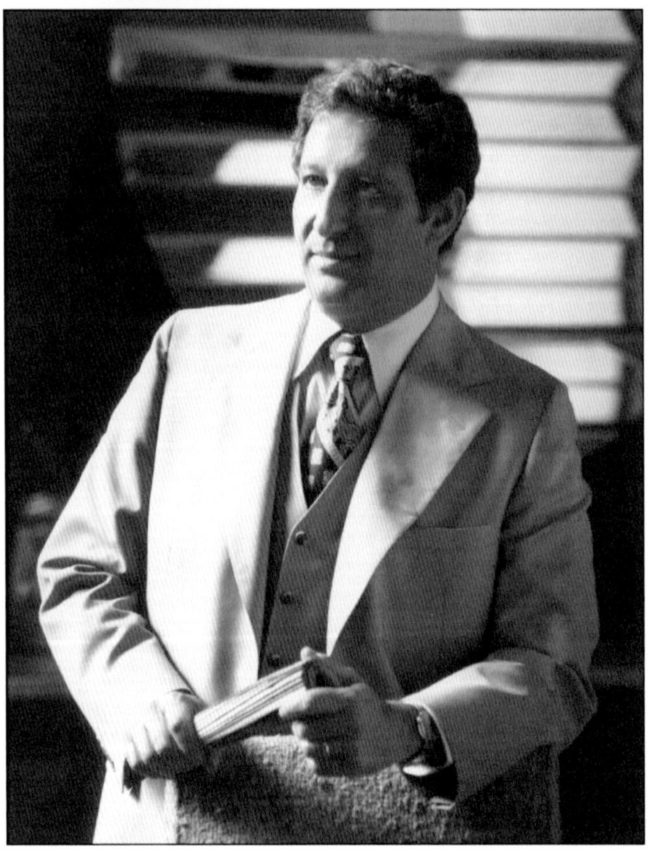

Harry Zimmerman (above), a Memphis native, built Service Merchandise into a business with locations in 28 states and net sales in excess of $1 billion by the early 1980s with his son Raymond (left). In addition to his many contributions to Nashville's Jewish community, Harry was known nationally for his support of Jerry Lewis's muscular dystrophy telethons, the state of Israel and Israeli-Egyptian peace efforts, and B'nai B'rith. He and his wife, Mary, also had two daughters, Sue and Doris. Raymond had two children: a son, Fred, who lives in Nashville and is an active member of the Jewish community, and a daughter, Robin.

Reuben Mills opened his first bookstore in Nashville in 1892. The son of Louis and Jettie Loveman Mills, he founded what grew to become Nashville's leading bookstore for 75 years and the first to open stores in suburban locations. His biggest competitor, before the national chains came along, was a store owned and operated by another well-known Jewish family, Zibart's.

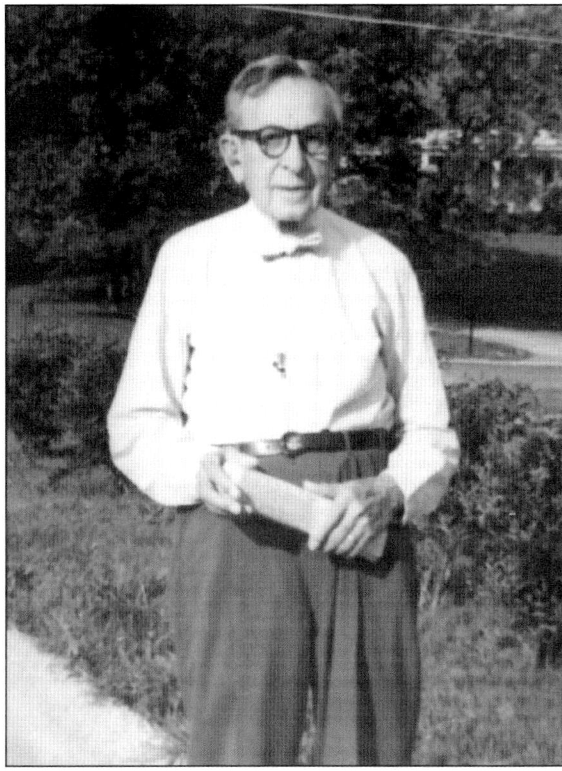

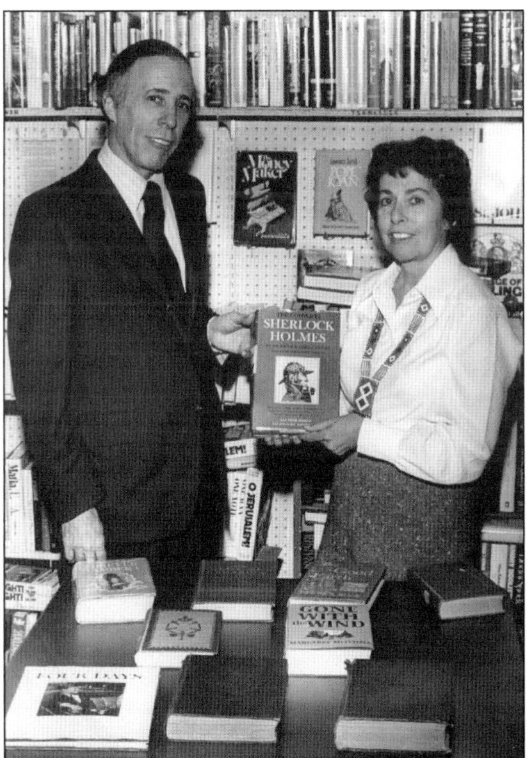

Reuben's daughter, Adele Mills, met her future husband, Bernie Schweid, at her father's store. Stationed near Nashville during World War II, Schweid was browsing through Mills Bookstore one day when he struck up a conversation with Adele, and the couple married in 1943. They operated the store and oversaw its growth and expansion for nearly 50 years. Making regular appearances on local television programs and writing numerous newspaper articles, they were familiar faces and voices to thousands of Nashvillians. They were also socially committed: Mills was the first retail store in Nashville to offer a sales position to an African American. Interestingly, one of their two sons, Richard, is a well-known author.

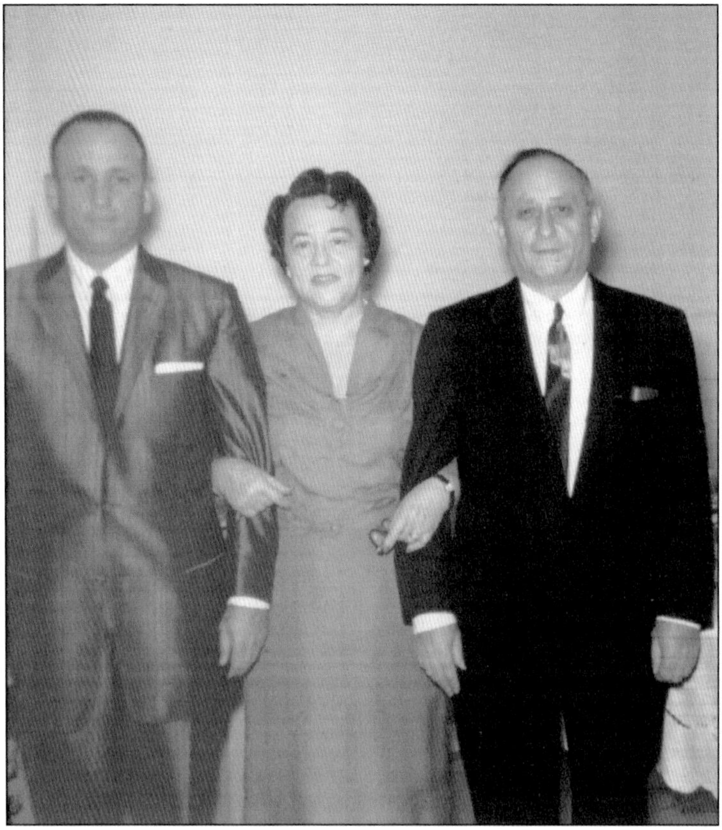

Ike Goldstein (above right) purchased Chattanooga-based Cumberland Manufacturing in 1939. At that time, Cumberland was known primarily for its Windsor brand of spices and extracts; Goldstein added a line of health and beauty products under the Swan Drugs label (right). He then moved the company to Middle Tennessee, setting up first in Nashville and later in Smyrna. When he retired, the company was run by his son Eddie (above left), who later brought his son, Randy, and daughter, Julie, into the business. Family members Raymond and Marilyn Simon were also involved in the company's ownership. The company was sold in 1992. (Both courtesy of Julie Boehm.)

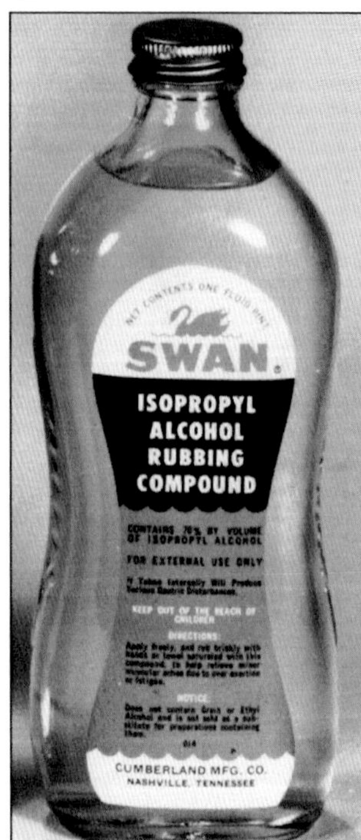

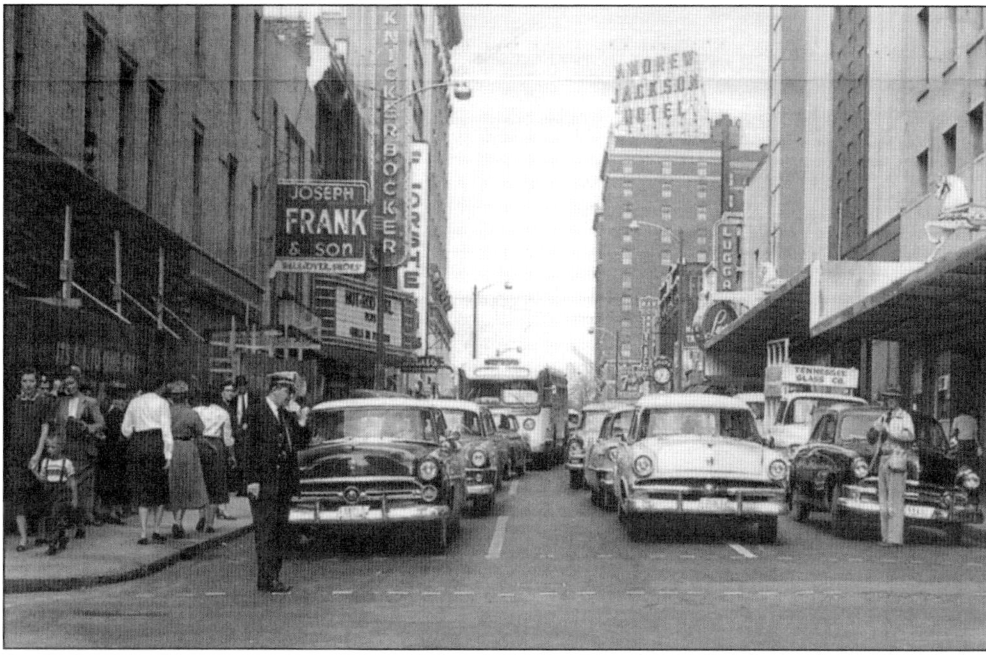

Downtown Nashville in 1954 still has a large number of visible Jewish-owned businesses. Levy's is next to Nashville Trunk and Bag, visible to the right with its "luggage" sign. Joseph Frank and Son, on the left, was another fine men's clothing store, and the delivery truck parked on the right is from Tennessee Glass Company, owned by the Isidore Schulman family.

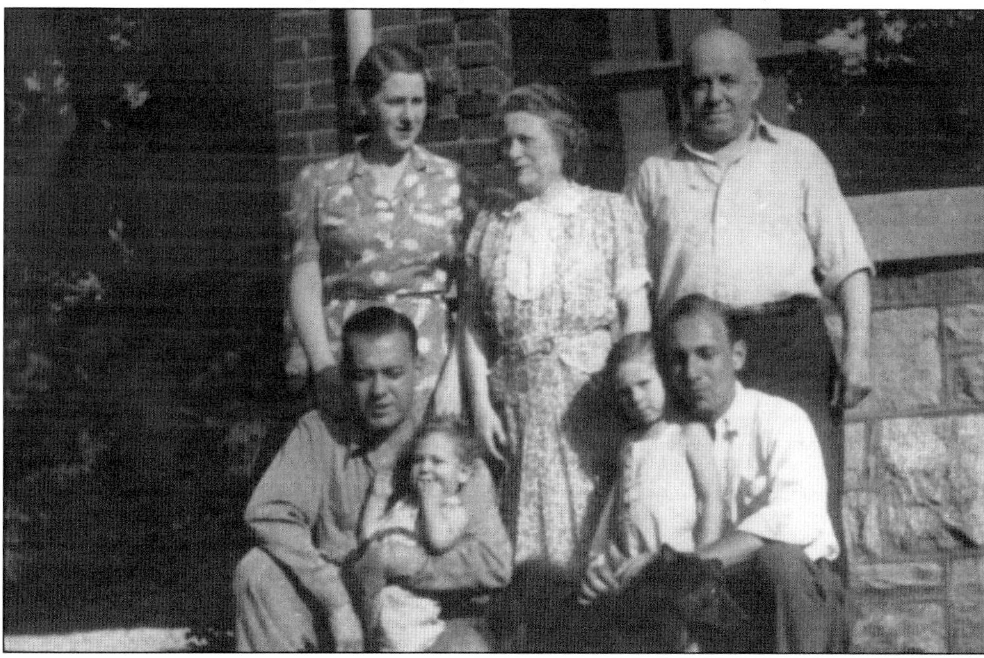

The Feldman family owned Nashville Trunk and Bag next to Levy's on Sixth Avenue. Manny and Daisy Feldman had two sons, Buford and Albert, who operated the store throughout the 1960s and 1970s. Buford and his wife, Rosalind, had two sons, Buford Jr. and Richard. Albert and his wife Phyllis had two sons, Tim and Ted.

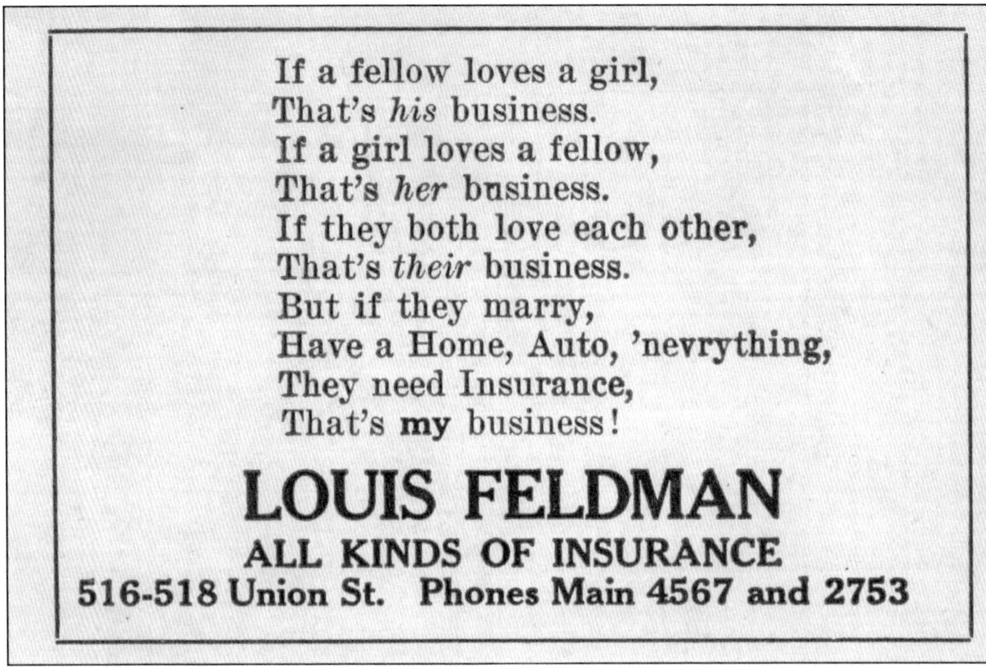

Louis Feldman was an insurance salesman in the 1920s, and according to information in old issues of the *YMHA News*, he was as proud of his advertising ideas as he was his sales ability. This clever ad is an example of his skills.

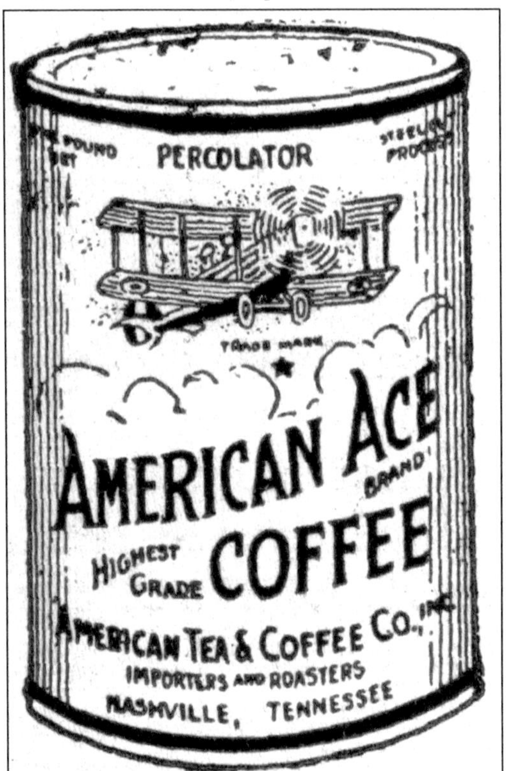

David Bubis, founder of the American Tea and Coffee Company, started like so many other early Nashville businessmen—as a peddler. He began roasting green coffee beans in 1919 and created Bluebird Coffee. But when he ran into problems registering that name and had to choose another, he selected American Ace Coffee as a means of honoring what he called "the exciting American aviator heroes of World War I."

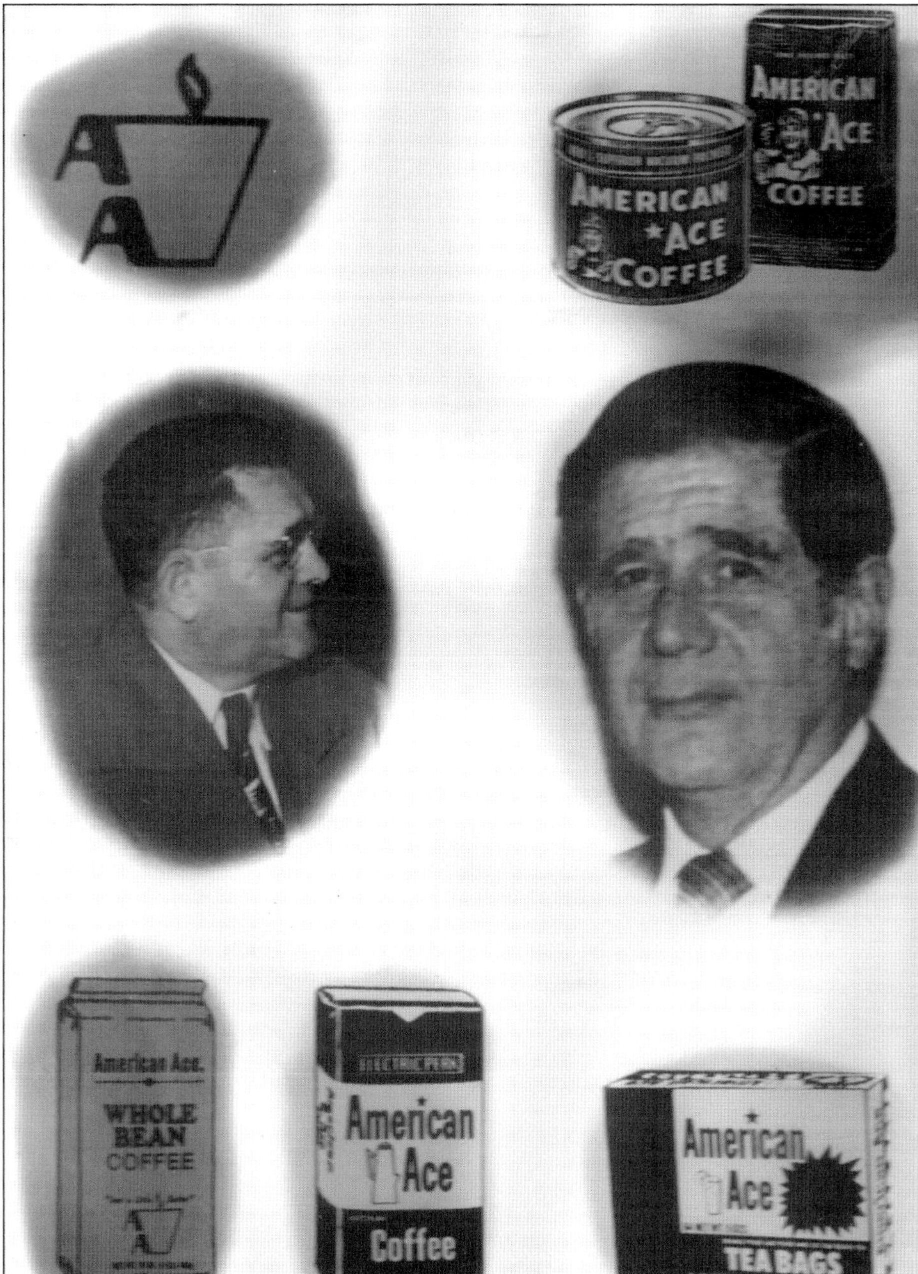

Marvin Bubis (right) took over running American Ace when his father David (left) died and continued to build on its success until he sold it in 1996. Starting as a teenager working part-time, he joined the company full-time following college and three years in service during World War II. Under his leadership, American Ace created exciting ad campaigns ("If you don't get your American Ace, go back to bed" and "Don't leave home without your American Ace") and for years advertised on the *Grand Ole Opry*, using Roy Acuff and Minnie Pearl as spokespersons. Under Marvin's leadership, the company expanded its institutional and restaurant coffee service and also marketed Big Chief peanut butter for a number of years.

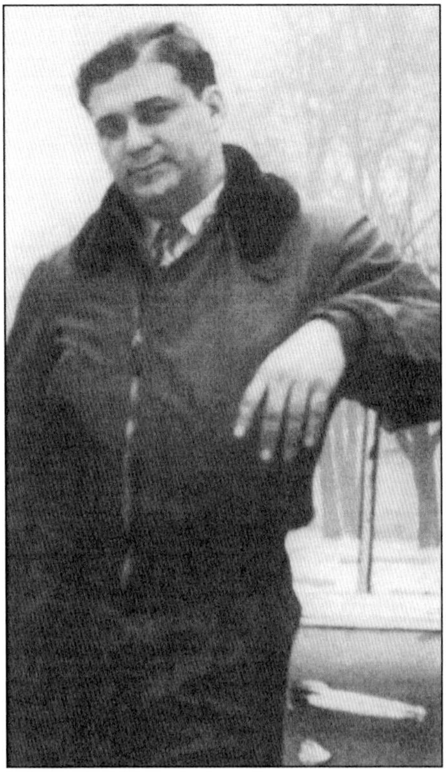

When David Bubis founded American Ace, he originally had two brothers as partners, but he later bought them out. His nephew, Reynold Bubis (left), became involved in the record business in the 1940s and 1950s. Reynold first worked for, then became partners with, several men who owned a record label and record distributorship. After dabbling in the business for several years, producing a few records and managing a few musicians, he started his own record label, Tennessee Records. While it never enjoyed overwhelming success, it did have a few moderate hits, mostly blues and gospel.

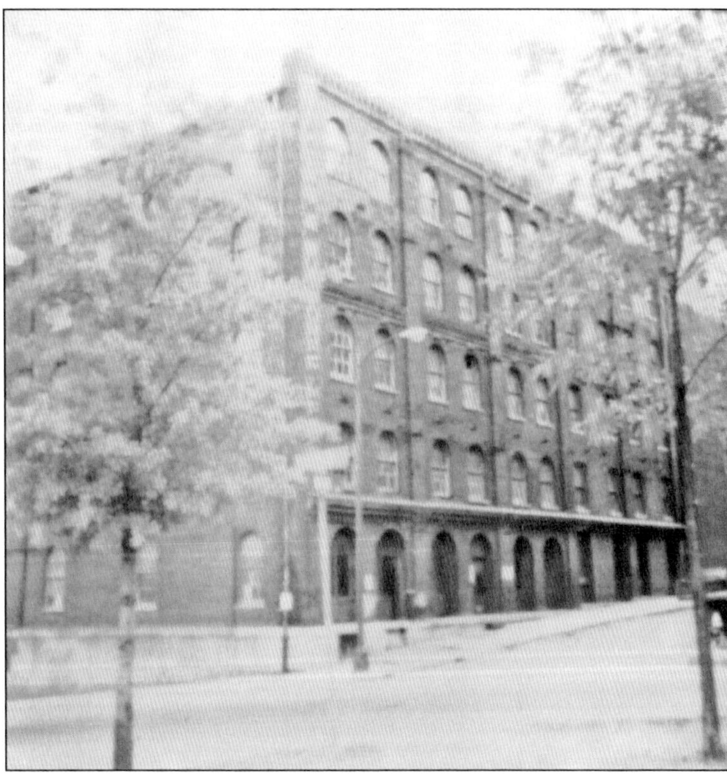

One of Nashville's more interesting businesses in the late 1800s was the Valentino Chewing Gum Company. Shown here in 1881, it was owned by Frank L. Blume, a Jewish Nashvillian, and his partner, Joseph Valentino. The factory and offices were originally located at 76 North Market Street, later moving to 8 Clark Street.

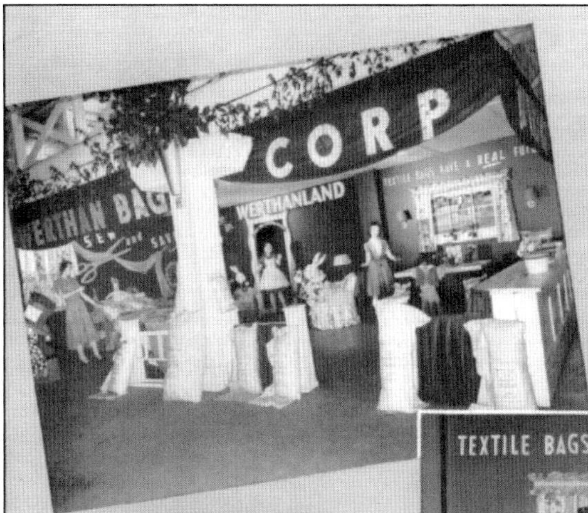

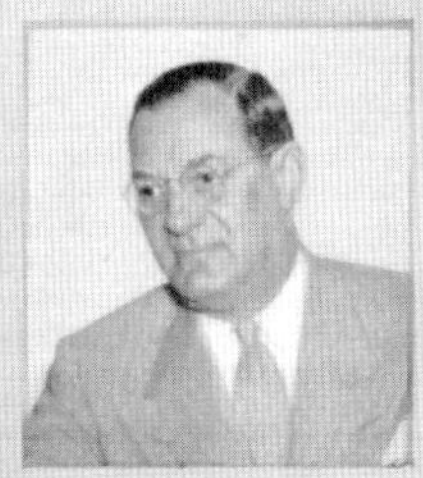

Joe Werthan

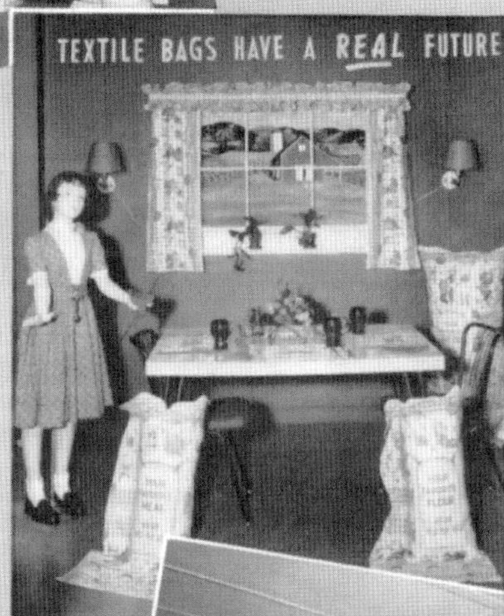

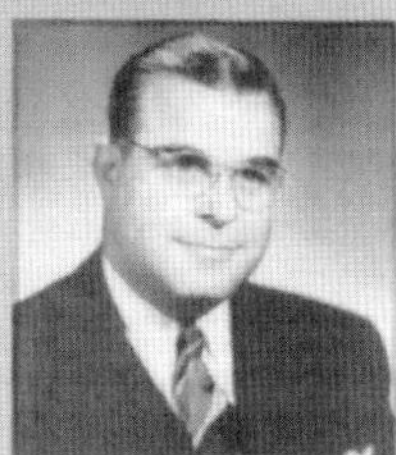

Bernard Werthan

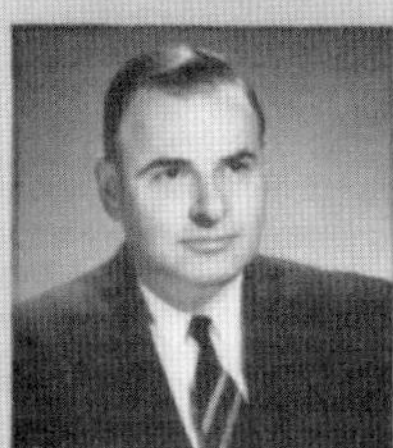

Albert Werthan

Howard M. Werthan

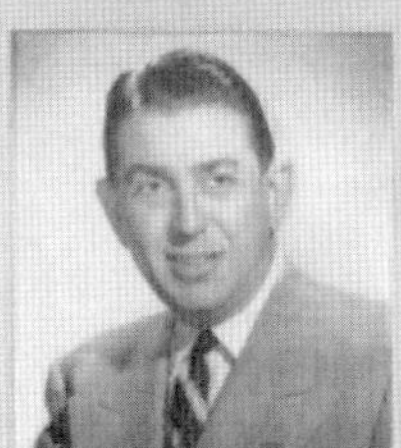

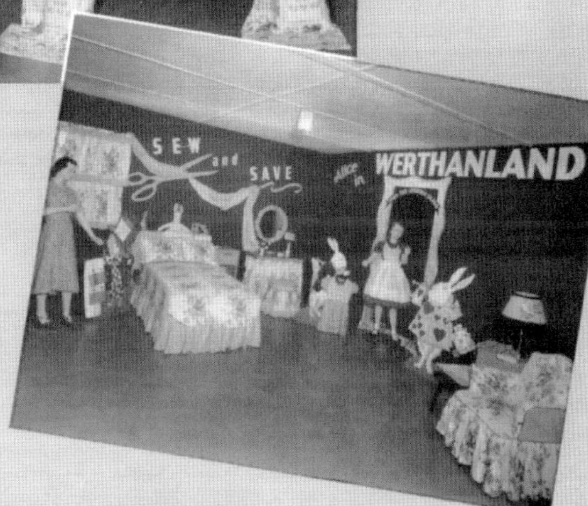

WERTHAN BAG CORPORATION
EXHIBIT, Tennessee State Fair, Nashville, 1954

One of Nashville's largest industries, Werthan Bag Company, began as a store in 1869 founded by Meier Werthan and his brother-in-law, Sigmund Godhelp. By the 1880s, the company was making most of its money selling reconditioned cotton and burlap bags. By 1890, it was dealing in scrap metal, burlap and cotton bags, and textiles. After Godhelp died in 1895, Meier brought his sons Morris and Joe into the business. In 1911, the company became Werthan Bag and Burlap and began manufacturing bags. During World War I, the company helped the war effort by producing sandbags. About 1920, Morris and Joe took over management of the company, and a few years later, Morris's sons Albert and Bernard and Joe's son Howard joined the business.

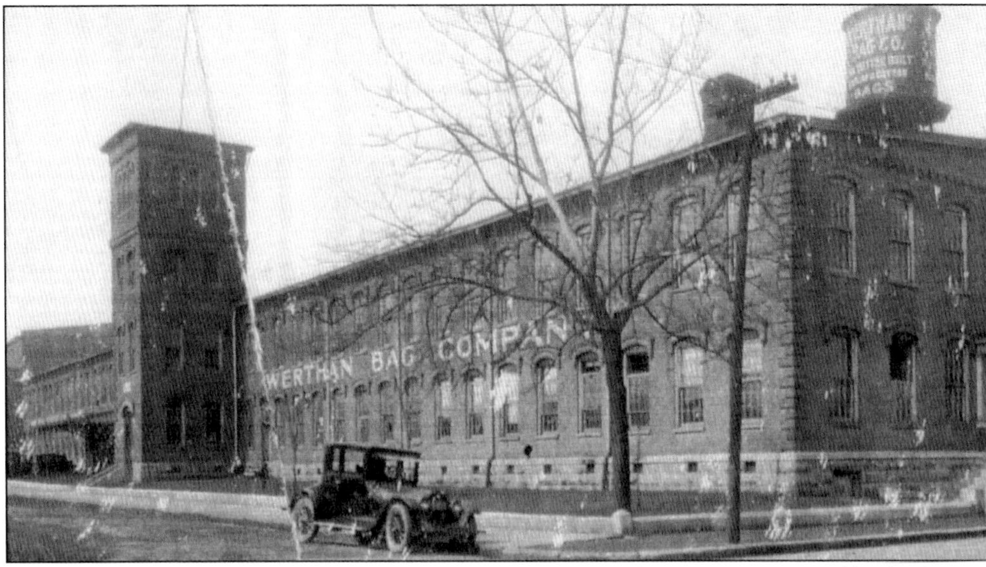

Werthan Industries has evolved over its 135 years from reconditioning cotton and burlap bags to manufacturing bags, textiles, plastics, and related products. In 1933, the company opened a textile mills office, and when World War II began, the company produced sandbags and camouflage material. Over the next 25 years, Bernard took over management of the company, and his two sons Bernard Jr. and Morris joined the business. Albert Werthan's son-in-law, Herb Shayne, came on board in 1968, and the company further diversified, becoming Werthan Industries in 1971.

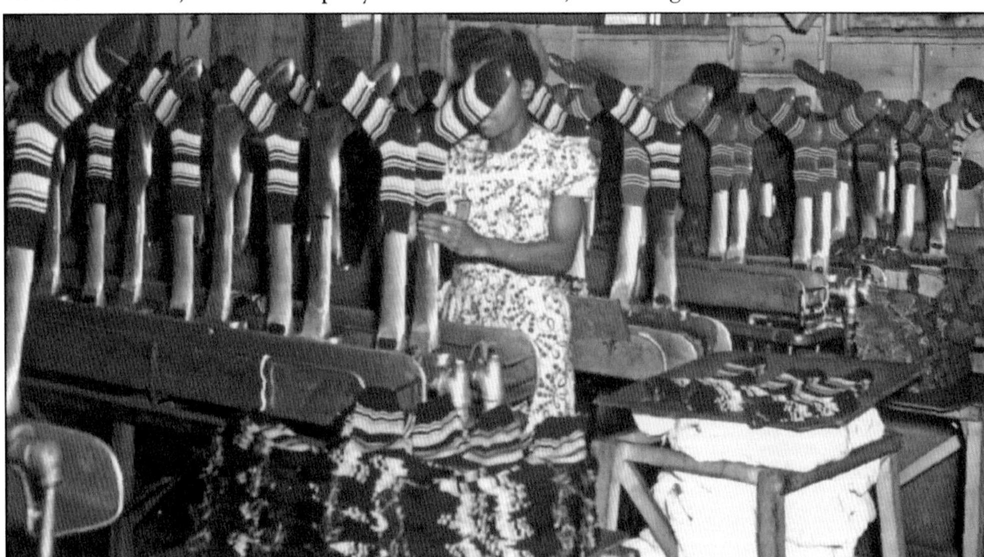

Rock City Hosiery Mills began more than 100 years ago, when Jacob May, a German immigrant then selling hosiery samples in New Hampshire, won a contract to provide labor at the Tennessee state penitentiary. The name of the business was changed to May Hosiery Mill in 1908, and the company became the primary supplier of socks to three major national retailers—Montgomery Ward, Marshall Fields, and Spiegel. During World War II, May's not only made socks and underwear for soldiers but also used their machine shop and 1,200 wartime workers to produce proximity fuses for mortar shells. The company later was chosen to produce the all-cotton crew sock for America's astronauts, who wore them when they landed on the moon.

Five

The Jewish Social and Cultural Community

There has always been a strong bond among Jews in every community, and Nashville is no exception. One of the by-products of anti-Semitism and prejudice against Jews has been that it drove them closer together and led to the creation of civic and social organizations, clubs, and other groups whose membership was entirely, or mostly, Jewish. The Jewish answer to the YMCA and YWCA was the YMHA and YWHA and eventually the Jewish Community Center. When Jews were excluded from membership in the Belle Meade and Richland Country Clubs, they created the Concordia, Standard, and finally Woodmont Country Clubs. When high school fraternities and sororities did not want Jewish boys and girls as members, they started chapters of Aleph Zadik Aleph and B'nai B'rith Girls. To create an awareness of their heritage and provide social and recreational activities that would bring them together, Young Judea, Temple and Synagogue Youth, and other organizations and clubs resulted. And for the adults, there was B'nai B'rith, Temple and Synagogue Men's Clubs and Sisterhood, Hadassah, and the Council of Jewish Women. The number of different organizations over the years that have provided opportunities for Jewish boys, girls, men, and women to serve their community and find productive and rewarding outlets for their energies and talents are many, now and in past years. Many of those are profiled here in a look at the social history of Nashville's Jewish community.

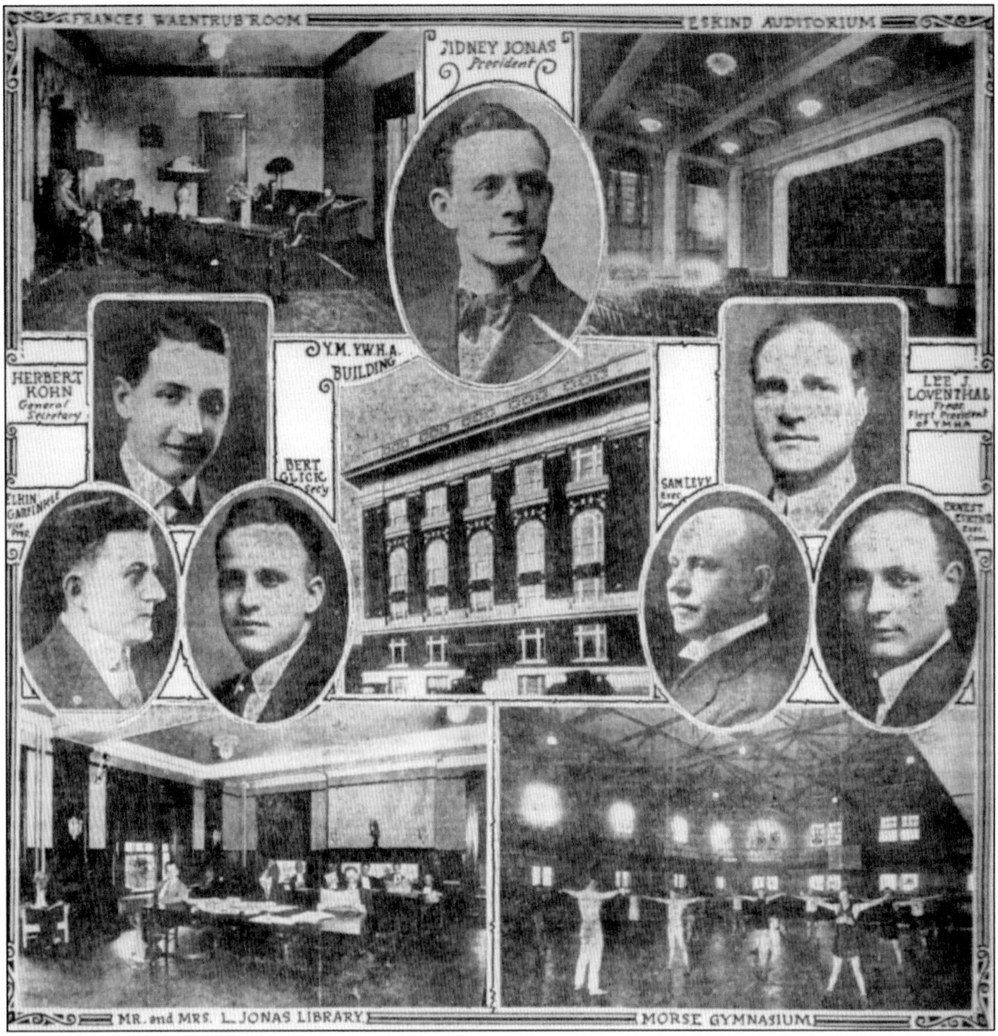

The YMHA, the center of social and recreational life in Jewish communities in the late 1800s and early 1900s, got its start in Nashville in December 1902. The organization obtained a charter in 1903, but it was not until 1908 that the first building opened downtown on Union Street. Patterned after the YMCA, it offered clubs for adults and children, sports teams, a swimming pool, games, dances, and literary and cultural activities. By 1916, the Young Women's Hebrew Association joined with the YMHA, and a larger facility opened in the same location in 1924. During World War II, an estimated 415,000 military personnel utilized the YMHA facilities.

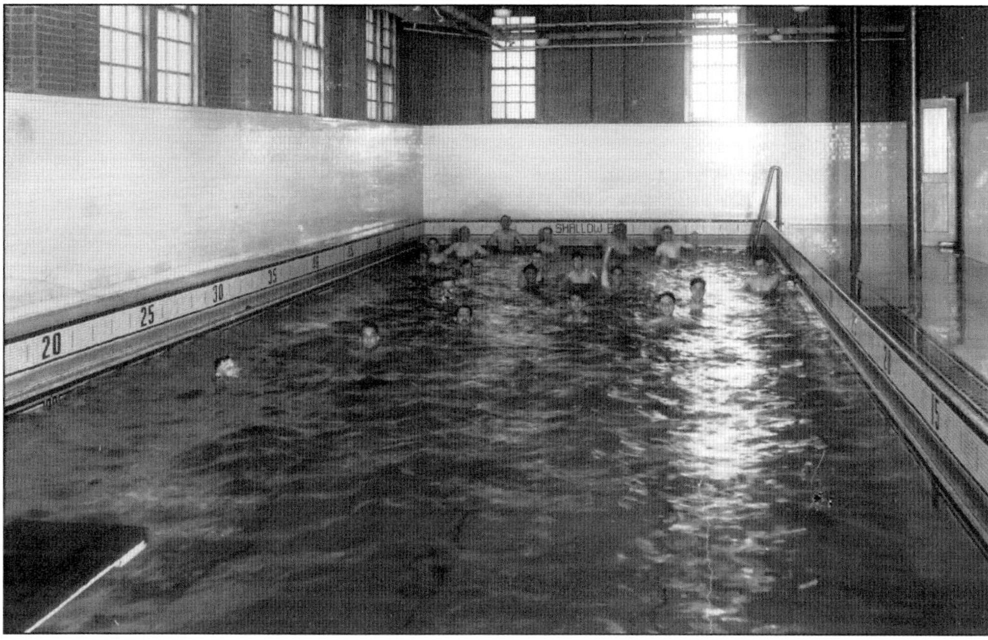

Swimming was always an activity members of the YMHA enjoyed, and the indoor pool in the original downtown location was a popular place. Through swimming classes for the children, swim activities for all ages, and exercise for seniors, everyone took advantage of the pool. Swimming at the outdoor pool of the Gordon Jewish Community Center continues to be one of the center's most popular activities today.

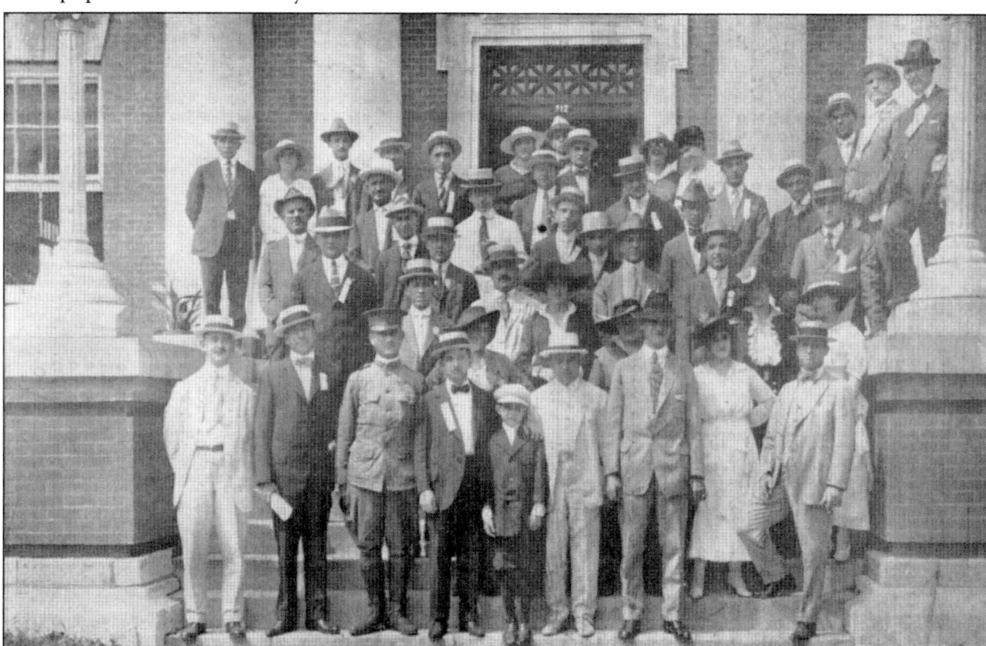

As both youth and adult groups today hold conclaves and conventions, so did the YMHA and YWHA members in 1916. In this photograph, members from the various branches of the organization throughout the South met in Nashville.

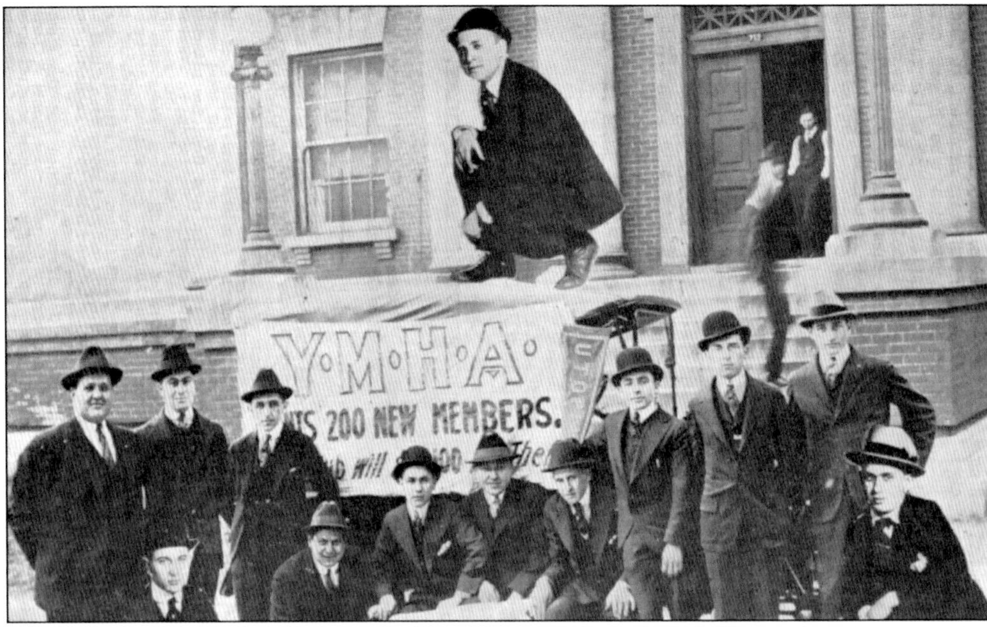

This photograph from 1916 shows the "winning team" in the YMHA's annual membership campaign, from left to right: (first row) Milton Friedman, Alvin Goldman, Sol Weise (captain), William Kirshner, Herman Morse, and Meyer Wolfe; (second row) Fred Kirshner, George Spiegel, Bernard Goldberg, Herman Hershkovitz, Sam Finklestein, and Sam Goldman. Bert Glick is on top of the car.

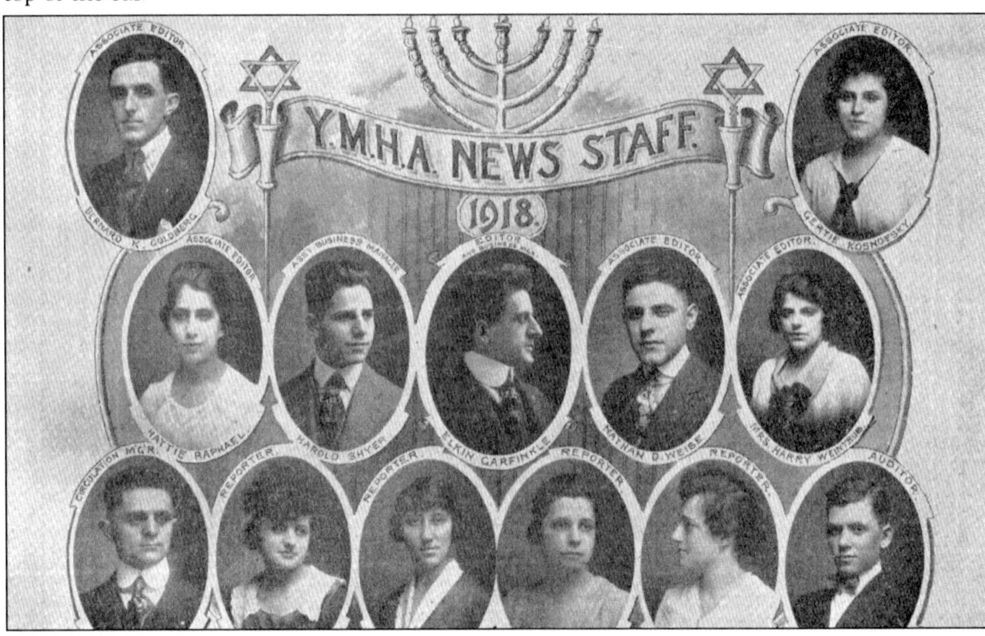

The members of the YMHA put out a monthly newsletter called the *YMHA News*. The front covers of several issues are reproduced in this book, each one featuring a different member of the organization. They were quite comprehensive, and included all of the social events and news of the day, along with interesting articles and profiles of the YMHA and YWHA members. This was the group that published the *News* in 1918.

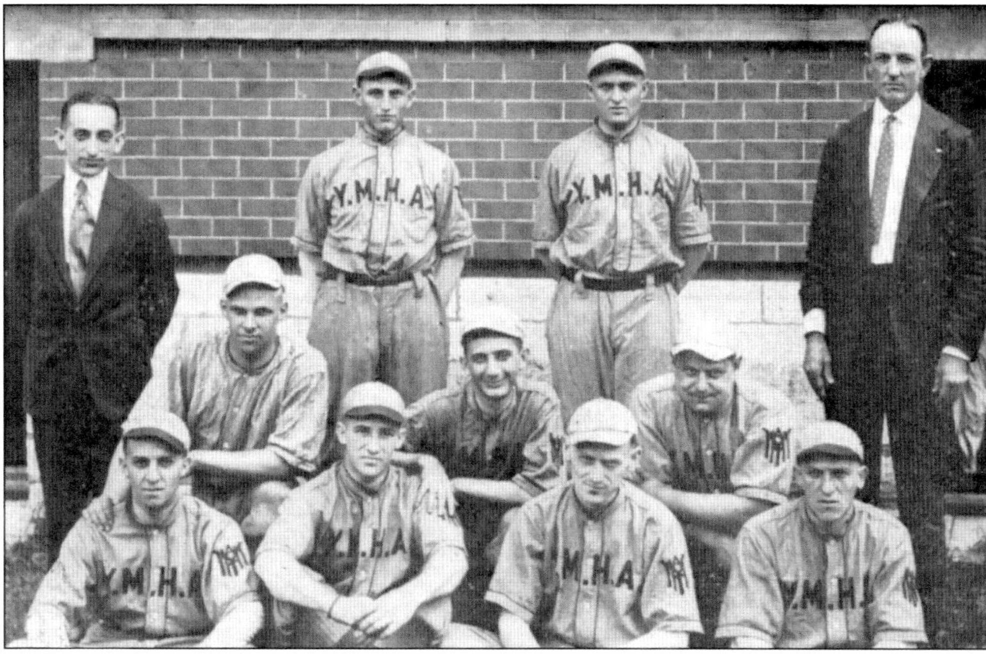

The YMHA, as part of its commitment to provide recreational activity for its members, regularly fielded athletic teams, including baseball and basketball. The 1917 team, pictured above, included Isadore Frank, Alvin Goldner, Sam Goldner, Ben Feldman, Herman Hershkovitz, Will Levy, Tib Lefkovitz, Totsy Grief, Ira Lusky, Max Feldman, Sol Moscovitz, Willie Kirshner, and Henry Weinberger. The bottom photograph shows the Peps basketball team that won the 1920 YMHA championship. Unfortunately, the members of the team are not identified.

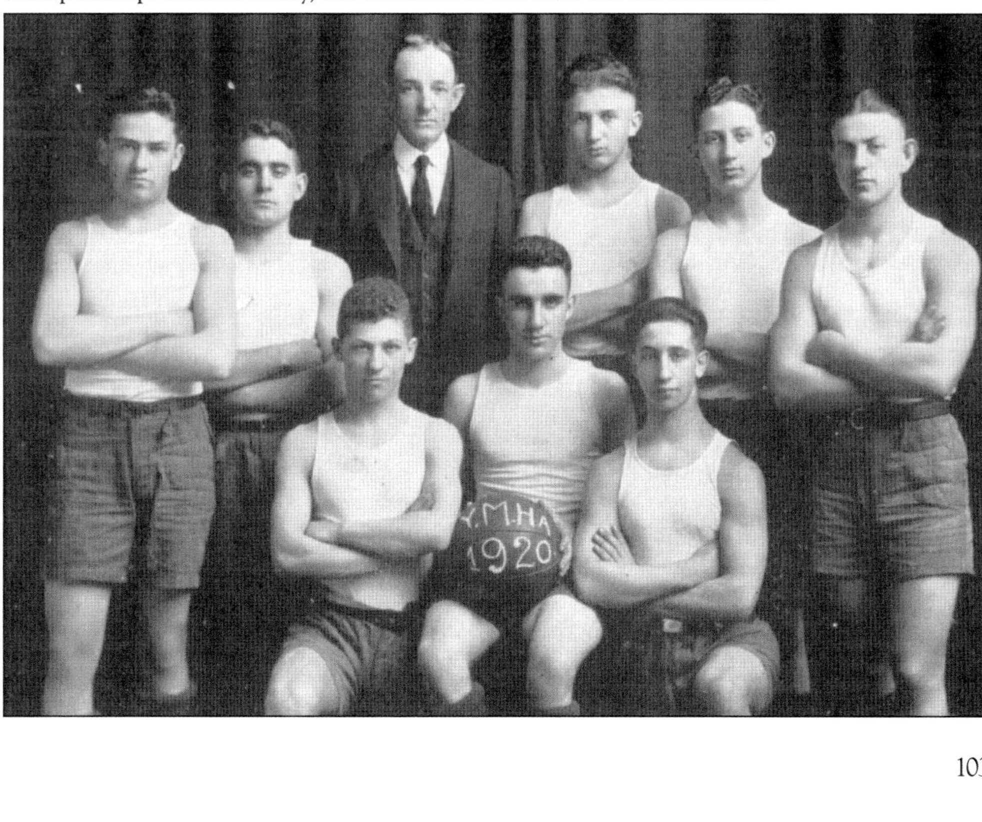

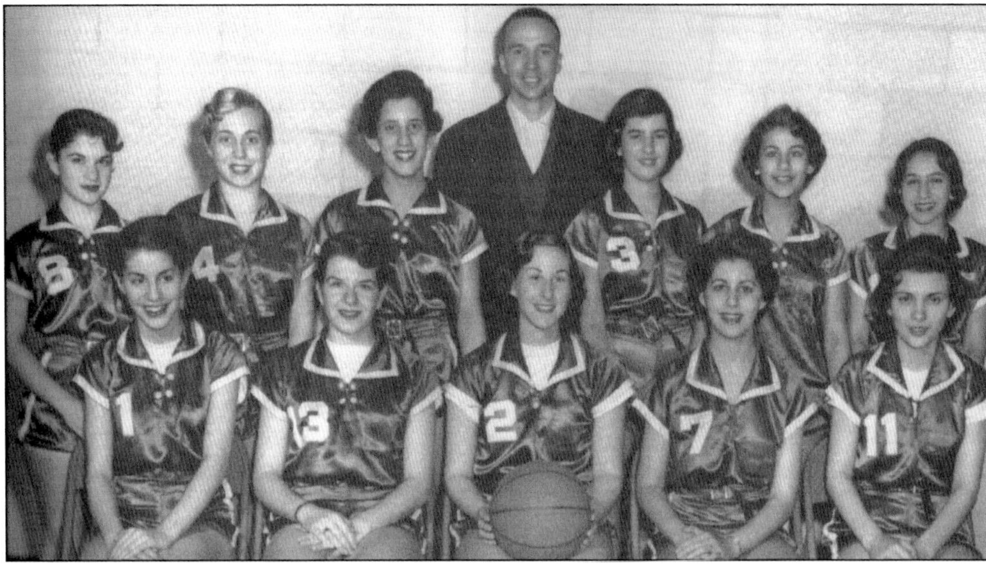

The women had athletic teams at the YMHA/YWHA and the Jewish Community Center, too. In the earlier days they were mostly swimming and volleyball. Later on, basketball became very popular, and a lot of girls took part in the program. Since the boys' team had been called the Peps, the girls' team was the Peppettes. This team, pictured with their coach in 1955–1956, includes, from left to right, (first row) Geri Lefkovitz, Jackie Finkelstein, Betty Lee Weinstein, Adrienne Glaboff, and Colene Cohen; (second row) Linda Lyon, Teryl Zeitlin, Joan Mendelsohn, coach Paul Aaron, Mary Schwartz, Carolyn Rosenblum, and Sheryl Feldman.

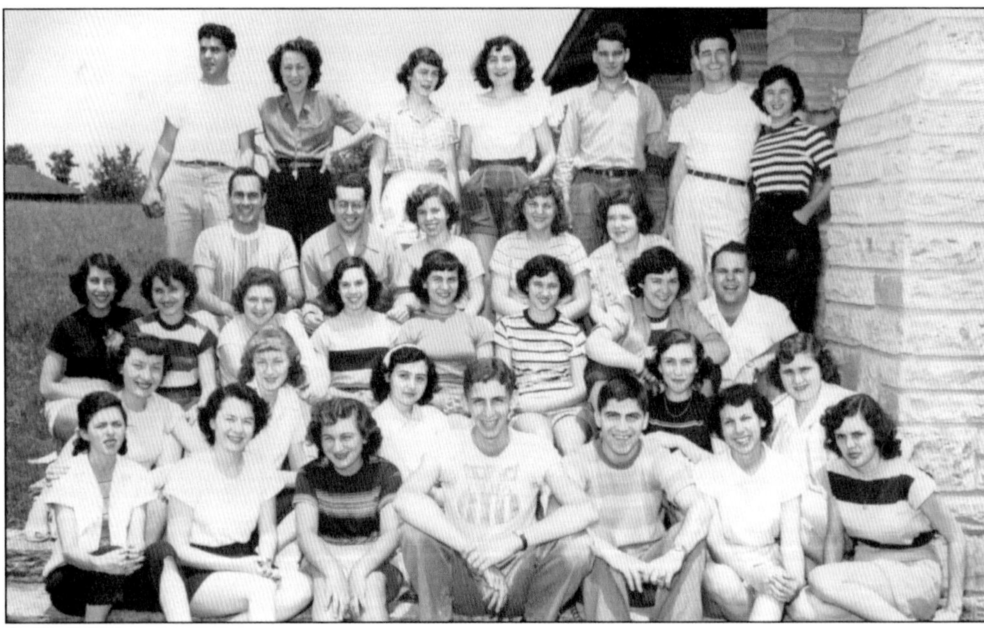

The Jewish Community Center (JCC) offered a day camp program during the summer, and hundreds of children participated every year in the outdoor activities, ball games, swimming, social activities, and snacks (including the "bug juice" all campers remember). High school students were counselors, and they looked forward to day camp as much as the campers did. This group photograph shows the counselors in 1948.

Most of the Jewish youth organizations, including Aleph Zadik Aleph (AZA), B'nai B'rith Girls (BBG), and Young Judea, held their meetings at the JCC, and when a Nashville chapter of one of those organizations was chosen to host a convention, that too was held at the JCC. Here a group of AZA and BBG members gathers in front of the JCC in 1980.

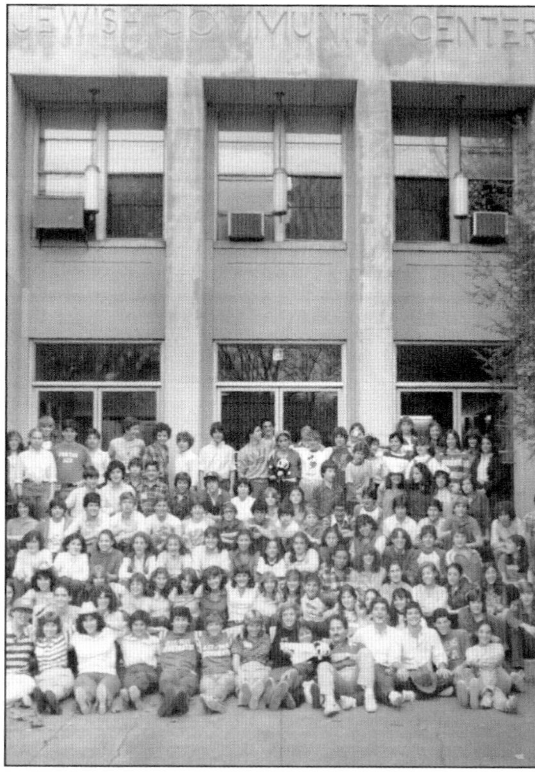

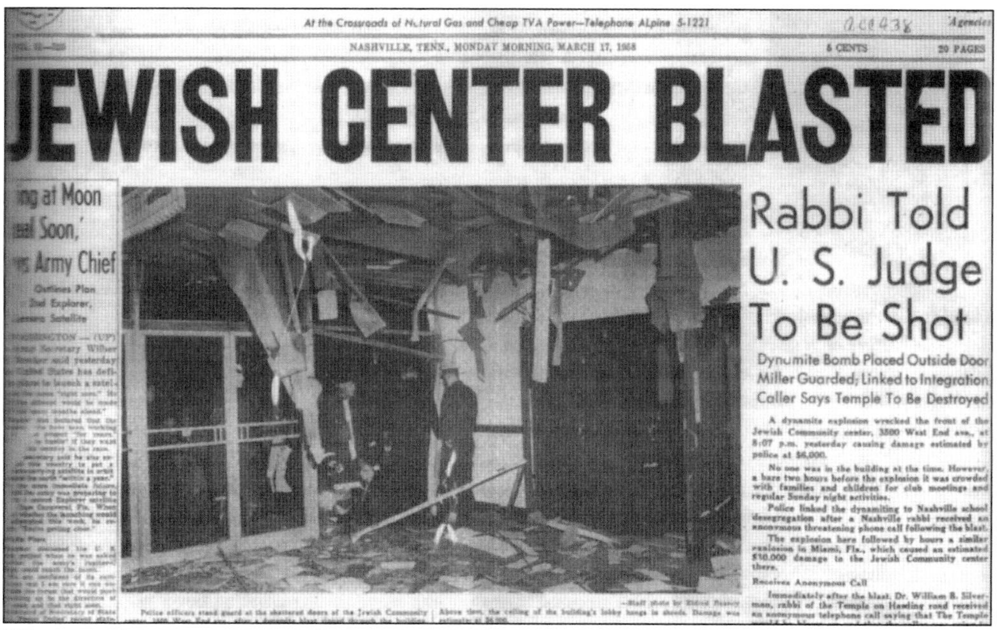

At the Crossroads of Natural Gas and Cheap TVA Power—Telephone ALpine 5-1221

NASHVILLE, TENN., MONDAY MORNING, MARCH 17, 1958 — 5 CENTS — 20 PAGES

JEWISH CENTER BLASTED

Rabbi Told U. S. Judge To Be Shot

Dynumite Bomb Placed Outside Door Miller Guarded; Linked to Integration Caller Says Temple To Be Destroyed

A dynamite explosion wrecked the front of the Jewish Community center, 3500 West End ave., at 8:07 p.m. yesterday causing damage estimated by police at $6,000.

No one was in the building at the time. However, a bare two hours before the explosion it was crowded with families and children for club meetings and regular Sunday night activities.

Police linked the dynamiting to Nashville school desegregation after a Nashville rabbi received an anonymous threatening phone call following the blast.

The explosion here followed by hours a similar explosion in Miami, Fla., which caused an estimated $10,000 damage to the Jewish Community center there.

Receives Anonymous Call

Immediately after the blast, Dr. William B. Silverman, rabbi of the Temple on Harding road received an anonymous telephone call saying that The Temple

When word got out in 1981 that an attempt had been made to bomb The Temple, those old enough to remember immediately thought back to the March day in 1958 when a dynamite bomb exploded at the Jewish Community Center. Fortunately, the building was empty and no one was hurt, but the sense of security that had enveloped the Jewish community less than one generation removed from the Holocaust was shattered.

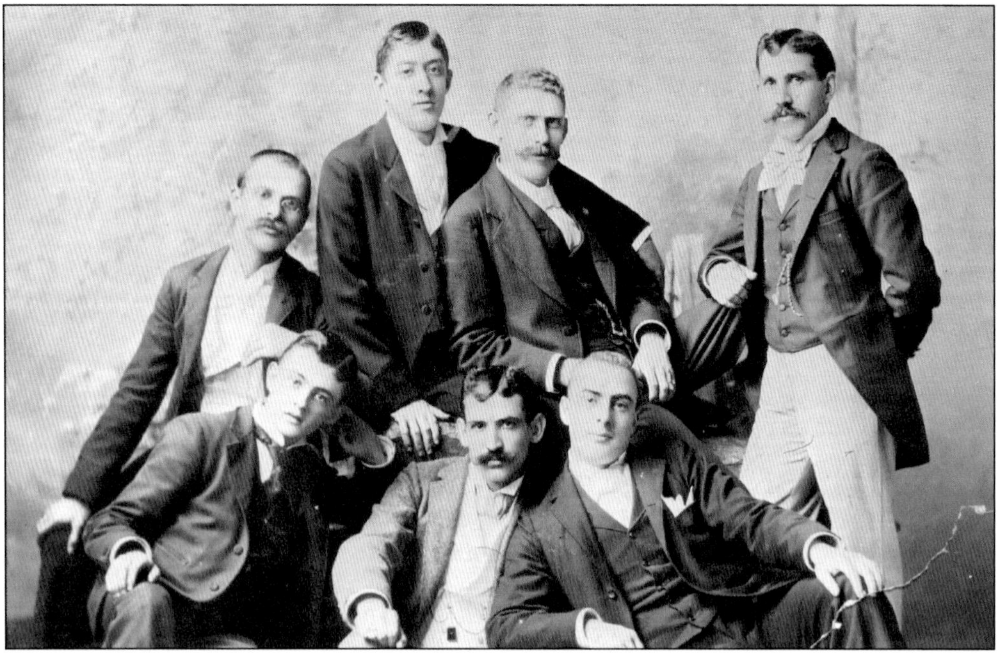

All of the Jewish employees of L. Jonas and Company gathered for this photograph in 1898, and the original caption was Nashville Beaus. There is no indication whether all of the "beaus" were eligible bachelors, but they include (not in order) Adolph Jonas, Adolph Meyer, Sol Klein, Alex Weinbaum, Sig Lowenstein, and J. Stein.

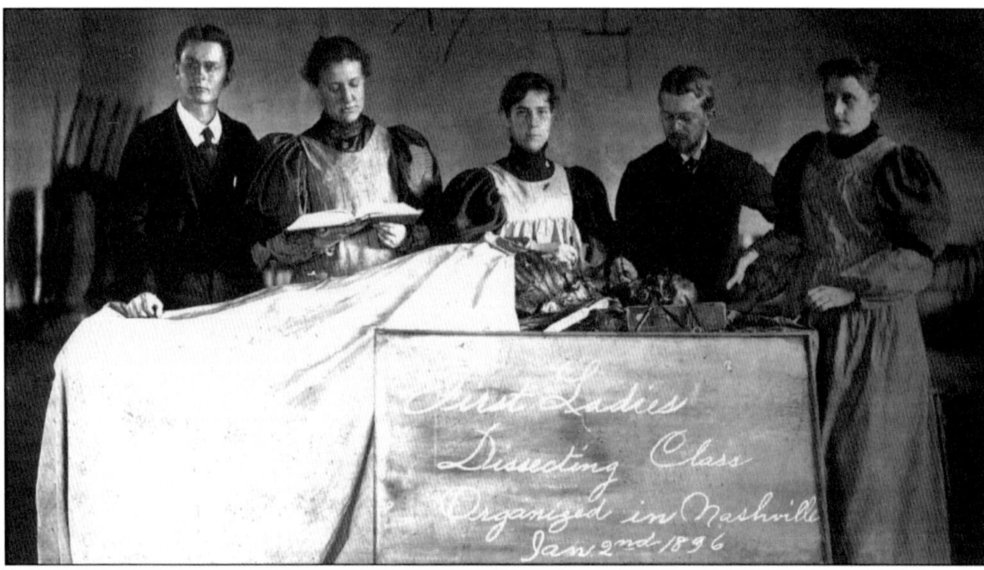

Dr. Celia Rich (center), who moved to Nashville from Atlanta in 1880, was a student in the first women's dissecting class in 1896, part of the training at Vanderbilt's medical school from which she graduated in 1898 as a winner of the Founder's Medal. She went on to become the first president of the National Association of Women Dentists (in 1922) and the Nashville Dental Society (in 1944). She and her brother, also a dentist, shared an office downtown. She and her brother, also a dentist, shared an office downtown. She was a member of the Jewish Welfare Center and the Nashville section of the National Council of Jewish Women and died in 1953.

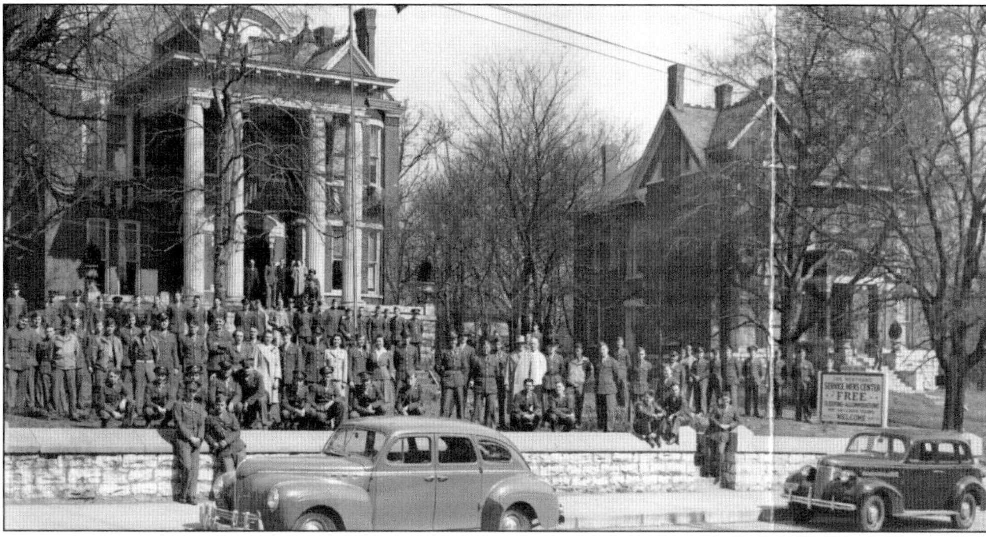

The Joe Werthan Service Center came about because Joe tired of seeing young American servicemen, on leave from Second Army training maneuvers in the area, sleeping outdoors. Some 800,000 troops trained at Fort Campbell in Clarksville and Camp Forrest in Tullahoma between 1942 and 1944. The center provided a much-needed service by giving the soldiers a place where they could relax, rest, sleep, and get a good meal and a little recreation. The facility had more than 250 beds, but sometimes even that was not enough. A count at the end of the war showed more than 2,000 Jewish soldiers used over three million services at the Werthan Center and four million at the YMHA.

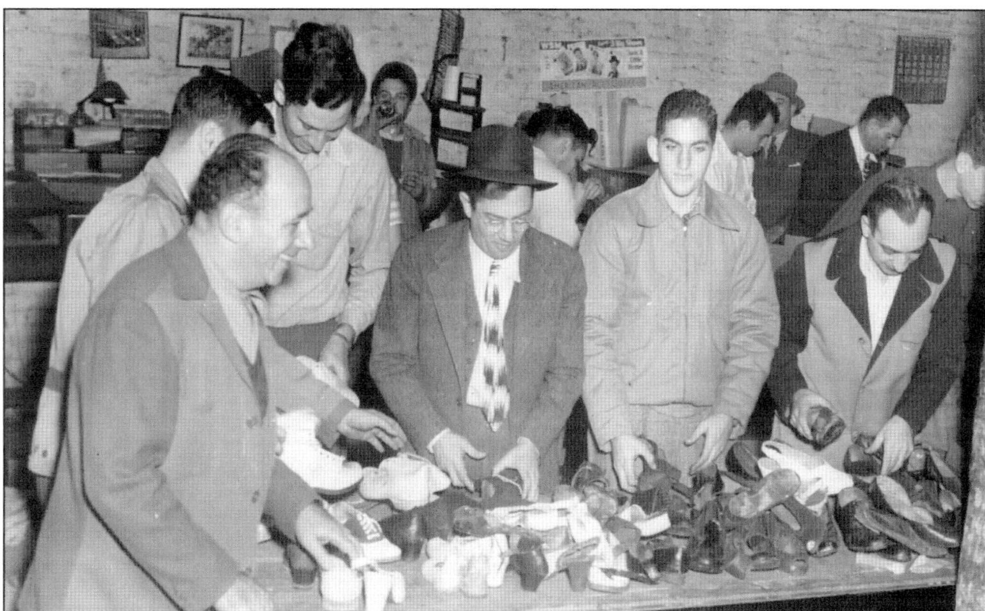

The turmoil in the Middle East was intensifying in 1947, a year before Israel was to become a Jewish state. European Jews displaced by World War II were in need of food, clothing, and a place to live. So more fortunate Jews, such as those in the United States, did what they could to help. In Nashville, an effort coordinated by local Jewish organizations collected 8,000 pounds of clothing and 4,000 pounds of food to send overseas.

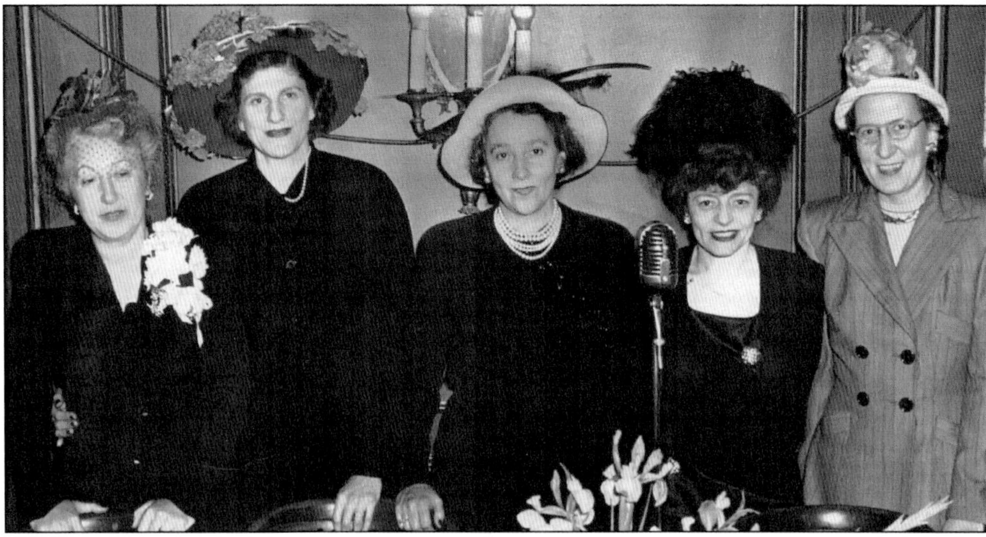

The Nashville section of the National Council of Jewish Women sponsored both the Home for Convalescent Children and the Bertha Fensterwald Settlement House, later known as the Bertha Fensterwald Social Center. It began in 1909 in a home purchased from Sam Levy at 503 Fifth Avenue South. Bertha Fensterwald, who had helped start the Nashville chapter in 1901, died in childbirth in 1903. The purpose of the center was to provide learning facilities and proper personal care for those who could not afford those advantages. Services included a library and reading room, a kindergarten, and classes in English, folk dancing, citizenship, housecleaning, Bible, and personal hygiene. About 300 people per week took advantage of the center's offerings, which included a kindergarten, baby, nutrition, and dental clinics, and sewing and embroidery classes for girls. In this photograph from 1948, the Nashville section of the National Council of Jewish Women was led, from left to right, by unidentified, Mrs. Albert Werthan, Mrs. Manual Eskind, Mrs. Alvin Keller, and Mrs. Percy Cohen.

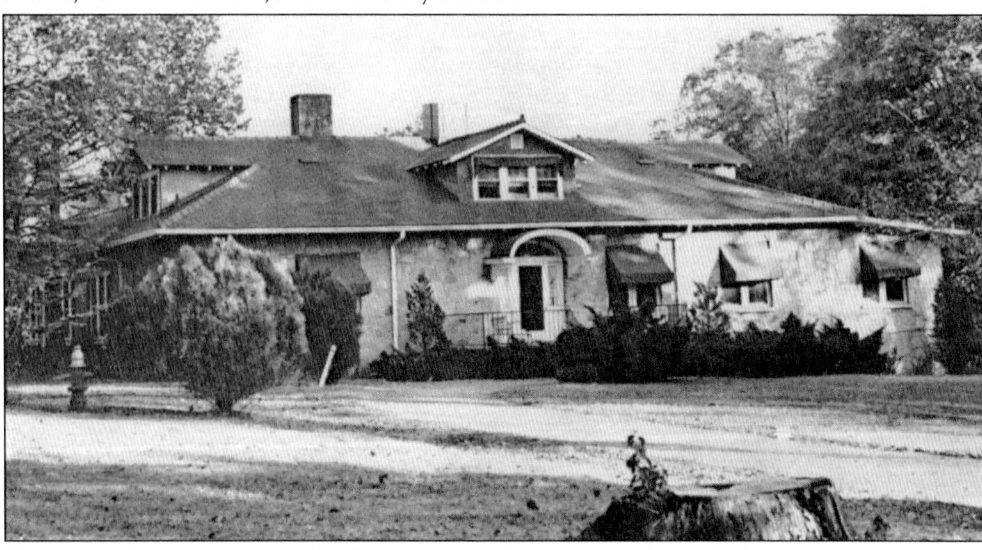

The Home for Convalescent Children was established in 1947 on Vultee Boulevard and was the first of its kind in Tennessee. Its purpose was "to take half-well children whose chances of recovery [from illness or injury] would be endangered by poor living conditions at home, and nurse them back to health."

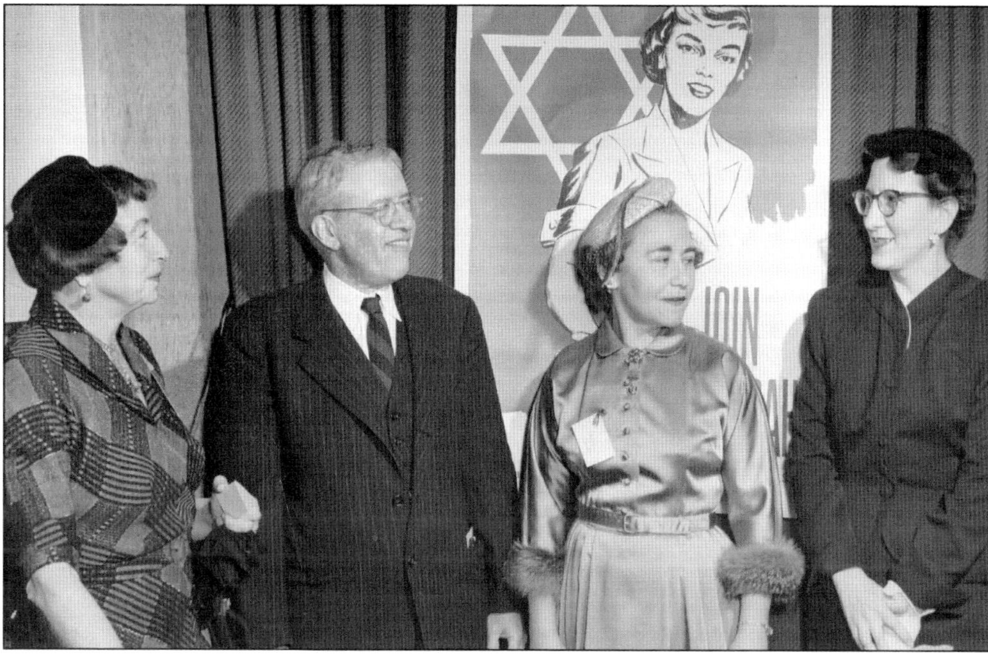

Hadassah has long been one the most important civic organizations for Jewish women in Nashville, as it has been elsewhere, providing many community services and supporting Zionism and Jewish causes for almost a century. Shown here in the 1950s, from left to right, are Blanche Fensterwald, Mortimer May, Peggy Tohrner, and Bea Cohen.

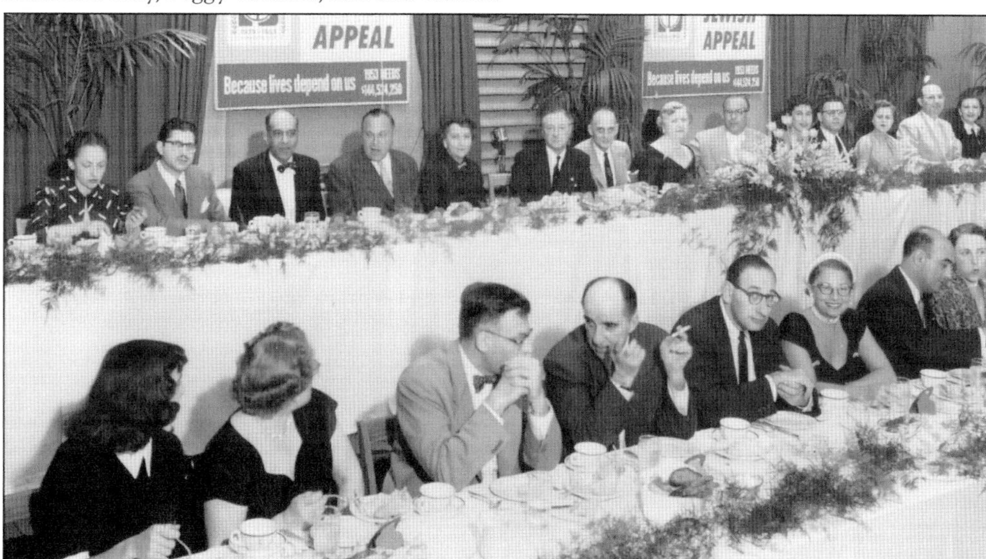

Community fund-raising for Jewish causes began in Nashville in 1916 at the Conference of Jewish Organizations. In 1937, Bernard Fensterwald led the Jewish Community Council's first fund-raising campaign after its 1936 inception. Their initial goal was $20,000, "three-fourths of which was to be sent to suffering 'Jewish foreign lands,' particularly the threatened Jews of Europe." In 1969, the group changed its name to the Jewish Federation, and in 1978, it began the split into three separate entities: the Jewish Federation of Nashville and Middle Tennessee, the Jewish Community Center, and Jewish Family Services. This photograph is from 1957.

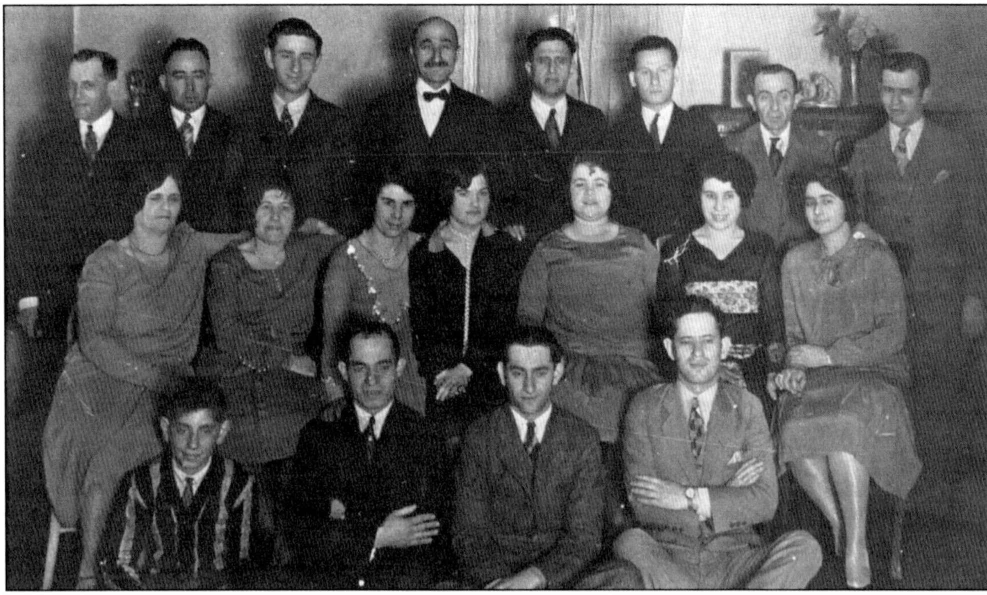

The Culture Club, shown here in 1926, was created in 1923 for the purpose of bringing "things Jewish" to Nashville. These included plays, concerts, musical programs, and the discussion of creative works of art and literature, including the first Yiddish play ever produced in Nashville. In its early days, the club met at Watkins Institute, then later at the Fensterwald Social Center. With an initial membership of just 17, the group grew to more than 100 members and also conducted classes in history and Yiddish.

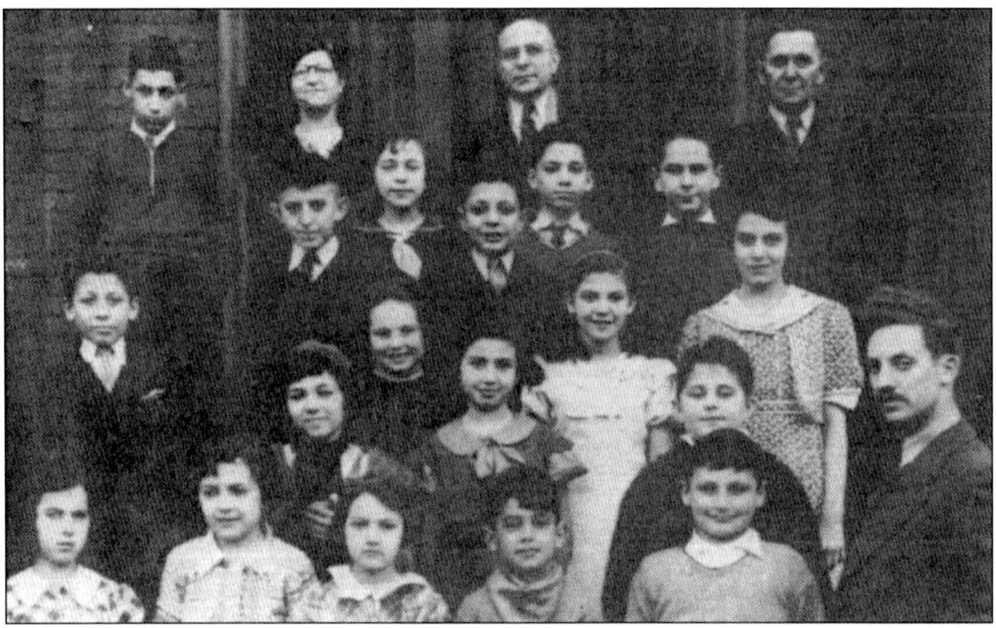

The Workmen's Circle was a secular Jewish fraternal and charitable organization that began in New York in 1900. Also political, it supported the labor and socialist movements and promoted Yiddish culture, including theater and music, and sponsored regular discussion groups. The Nashville chapter also started a kindergarten in 1924. (Two familiar faces are Julius Doochin, top left, and Joe Kraft, below Doochin.)

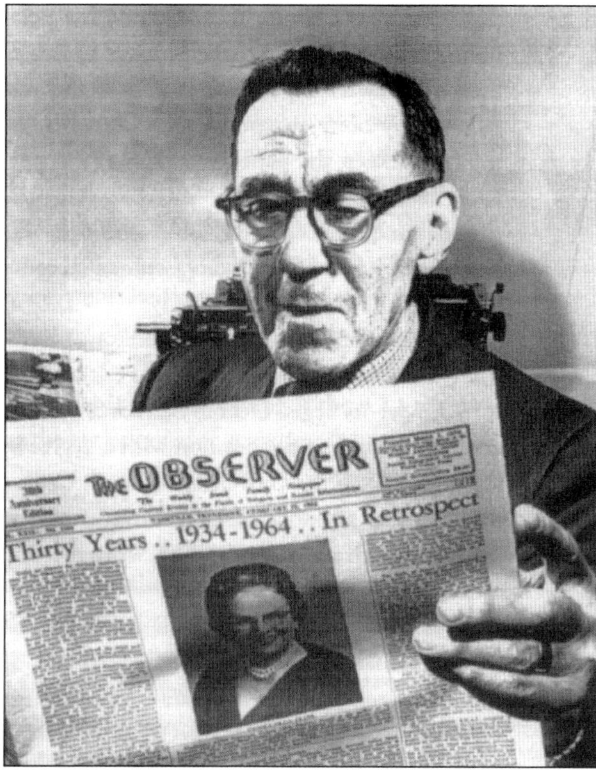

Jacques Back, who came to the United States from Alsace-Lorraine in 1884 at age 17, founded Nashville's Jewish community newspaper, the *Observer*. Back, who had attended college in Switzerland and lived in St. Louis before moving to Nashville, previously worked with two other local publications, the *Peabody Reflector* and the *Nashville Review*, before starting the *Observer*, which took over the function previously provided by the *YMHA News*. Aiding him in publishing the paper were his wife, Virginia, and one of his two daughters, Adele. Active in a number of Jewish organizations, Back died in 1975. The *Observer* continued under the leadership of a number of other owners and editors for 11 years before being purchased by the Nashville Jewish Federation in 1986.

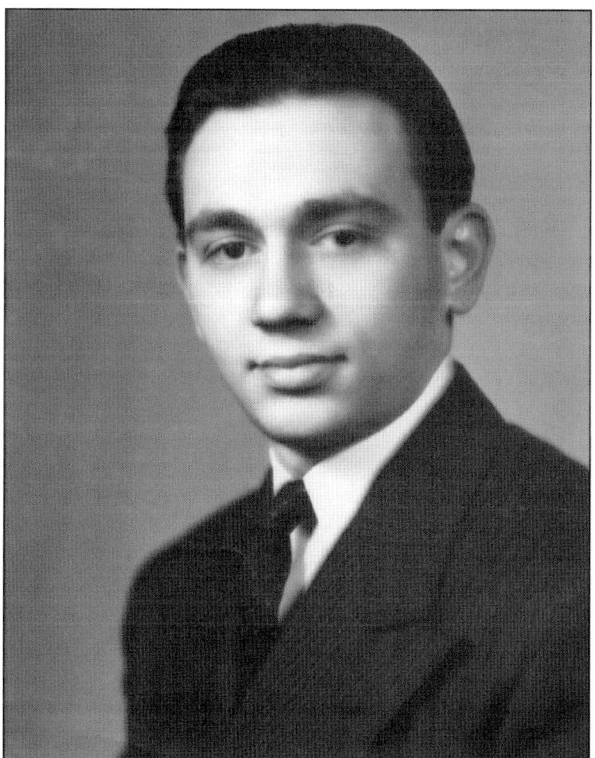

Ralph Shepard was part of a group that created the Promote the General Welfare (PGW) Club in 1935. When World War II began, Ralph, like many other young Jewish men in Nashville, went off to fight. Unfortunately, he never returned, losing his life in the Battle of the Bulge in January 1945. In his memory, the Ralph Shepard Award was created in 1946 to honor outstanding Jewish youth who represent the principles and character embodied by Shepard.

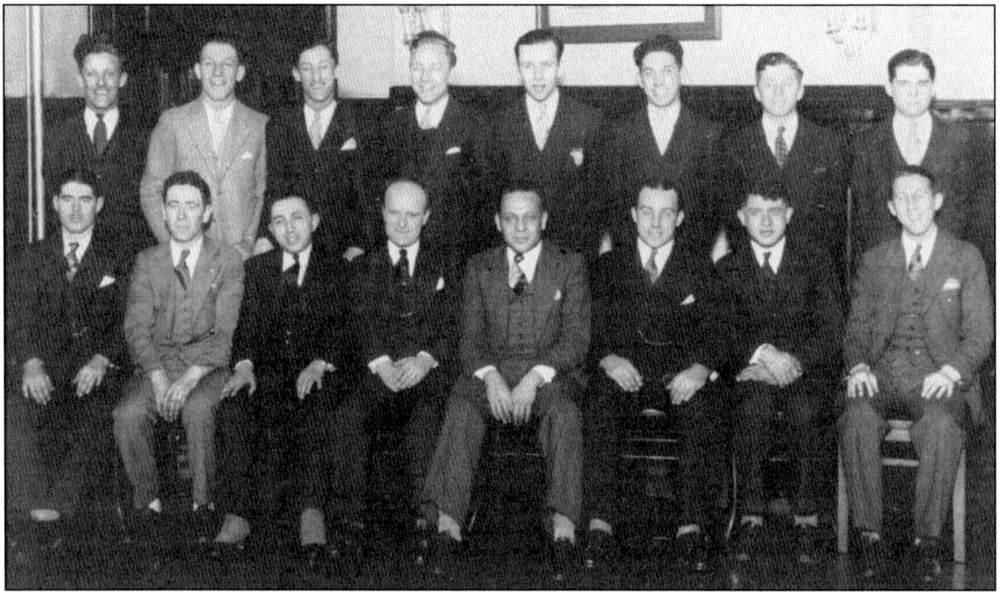

Shin Aleph was a Jewish men's fraternity (seen here in 1933) organized by seven friends in 1925. Original members included Charles Feigenbaum, Mahlon Ritt, Lazarus Cohen, Abe Kaplan, Jake Gilberman, Julius Glaboff and a Mr. Lefkovitz. Minutes of early meetings indicate Shin Aleph began as a way for the friends to get together. In 1939, some of the men's wives formed the Shin Aleph Auxiliary. The group continued to meet on a regular basis for more than 70 years, finally disbanding in 1997.

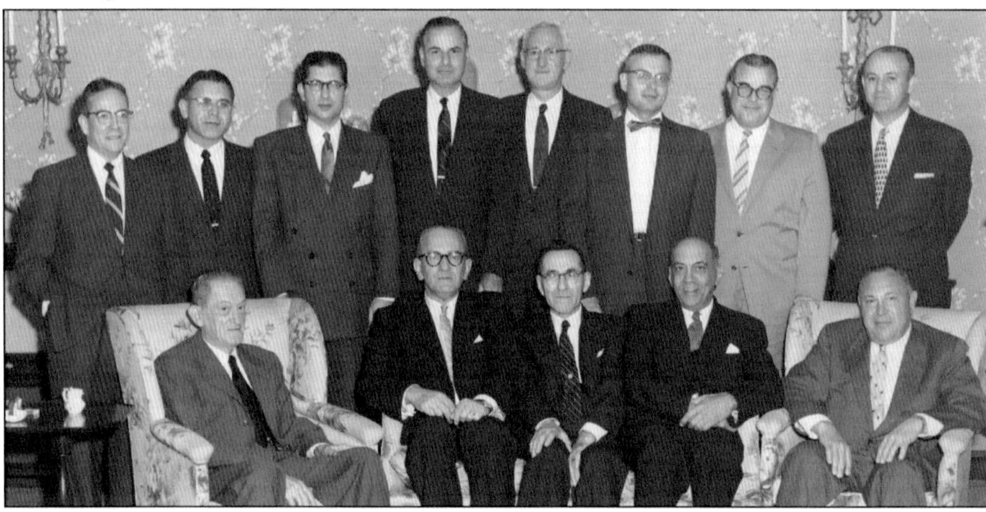

The Shamus Club was created in 1927 by a group of Jewish men who were seeking to start a social literary club. In 1933, it had 13 members, and it was never to go over that number during the years it remained in existence. The club held regular monthly dinner meetings at which a different member presented a program, even though the club proudly boasted that it had "no by-laws, no officers, and no program committee." Topics of the papers presented ranged from Longfellow's *Hiawatha* to the merits of Bacardi Rum. The 1933 membership consisted of two manufacturers, two merchants, two lawyers, one judge, one doctor, one dentist, one rabbi, one social worker, one music professor, and one advertising agency owner. This photograph shows the club's members in 1956.

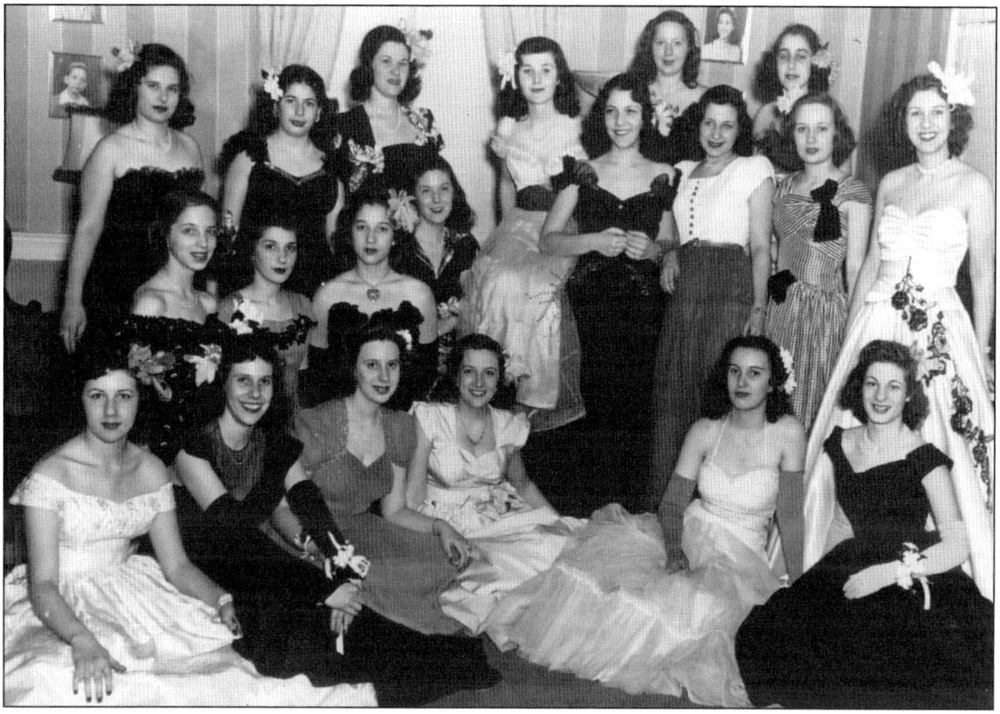

Tau Lambda Phi was a Jewish girls' social sorority that reached its peak of popularity in the 1940s. While a similar organization, BBG, was known primarily for its services to the community, Tau Lambda Phi was geared more toward social activities.

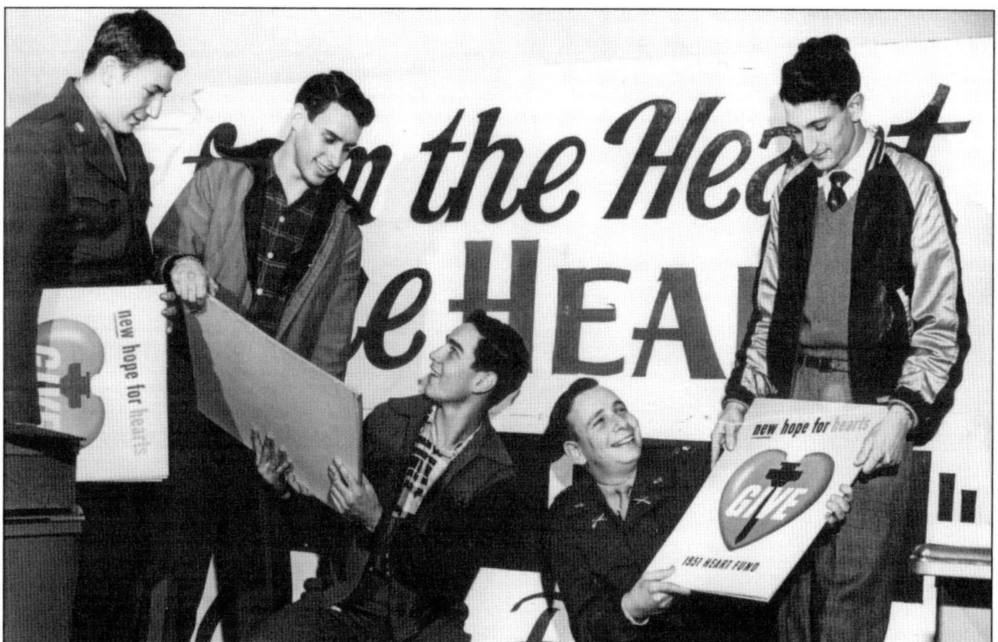

The No Name Club was another one of Nashville's organizations created by a group of friends within the Jewish community. In this photograph from 1951, the young members are working on a campaign to raise money for the Heart Fund.

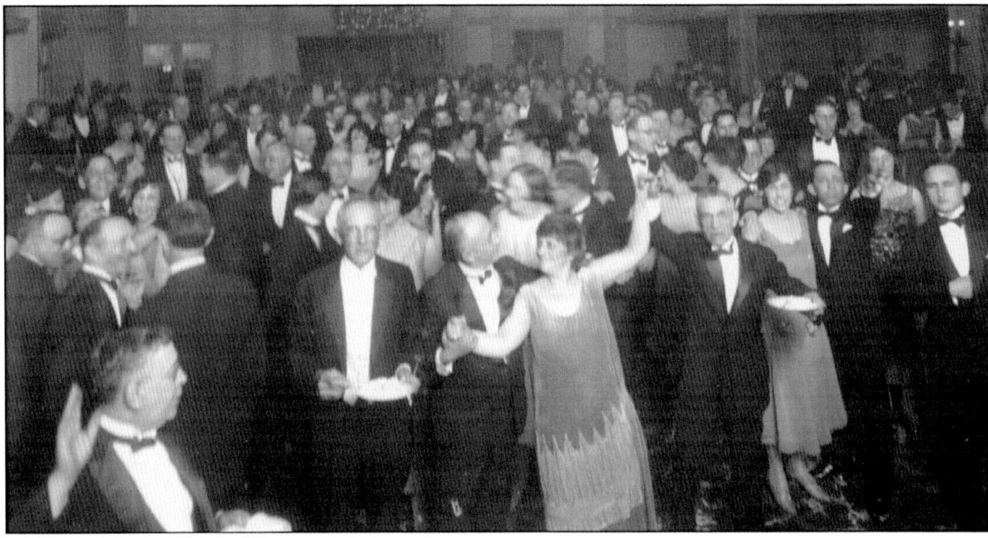

Nashville's first Jewish social club was the Eureka, founded in 1863. In 1866, it moved to a building at Cedar and Cherry Streets and changed its name to the Concordia Club. In 1876, it dissolved, and the Standard (Country) Club (above) was born. The club continued to be the center of the Jewish community's social activities until it purchased land on Woodmont Boulevard in the Belle Meade area in 1923 and built a new club that was dedicated in 1925. At that time it became the Woodmont Country Club. In this photograph below from 1932, members and their guests enjoy the dancing, including 17-year-old Fanny Rose Shore (in white at the center of the photograph, touching her ear).

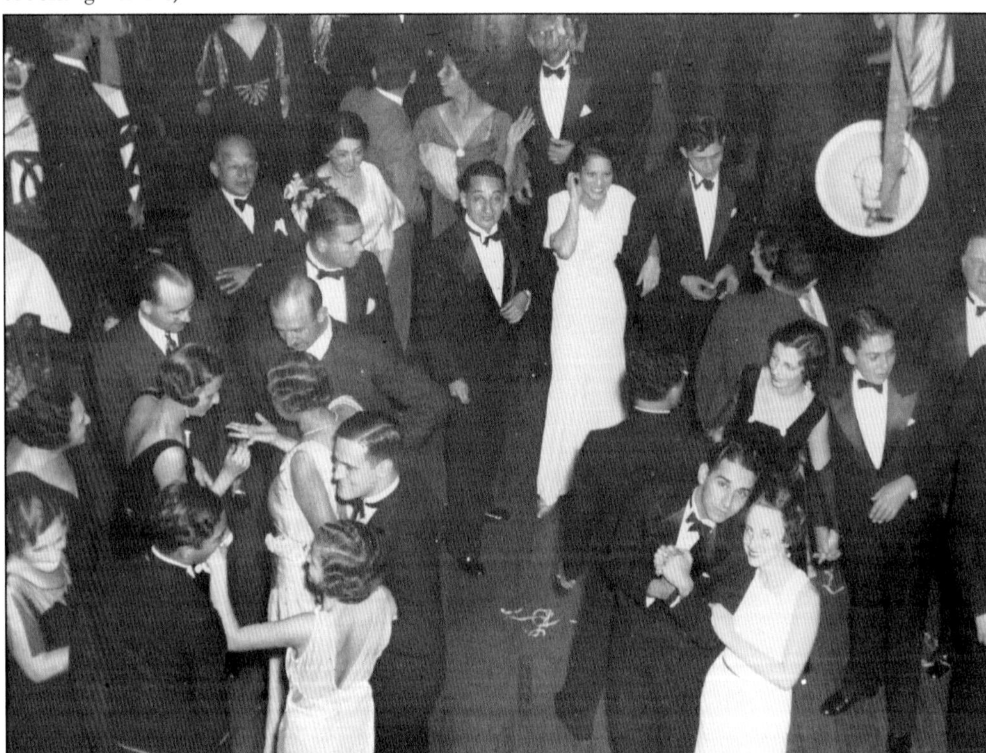

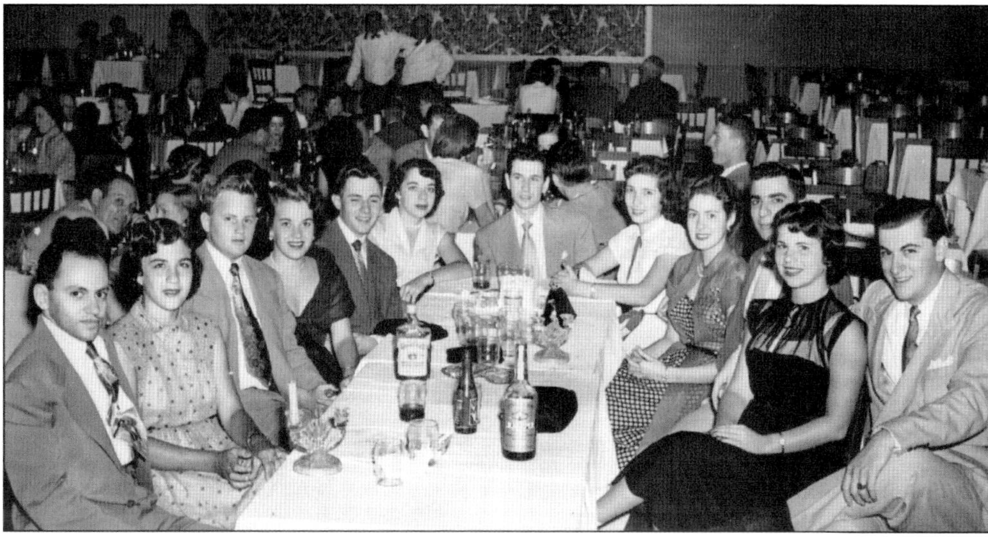

In addition to all of the so-called Jewish events—parties, dances, dinners, and social gatherings at the YMHA, JCC, Woodmont Country Club, The Temple, or one of the other synagogues—there were a number of favorite places where Jewish couples regularly gathered for dinners, dancing, or a night out. One of those, seen in this photograph from the late 1940s, was Club Plantation, located on Dickerson Pike north of Nashville.

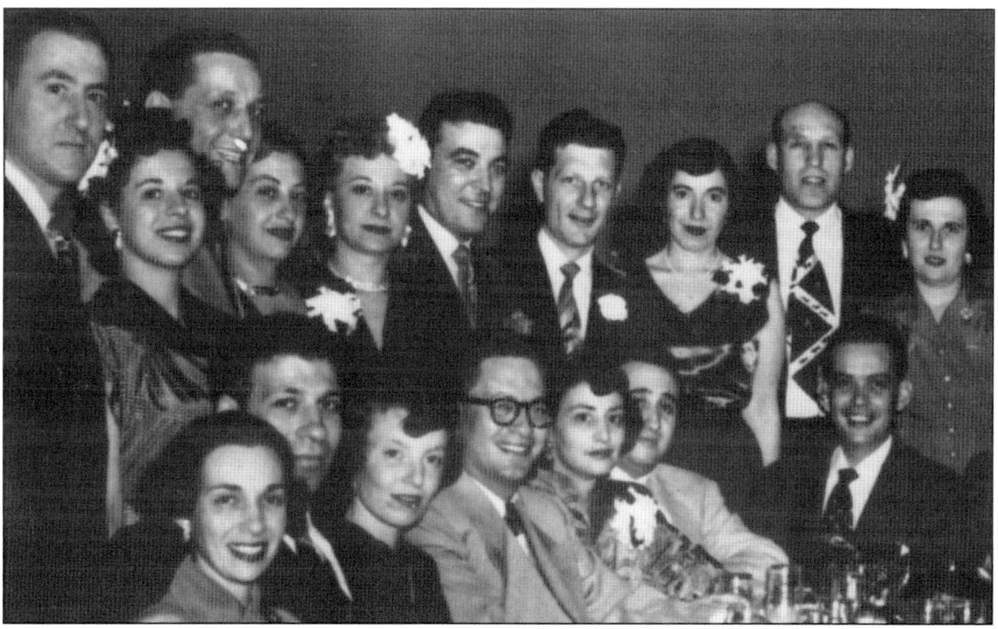

The PGW Club was formed in 1935 by a group of young Jewish Nashvillians, including Ralph Shepard, David and Willie Levine, Ernest Davis, Chuck Gross, Paul Flexer, Charlie Lapidus, Irwin Wolf, and Leo Wise. Originally designed as a social club and to field a basketball team, the group met regularly on Sundays at the YMHA until interrupted by World War II, when most members were called away to fight. One of those who joined the club shortly after it was started, Bernard Sanderson, recalled later that while the initials *PGW* stood for "Promote the General Welfare," "We were a bunch of teenagers who did anything we could get by with. I don't think we promoted the general welfare too much."

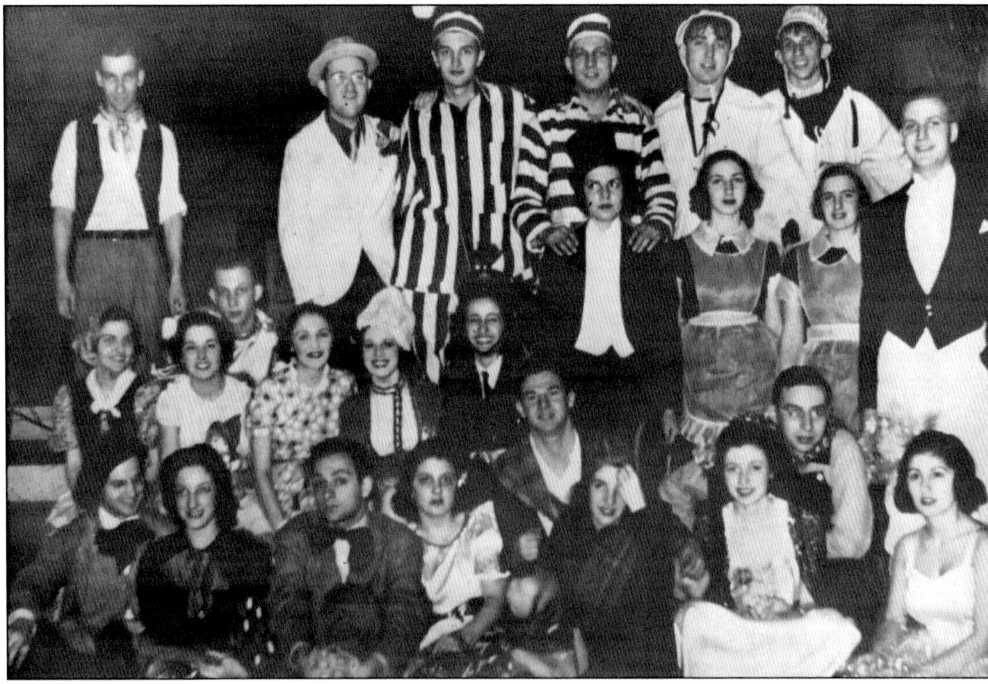

The Gaylord Club was primarily a social organization that boasted a membership of many prominent Jewish men throughout the 1930s, 1940s, and 1950s—its peak years. This photograph shows the members and their wives (or dates) at one of the musical or dramatic programs it regularly produced in the 1940s.

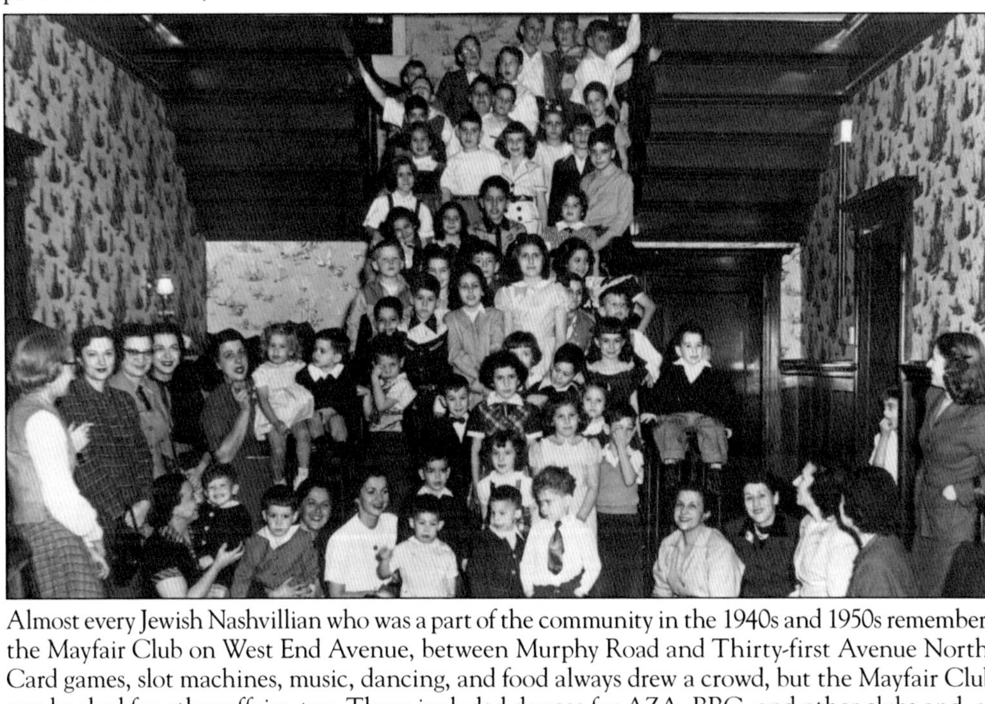

Almost every Jewish Nashvillian who was a part of the community in the 1940s and 1950s remembers the Mayfair Club on West End Avenue, between Murphy Road and Thirty-first Avenue North. Card games, slot machines, music, dancing, and food always drew a crowd, but the Mayfair Club was booked for other affairs, too. These included dances for AZA, BBG, and other clubs and, as seen in this photograph from 1951, even parties and other events for children.

Six

Highlights of Jewish Nashville

It is impossible to fully cover the expanse of nearly 200 years of Jewish history in Nashville in 128 pages with 225 photographs. For that reason, this account of Nashville's Jewish community has tried to focus on the first 100 years—1850 to 1950. Almost every photograph and all of the stories in the first five chapters of this book have covered those years. The obvious exceptions are where certain families, businesses, organizations, or congregations had their origin during those years but have continued into the present day. This final chapter takes a brief look at the more recent history of the Jewish community—some of the events and people that have played an important role in this history in the past 50 years. In addition to the names and faces included in this chapter, it is important to point out that there are many other members of the Jewish community—some well known and others more obscure, some high profile and some who prefer to remain behind the scenes—not pictured here. Among this group are a number of professors and educators at Vanderbilt and other area universities and colleges, some of whom are known for their scientific, medical, and literary achievements; several attorneys and judges who have played major roles in Nashville's legal community; and a sizable number of men and women who have contributed greatly to the city's political, civic, and social structure, including the fight for racial harmony and civil rights, women's rights, gender equality, and gay rights, not to mention the thousands of hours and millions of dollars they have raised for many good causes, secular and otherwise, in Nashville. It is not because they or their accomplishments are not worthy of inclusion. Rather it is because time and space constraints limit the number that can be included. It is safe to assume that there will be some that readers feel should or could have been included, so it is important to point out that it is the writer's intention that those people and their contributions to the community be included in a future work that will cover the years 1950 to the present day.

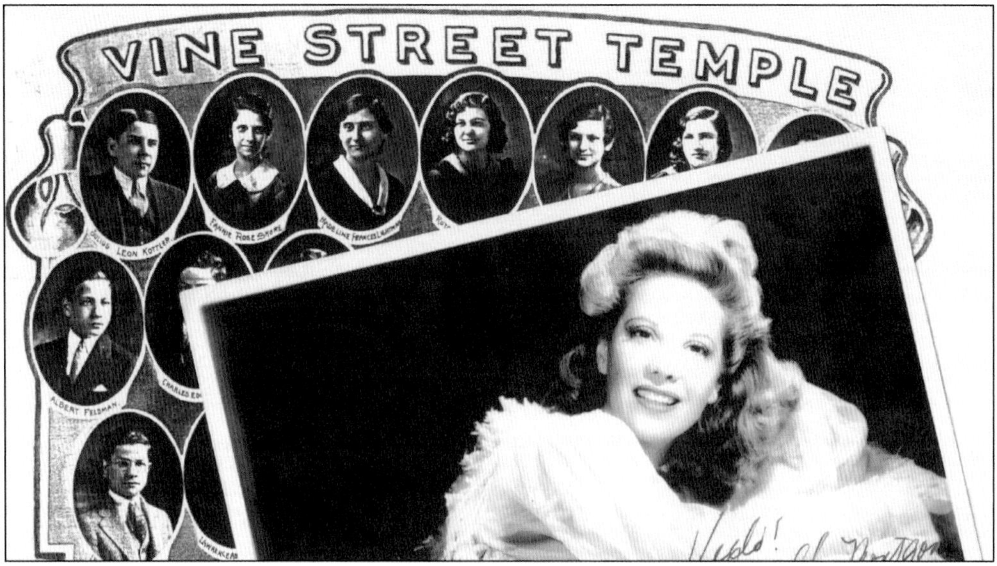

Fannie Rose Shore, as she was known during her childhood and adolescent years, was born in 1917 in Winchester, where her father owned a dry goods store. In 1923, Sol Shore moved the family to Nashville, where Fanny attended Hume-Fogg High School and was confirmed at Vine Street Temple. After graduation from Vanderbilt and a career start at WSM radio, she moved to New York and joined the cast of NBC's *Eddie Cantor Show*, rooming with another Jewish girl, singer Kitty Kallen. Dinah Shore, as she became known, went on to become one of America's most popular singers and television personalities of the 1950s and 1960s.

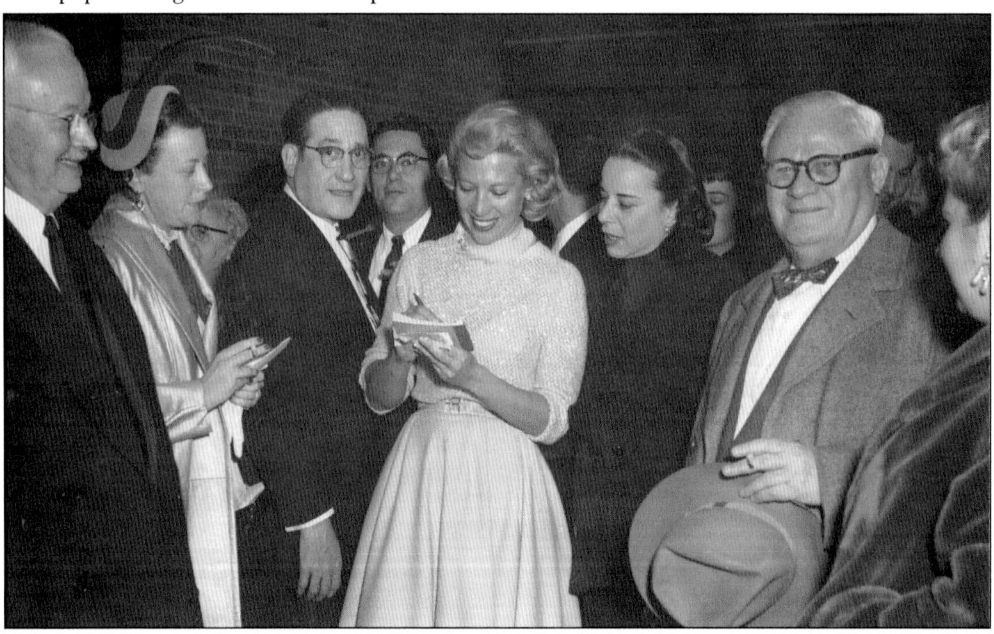

Despite reaching the highest levels of fame and fortune, Dinah Shore never forgot her Nashville roots. She was a frequent visitor to the city where she grew up, and she never passed up an opportunity to lend her support to local and national Jewish causes, as she did when she came to Nashville in 1957 for the United Jewish Appeal. Pictured here, from left to right, are Morris Steiner, Selma Goldstein, Ike Barnett, Jack Speller, Dinah, Helen Rosenfeld, and Abe Olshine.

Dinah also was always willing to help out the Nashville's Jewish community in other ways. When a cookbook she wrote was published in 1990, she came to the annual Jewish Community Center Book Fair to promote the book and sign copies of it.

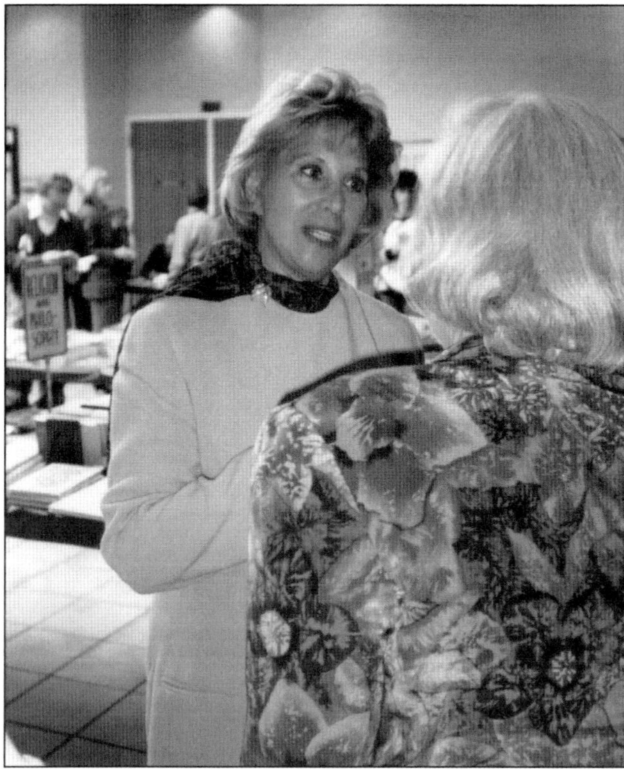

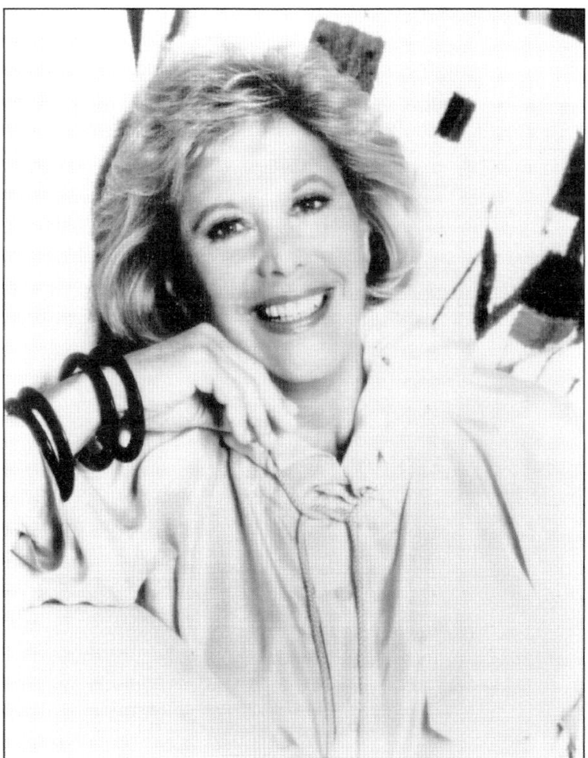

Her cookbook became a best seller, and Dinah the singer and the actress of stage and screen became Dinah the author. A number of Nashvillians have pointed out to the author how warm and friendly she was whenever she came back home to visit old friends.

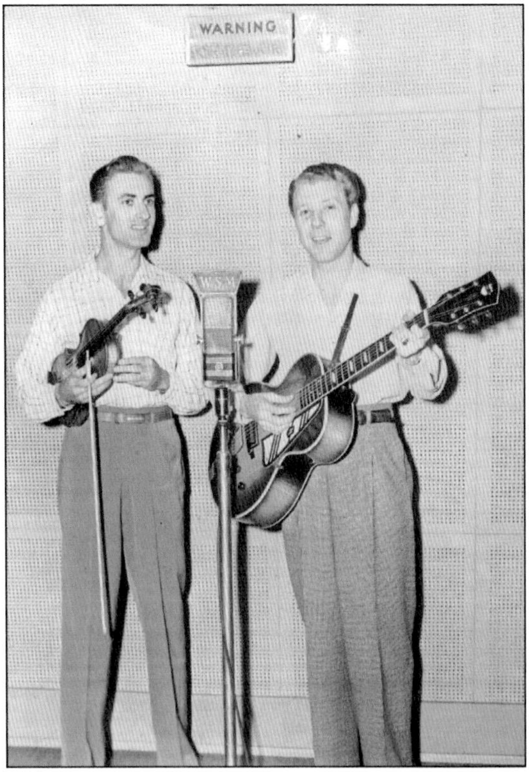

Musician Maurice (Mutt) Blumen, a longtime Nashville resident, was born in Birmingham in 1919. After making appearances on the *Louisiana Hayride*, he moved to Nashville in 1933, appearing on the *Grand Ole Opry* and touring with such stars as Bill Monroe. He is pictured at left with fellow musician Jimmy Selph at WSM. He died in 2006. (Courtesy of David Blumen.)

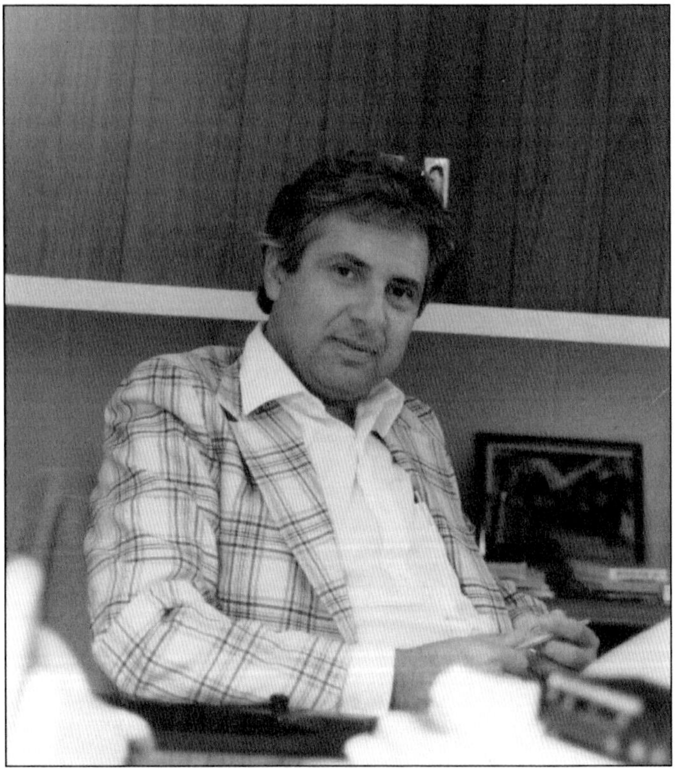

Teddy Bart (see page 28) has been a well-known fixture in Nashville's Jewish community since moving from Philadelphia in the early 1960s. While his first job was singing in Printers Alley, he went on to become a staff singer at WSM radio and television, host of the popular *Noon Show* on Channel 4, talk show host and newspaper columnist, and author of several books. He and his wife, Jana, also published Nashville's Jewish community newspaper, the *Observer*, for several years in the late 1970s after purchasing it from George Barker. (Courtesy of Teddy Bart.)

Morris Frank grew up in Nashville and attended Montgomery Bell Academy, where an injury in a boxing match caused him to lose his sight. After attending Vanderbilt, he heard about a woman in Europe who was training dogs to lead the blind. He went there to meet her and find out more about her work and ended up obtaining Buddy, his first guide dog, and returning to the United States to help other sightless people benefit from the program. The woman who trained Buddy went on to found the Seeing Eye program.

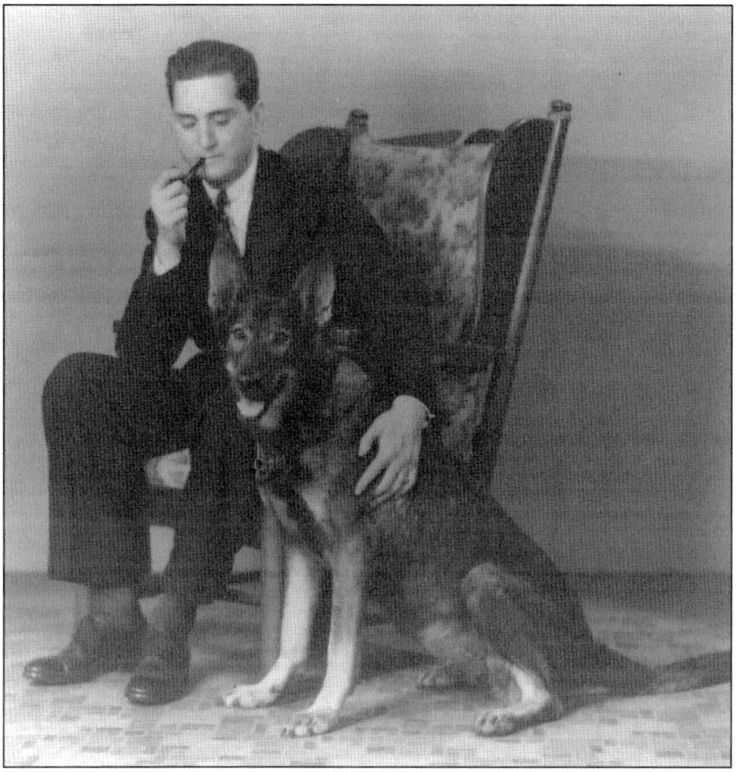

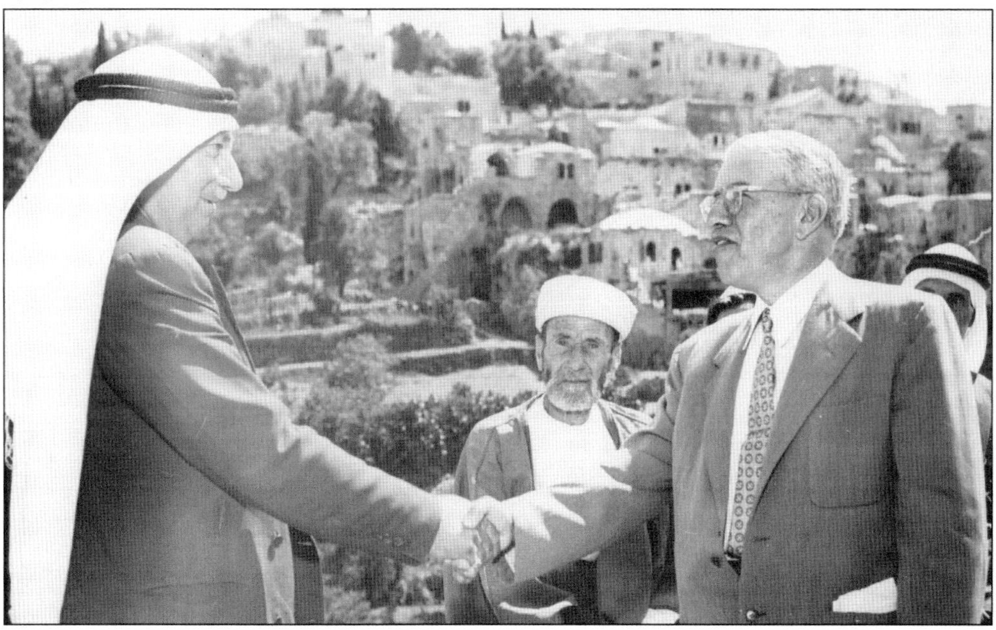

Mortimer May was the son of Jacob May and the father of Dan and Leon May. An ardent Zionist, he worked tirelessly on behalf of Israel and Jewish causes throughout the world. In 1954, he was elected president of the Zionist Organization of America, and he was also a board member of the Union of American Hebrew Congregations. The May family saved hundreds of lives in the late 1930s by agreeing to sponsor Jewish immigrants trying to escape the Nazis.

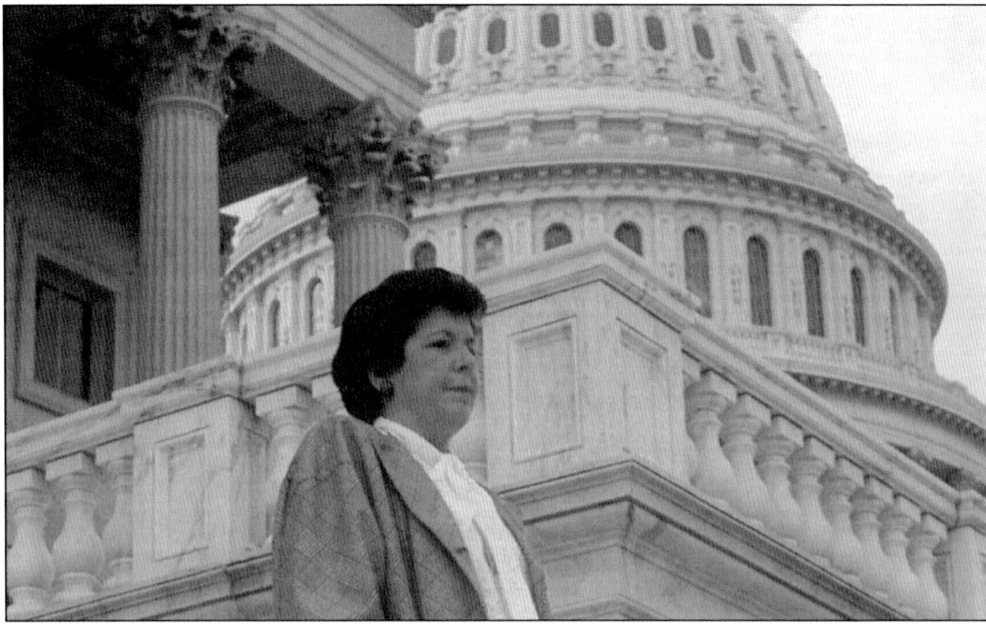

Jane Eskind has long played a major role in local Democratic politics. She was the first woman elected to statewide office in Tennessee when she won a seat on the Public Service Commission. She also ran unsuccessfully for the U.S. Senate in 1978 and in the Democratic primary for governor in 1986. She is married to Dick Eskind and has been very active in Jewish community organizations for many years.

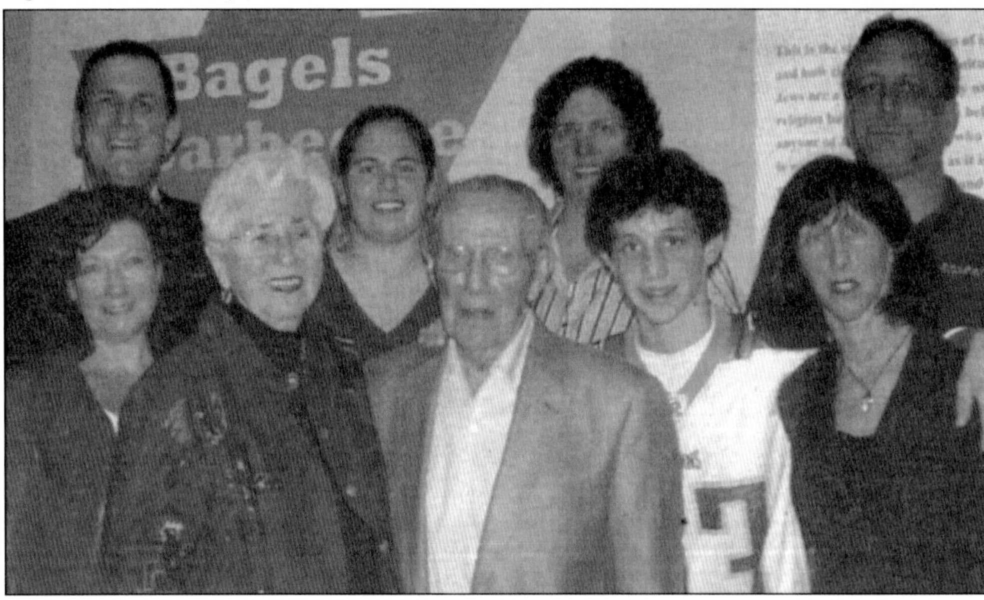

Annette Levy Ratkin has done more to chronicle the development of Nashville's Jewish community in the past 30 years than anyone else. She is shown in this photograph with her family. Her first husband, Ralph Levy Sr., died in 1976, and she later married Ruben Ratkin (fifth from left). Working first in the JCC library in the 1970s, she went on to build the archives into a repository of local Jewish history rivaling that of any other Jewish community in this country. (Courtesy of Annette Levy Ratkin.)

Fedora Frank, the daughter of Louis and Rosa Small, was the first person to write a book detailing the history of Nashville's Jewish community, and she wrote two. *Five Families and Eight Young Men*, published in 1962, started with the first Jewish settlers around 1850 and ended with the beginning of the Civil War. The second volume, published in 1976, covered the period from 1861 to 1901. Fedora was married to Isadore Frank and was also a member of several book, magazine, and discussion clubs and other Jewish organizations.

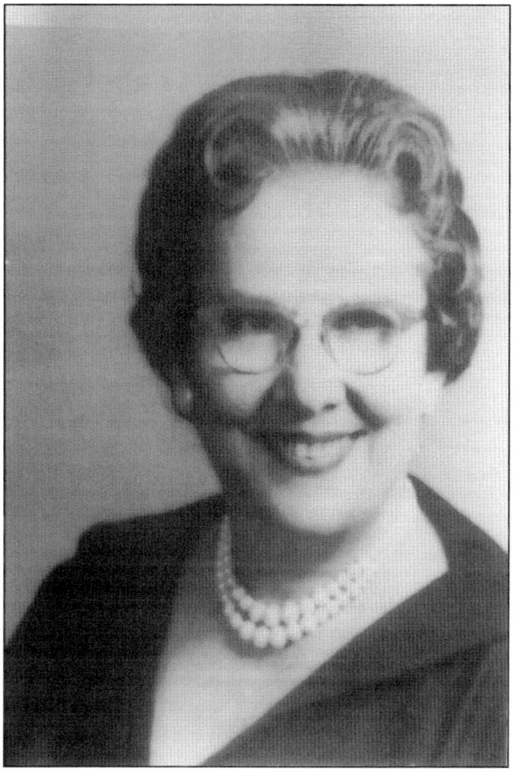

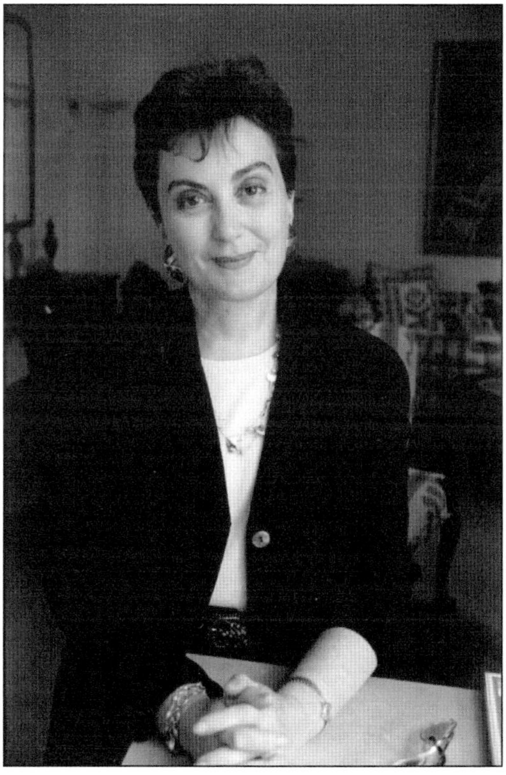

Libby Werthan is the daughter of Herman and Baylie Rosenblum and is married to Morris Werthan Jr. A Nashville native, she decided she wanted to tell the story of growing up Jewish in a fictional account, so she wrote *The Fourth Corner*, published in 2001. It served as an opportunity for Libby to "describe the differences between a Jewish girl and her non-Jewish neighbors, as well as how the Southern Jewish experience was different from that of a Jewish girl growing up in New York or another northern city." The decision to write the book came after taking creative writing classes at Vanderbilt and after she and her husband moved to Israel in 1990. While both Libby and Morris have become involved in a variety of social, civic, and business activities in Jerusalem, they still come back to Nashville regularly. (Courtesy of Libby Werthan.)

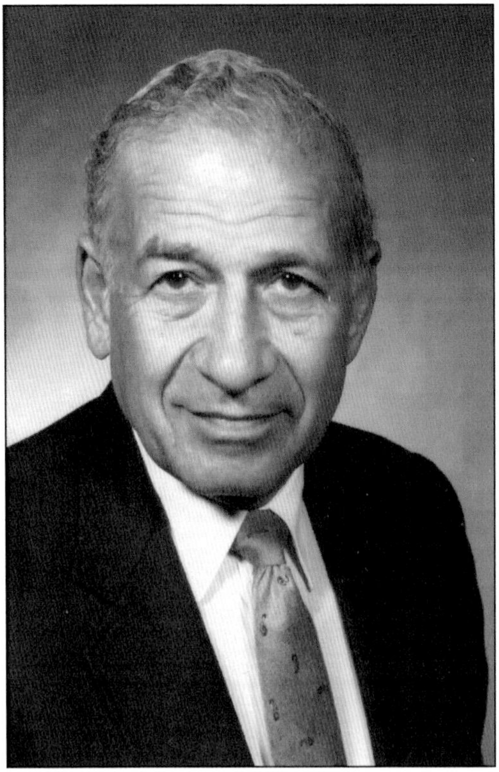

Joe Kraft, the son of Boruch (Boris) and Fannie Kraft, was born at his parents' home in South Nashville in 1925 (later the site of Joe's brother Morris's 5 and 10¢ store and Joe's first office when he became a certified public accountant). He graduated from Vanderbilt University, playing on the Commodores basketball team as one of its first Jewish players. In 1958, he founded Kraft Brothers, one of Nashville's most respected CPA firms. Joe passed away in 1993, and the Joe Kraft Humanitarian Award was created that same year in recognition of the many civic and community contributions he made during his life. It perpetuates the memory of "a special person who made Middle Tennessee a better place to live through his dedication to community, home, and hearth and individuals in need." Both Joe and his wife, Elsie, worked tirelessly on behalf of many causes, both Jewish and secular, during their lives. They had a daughter, Julie, and a son, Lee, who is a partner with Kraft Brothers. Both live in Nashville.

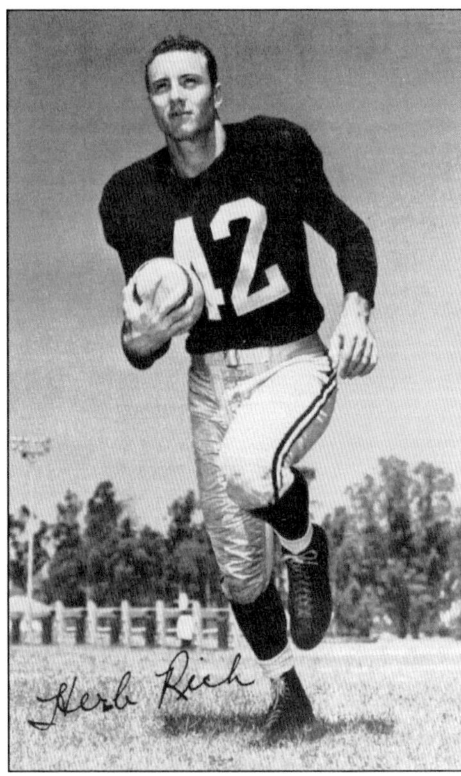

Herb Rich was a well-known Nashville attorney for many years. But before that, he was a seven-year veteran of the National Football League, playing for the New York Giants, Baltimore Colts, and Los Angeles Rams. Coming to Nashville from Florida to attend Vanderbilt, he was a football standout for the Commodores and also played basketball and baseball. He still holds the NFL record for best punt return average in a single season, and was inducted into the Tennessee Sports Hall of Fame in 1992. He died in 2008 at 79.

Mickey Kantor was born in Nashville in 1939, the son of Mr. and Mrs. Henry Kantor. He graduated from West End High School in 1957 and Vanderbilt in 1961, then earned a law degree from Georgetown University. Feeling a strong commitment to social causes, much of which he learned growing up in a close-knit Nashville Jewish family, one of his first jobs was providing legal assistance to migrant farm workers. Becoming active in Democratic Party politics while still practicing law, he was chair of the 1992 Clinton-Gore campaign and later served as U.S. trade representative under Pres. Bill Clinton. Kantor is married to broadcast journalist Heidi Schulman, and they have one daughter, Alix, and three grandchildren. He also has two children from his first wife, Valerie, who died in a plane crash in California in 1978; a third, his son Russell, died in an automobile accident in 1988. Growing up in Nashville, he was an outstanding baseball and basketball player at West High. He has two brothers, Carl and Charles, and a sister, Sonya Kantor Eskind. (Courtesy of Mickey Kantor.)

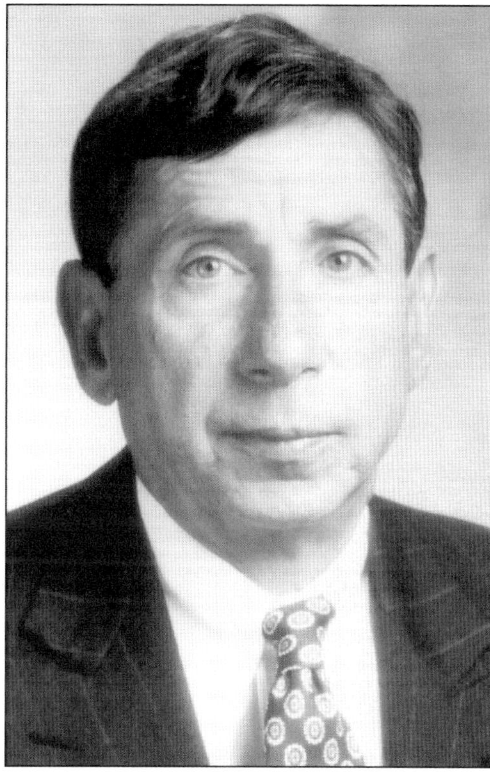

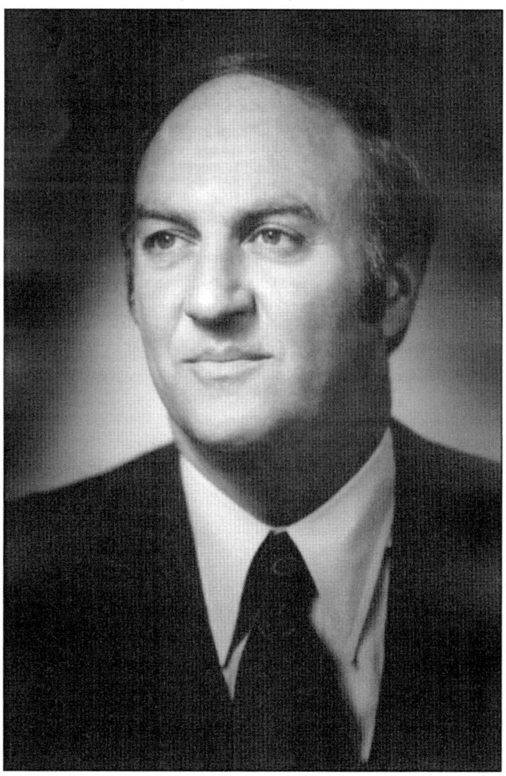

Joel Gordon came to Nashville in 1954 from Crofton, Kentucky, where his parents ran a small general store. After spending 11 years in retail with Harvey's and Cain-Sloan, he founded General Care Corporation, a health care–related business, in 1969 and Surgical Care Affiliates in 1982. He married the former Bernice Weingart, daughter of Mr. and Mrs. Harry Weingart (Harry Weingart had a tailor shop on West End Avenue near Vanderbilt), and the couple has four children. Because of Joel's contributions to the JCC, it was renamed the Gordon Jewish Community Center in 1999, and the Joel C. Gordon Honor Scholarship was endowed in 1998 as a tribute to Gordon in recognition of his contributions to health care.

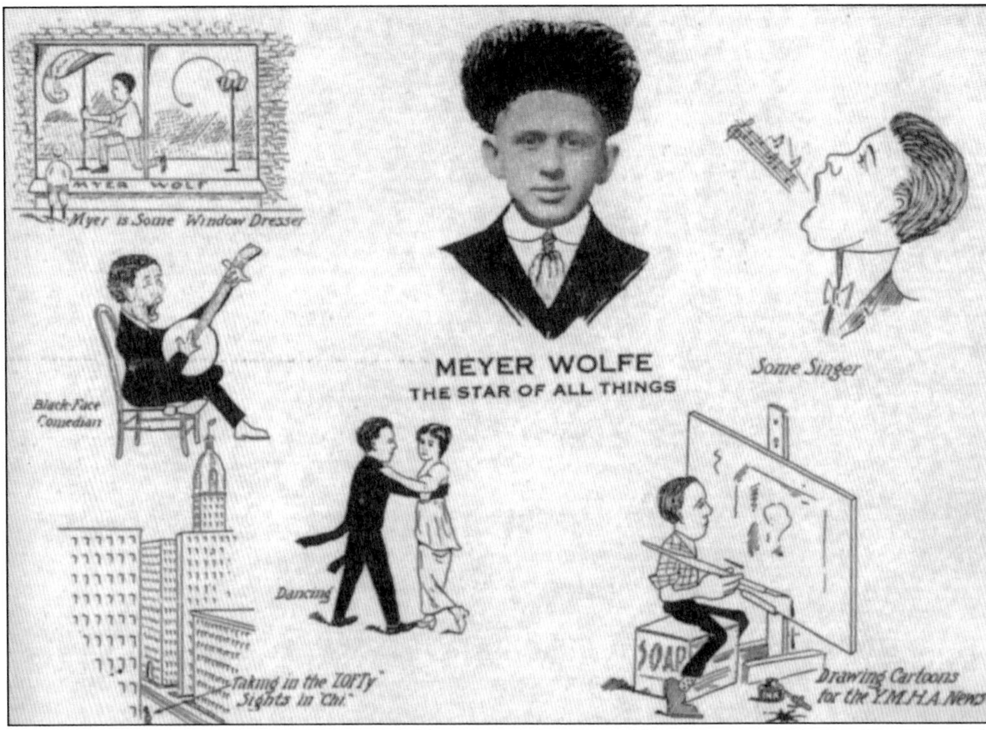

Born in Louisville in 1897, artist and illustrator Meyer Wolfe grew up in Nashville. His early sketches were seen throughout the *YMHA News*. After high school, he studied in Chicago at the Academy of Fine Arts and in New York at the Art Students League, and in 1926, he went to Paris to train at the Academie Julian. One of his better-known works is "Red Eye's Hall," his 1934 portrayal of African Americans in a Nashville dance hall. Wolfe, who was married to New York photographer Louise Dahl, died in 1985.

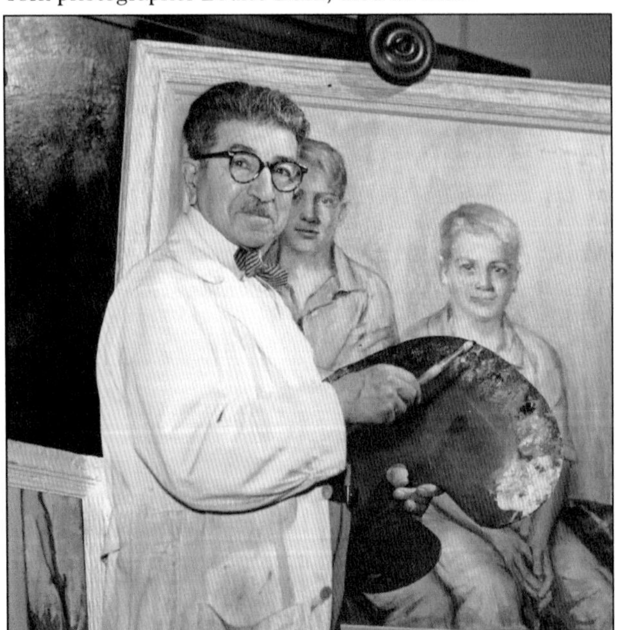

Max Westfield came to Nashville in 1940 after escaping from Nazi Germany. One of his brothers, Walter, an art dealer, died in the death chambers at Auschwitz. Another brother, Dietrich, a well-regarded lawyer before the Nazis rose to power, fled the country and ended up in Nashville without a profession and penniless. Max and Dietrich took odd jobs, including selling cola at the May's Hosiery Mill. Max painted a number of portraits during his years in Nashville, including a very well-known one of Albert Einstein. He also painted portraits of several notable Jewish Nashvillians, including the one of Barbara Jacobs Kuhn on page 70.

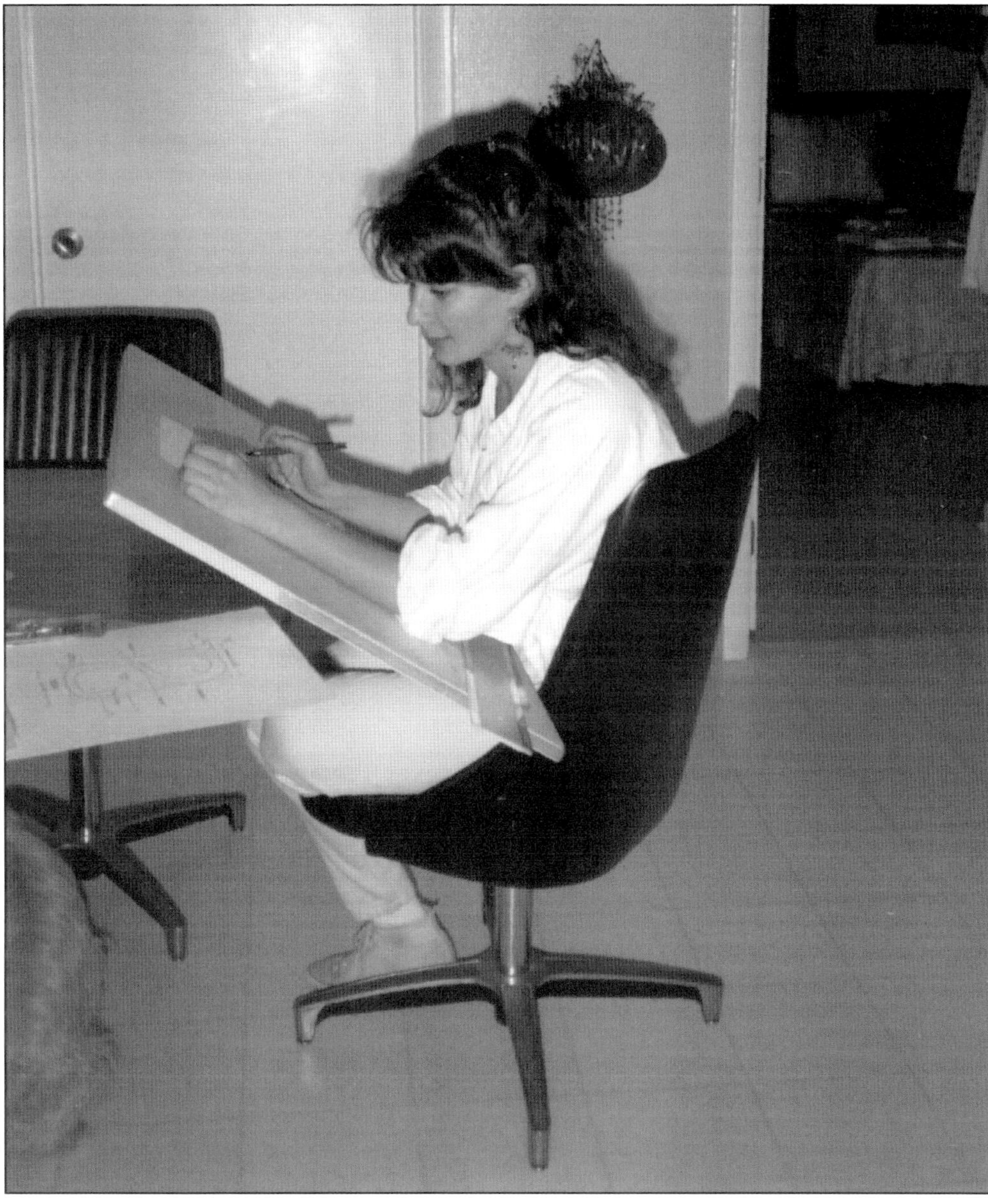

Sadly, the history of Nashville's Jewish community cannot be fully told without the story of the tragic disappearance and death of Janet Levine March. The daughter of Carolyn (Rosenblum, see page 104) and Larry Levine, she grew up in Nashville, attending University School before going away to college at the University of Michigan. After graduating, she returned to Nashville and in 1987 married her college sweetheart. They had two children, son Sammy and daughter Tzipi. Janet's love of art led her to realize a lifelong dream when she was chosen to illustrate a number of children's books. Suddenly in the summer of 1996, at just 33 years old, she disappeared. For the next 10 years, while no one knew for certain what happened, everyone feared the worst. Finally, in 2006, after a long, tense, and dramatic legal ordeal, her husband, Perry March, was convicted of murdering her and was sentenced to life in prison. To honor the life of this talented and beautiful young woman, the Janet Levine March Art Gallery at the Gordon Jewish Community Center was named in her memory. (Courtesy of Carolyn Levine.)